The Complete Idiot's Command Reference

Network Troubleshooter's Checklist

If your network is broken, use this checklist to trou

Troubles Reaching Your LAN?

➤ **Check that the light on the hub is green for your connection to the hub** On some hubs, a yellow light means the hub and NIC can't communicate. You may need a new NIC.

➤ **Check that the cable is connected to your NIC and your hub** With RJ-45 ports, the connector clicks when it is inserted in the port properly.

➤ **Check that your NIC has a working driver and settings** In Windows 95/98, right-click **My Computer**, click **Device Manager**, click "+" next to Network Adapter, and double-click the entry for your NIC. On this window, check that the device is working properly and that there are no conflicts in resources.

➤ **Check that you can reach another computer on the LAN** Get the IP address for a computer (such as 10.0.0.5) and use it with ping as follows:

`ping 10.0.0.5`

➤ **Check that the network interface card (NIC) is inserted properly** This usually entails opening the case on your computer and pressing the NIC firmly into its slot.

Troubles Reaching the Internet?

➤ **Check that your IP address is configured properly** In Windows 95/98, go to **Start, Settings, Control Panel, Network**. Select **TCP/IP** and choose **Properties**. On the IP Address tab, click **Obtain an IP address** (if there is a DHCP server available) or click **Specify an IP address** and type your computer's IP Address and Subnet Mask.

➤ **Check that your computer has the correct DNS server address** In Windows 95/98, go to **Start, Settings, Control Panel, Network**. Select **TCP/IP** and choose **Properties**. On the DNS Configuration tab, add the addresses of one or more DNS servers.

➤ **Check that the gateway is set properly** In Windows 95/98, go to **Start, Settings, Control Panel, Network**. Select **TCP/IP** and choose **Properties**. On the Gateway tab, add the IP address for the gateway. This is the address where your router connects to your LAN.

➤ **Check that you can reach your router on the LAN** Get the IP address for the router (such as 10.0.0.1) and use it with ping as follows:

`ping 10.0.0.1`

➤ **Check that your network's router is configured properly** The router needs to have a connection to your LAN and one to the Internet.

➤ **For dial-up connections, check to see if the connection is failing** Make sure you are getting a dial tone, that the ISP phone number is correct, and that you have the correct account name and password.

Network Setup Checklist

Write down information about your network (and keep it locked up!). Use this list to keep track of names, addresses, and hardware information for each computer on your network.

Internet Connection Information

DNS Server #1 (IP address):

DNS Server #2 (IP address):

If LAN Internet access (DSL, Cable Modem, and so on):

    Gateway (router) IP Addresses

        On LAN:

        To Internet:

If dial-up Internet access (telephone modem):

    Telephone # to ISP:

    Account name:

    Password:

Table 1   LAN Workstation Information

Workstation #1	Workstation #2	Workstation #3
Type of NIC:	Type of NIC:	Type of NIC:
IRQ & I/O Range:	IRQ & I/O Range:	IRQ & I/O Range:
Hub connection #:	Hub connection #:	Hub connection #:
Windows Network:	*Windows Network:*	*Windows Network:*
Computer name:	Computer name:	Computer name:
Workgroup name:	Workgroup name:	Workgroup name:
Access control:	Access control:	Access control:
WINS Server:	WINS Server:	WINS Server:
TCP/IP Network:	*TCP/IP Network:*	*TCP/IP Network:*
DHCP Server:	DHCP Server:	DHCP Server:
Host name:	Host name:	Host name:
Domain name:	Domain name:	Domain name:
IP Address:	IP Address:	IP Address:
Subnetwork Mask:	Subnetwork Mask:	Subnetwork Mask:
Gateway:	Gateway:	Gateway:
Workstation #4	**Workstation #5**	**Workstation #6**
Type of NIC:	Type of NIC:	Type of NIC:
IRQ & I/O Range:	IRQ & I/O Range:	IRQ & I/O Range:
Hub connection:	Hub connection:	Hub connection:
Windows Network:	*Windows Network:*	*Windows Network:*
Computer name:	Computer name:	Computer name:
Workgroup name:	Workgroup name:	Workgroup name:
Access control:	Access control:	Access control:
WINS Server:	WINS Server:	WINS Server:
TCP/IP Network:	*TCP/IP Network:*	*TCP/IP Network:*
DHCP Server:	DHCP Server:	DHCP Server:
Host name:	Host name:	Host name:
Domain name:	Domain name:	Domain name:
IP Address:	IP Address:	IP Address:
Subnetwork Mask:	Subnetwork Mask:	Subnetwork Mask:
Gateway:	Gateway:	Gateway:

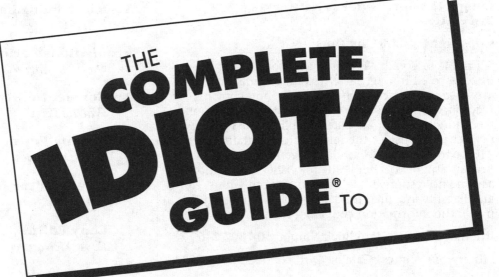

THE COMPLETE IDIOT'S GUIDE® TO

Networking

3rd Edition

by Chris Negus
and
Bill Wagner

201 W. 103rd Street, Indianapolis, IN 46290

que®

Trademarks

Warning and Disclaimer

Associate Publisher
Jeff Koch

Acquisitions Editor
Vicki Harding

Development Editor
Valerie Perry

Managing Editor
Thomas F. Hayes

Project Editor
Heather McNeill

Copy Editor
Julie A. McNamee

Indexer
Bill Meyers

Proofreader
Benjamin Berg

Technical Editor
Jim Kelly

Illustrator
Judd Winick

Interior Designer
Nathan Clement

Cover Designer
Michael Freeland

Production
Darin Crone

Contents at a Glance

Table of Contents

vii

ix

About the Authors

Bill Wagner currently runs an Internet security consulting company. His sordid past includes NetWare, Linux, and UNIX system administration. Bill lives on the southern California coast with his wife, Michelle, who has been certified Y2K compliant.

Chris Negus has written about networking and UNIX for nearly two decades. His *Red Hat Linux Bible* spent most of 2000 near the top of the *Publisher's Weekly* computer operating systems bestseller list. Other books by Chris include *Internet Explorer 4 Bible*, *Netscape Plug-ins for Dummies*, and the *Caldera OpenLinux Bible*. Chris lives with his wife Sheree (the best teacher around), Caleb (the kid with cool braids), and Seth (who aspires to be a Pokémon™ master) somewhere in the Pacific Northwest.

Dedication

Bill Wagner

In memory of Lewis Herschler, soldier, political scientist, and all-around cool cat.

Chris Negus

In memory of Joan Negus: the world's greatest astrologer, baseball coach, and mom.

Acknowledgments

Bill Wagner

The following persons were indispensable: Michael Mikaleczko, David Sale, David Pennells, David Fugate, Margot Hutchison, and Marty Rush.

Chris Negus

I'd like to thank Sheree for setting up our new home in Washington State as I spent the last few weeks polishing off this book. Leave the light on...I'll be there in a couple of days!

Thanks to Bill Wagner, Vicki Harding of Que, and Margot Hutchison of Waterside for bringing me into this project. I'd also like to thank Scott Cowan of Salt Lake City for his perspective on Internet services and the fine people at Que who make words into real books.

Tell Us What You Think!

As the reader of this book, *you* are our most important critic and commentator. We value your opinion and want to know what we're doing right, what we could do better, what areas you'd like to see us publish in, and any other words of wisdom you're willing to pass our way.

As an associate publisher for Que, I welcome your comments. You can fax, email, or write me directly to let me know what you did or didn't like about this book—as well as what we can do to make our books stronger.

Please note that I cannot help you with technical problems related to the topic of this book, and that due to the high volume of mail I receive, I might not be able to reply to every message.

When you write, please be sure to include this book's title and author as well as your name and phone or fax number. I will carefully review your comments and share them with the author and editors who worked on the book.

Fax: 317-581-4666

Email: jeff.koch@macmillanusa.com

Mail: Associate Publisher
          Que
          201 West 103rd Street
          Indianapolis, IN 46290 USA

1, 2, 3, Go!

The Internet is everywhere. Most offices with more than two PCs have a local area network (LAN). Prices for using computer networks are getting lower every day. People with the skill to set up and work with computer networks are at a premium.

So what are you waiting for? It's time to jump into computer networking!

This book takes you on a journey through the world of computer networking. It contains a mixture of information to not only help you understand networking, but to get your hands on it as well. Simple descriptions teach you how to choose networking hardware, design network layouts, and make decisions about choosing Internet services.

If you're still a bit shaky about what to do with your network, there's a chapter to tell you about the most popular networking software. It describes Web browsers, email readers, and even exciting multi-user games!

If you have never set up a network before, don't worry. Simple steps will take you through the process of building your first home or small office network. If you feel brave, you can go even further by looking into topics such as network administration, security, and troubleshooting.

Today, networking visionaries are promising that millions of new wireless handheld devices will soon flood the world. Old economy appliance manufacturers are preparing to put your coffee maker on a network. Low-cost broadband Internet access is expected to open homes and businesses to high-quality streaming video and audio. So you don't get left behind, we take you on a tour of how these bright ideas might rule your future or simply end up in the trash bin.

How the Book Is Organized

This book is divided into the following five parts and one appendix:

Part I: Scouting Out Your Network

Because the focus of this book is on LANs in Chapter 2, "Having Your Own Network (LAN)" (for connecting home or small office networks), and the Internet in Chapter 3, "Using a World-Wide Network (the Internet)" (for connecting to a world-wide network), those two technologies are described in the first part. Before that, Chapter 1, "What Is a Network?" begins with an even simpler network: two cans and a string.

Part II: Gathering Your Network Gear

Before you can build a network, it's best to choose the type of networking equipment you need, the types of computers to connect (clients and servers), and how it will all be connected (topologies). Chapters 4, "Choosing Your Networking Hardware," 5, "Network Servers and Clients at Your Service," and 6, "Take a Bus, Hitch a Star, Ring Around Network Topologies," help you make those choices.

Part III: Building Your Network Base

This part is the "do it" section. Chapter 7, "Making Those Internet Connections," tells you how to evaluate your needs for connecting to the Internet. Chapter 8, "Building Your Home Network," steps you through creating your first home LAN. Chapter 9, "Hooking Up Your Small Office Network," covers topics that are important to someone creating an office network. Chapter 10, "Taking Your Network for a Drive," takes you through many of the most popular tools for using the Internet. Chapter 11, "Linking Your Home and Office Networks," describes issues related to telecommuting and accessing your work network from home.

Part IV: Defending Your Network Turf

Connecting computers to a network opens them up to potential abuse. This part describes how to protect your network resources. Chapter 12, "Your Fearless Leader: The System Administrator," describes the duties of a system administrator. Chapter 13, "Devising a Backup Plan," describes how to create and implement plans for backing up your data. Chapter 14, "Securing Your Fortress," describes ways of securing your computers from malicious visitors. Chapter 15, "Troubleshooting from the Trenches," describes tools and techniques for troubleshooting a network.

Part V: Charting Your Networking Future

This part describes new and possible future networking features. Chapter 16, "To the Internet and Beyond," describes the direction of change for the Internet. Chapter 17, "Preparing for an Explosion of Network Content," describes new types of Internet content that are becoming available. Chapter 18, "Networking Your Kitchen Appliances?" talks about new devices and appliances that are being connected to computer networks.

Appendix: Speak Like a Geek: The Networking Bible

This contains a glossary of networking terms.

Let's Go...

If you are ready to begin making the connections that speed bits of information around your home, around the office, or around the world, we invite you to turn the page and step into the journey with us.

We sincerely hope that you enjoy this book. If you have any questions, or answers, feel free to contact us at:

Chris Negus   chris.negus@iname.com

Bill Wagner   bwagner@altavista.net

Part 1

Scouting Out Your Network

You've been getting along just fine without a network. The tin cans and string between you and your employees' offices work great. Paper airplanes are fine for distributing memos. "If it ain't broke, don't fix it," you always say...

...Okay, so you have a sneaking suspicion that communication in your organization could be more efficient. The chapters in this part describe networks (Chapter 1, "What Is a Network?"), Local Area Networks (Chapter 2, "Having Your Own Network (LAN)"), and the Internet (Chapter 3, "Using a World-Wide Network (the Internet)").

What Is a Network?

In This Chapter

➤ Understand how computer networks began

➤ Learn what a network consists of

➤ Understand how networks can grow

➤ Learn about network layers and OSI

Computer networks are used to share information. With a network, you can open a document from a computer in the next room or view a Web page from another continent. You can grab movie clips or music from remote sites and play them on your computer. You can even participate in real-time discussions, multi-user games, or conferences.

With easy-to-use applications (such as Web browsers and email readers) and a bit of practice, using a computer network isn't much more complicated than using a telephone. However, to most people, the way that networks bring information to their computers is a mystery.

The aim of this book is to help unlock that mystery. When you are done reading, you should understand how information gets around on computer networks, be able to make intelligent decisions about using and purchasing network products, and even set up and manage a simple network yourself. The first step is to understand what the pieces are that make up a computer network.

How Computer Networks Began

Computer networking as it is today didn't just drop from the sky, fully configured and ready to run. In fact, it all started out rather messy. A little bit of history about the development of computer networks should help put this technology into perspective for you.

Computer networks came about as an afterthought. Mainframes, which are large, multi-user computers, were the first computers used by corporations. The first computers for home use were Apple Computers (IIe, Lisa, Macintosh, and so on) and IBM-compatible PCs designed for personal use.

Companies that created these computers were slow to create products to connect their computers together on a network (let alone to communicate with other computers). When it came right down to it, however, it was the U.S. government that came up with the solution that would allow internetworking of the different kinds of networks.

Networks for Mainframes

At first, large mainframe computers ruled the world. Users could share a database, exchange email, or run the same applications because everything was stored on the same massive computer. Instead of everyone having a PC at their desks, they would each have dumb character terminals hard-wired to the mainframe. These character terminals had no graphics or colors. There was only text on the screen.

When a company needed to add more computers, each computer vendor had its own way of networking its own computers together. And, as you might guess, the networks didn't talk to other vendors' computers. Why should a computer vendor create networking that might encourage you to buy someone else's computer?

IBM created some of the earliest networking protocols. Binary Synchronous Protocol (BSC) existed in the 1960s and was later replaced by Synchronous Data Link Control (SDLC) protocol. With SDLC, communication with other computers was available across wide-area networks, as well as among computers that were located behind the fishbowl of massive company computer centers.

The problems started when diverse computing equipment was preventing a company's own hardware components from talking to each other. In response, large computer vendors began creating their own internetworking strategies to interconnect their computers. IBM came up with its Systems Network Architecture (SNA) whereas Digital Equipment Corporation (which is now part of Compaq Computer Corp.) created DecNet to connect its computers.

Little was being done, however, to interconnect equipment from different vendors. Although this was a problem for many computer companies and their customers, it was seen as a larger problem by the U.S. government, which didn't want any single computer vendor controlling the future of network computing.

The Government Steps In

By the 1960s, the U.S. government was having its own problems interconnecting its computers. This was seen not only as an inconvenience, but as a potential threat to national security. In 1969, the Advanced Research Project Agency (ARPA), which was part of the Department of Defense, was given the task to develop an experimental computer network. That network would have to

➤ Keep working in the event of war or natural disaster.

➤ Have no single point of failure. So, if part of the network were destroyed, information could find another route to its destination.

➤ Interconnect a variety of computer systems and network protocols.

The result of this effort was a network architecture referred to as ARPAnet (Advanced Research Projects Agency Network). At first ARPAnet was used to connect four universities (UCLA, Stanford Research Institute, UC Santa Barbara, and University of Utah) that were doing government research. The network could be used to transfer files, log in to another computer on the network, and run applications on another computer on the network. However, there were not yet protocols that would allow networks of different types to be interconnected. That wouldn't happen until 1973.

In 1973, the Stanford Research Institute was commissioned by ARPA to create the protocols that would allow the interconnection of different types of networks. The result was the Transmission Control Protocol/Internet Protocol (TCP/IP). This set of protocols defined some of the most basic requirements of ARPAnet:

➤ How networked computers are named and addressed

➤ How messages are routed across multiple subnetworks

➤ How diverse networks are connected together

The early development and growth of what would become the Internet mostly interconnected universities, government agencies, and defense contractors. By 1985, the National Science Foundation (a U.S. government agency) took over ARPAnet. One of its major contributions was to interconnect six U.S. government-supported supercomputer centers. This was done through the creation of NSFNET: a high-speed, high-capacity network backbone.

With the creation of the World Wide Web in the mid-1980s, Internet growth shifted toward commercial sites (.COMs) and began heading toward its most explosive growth. Commercial networks began to take over the long-haul traffic previously handled by NFSNET (which was phased out in 1995). Today, the Internet is by far the world's most popular wide area network (WAN).

PCs Take the LAN Route

Personal computer networks came about from a completely different direction. Personal computers gained popularity in homes and small offices, rather than massive corporate computer rooms. So, when the economics of connecting PCs to share files, printers, and other devices became apparent, *Local Area Networks (LANs)* became the network medium of choice.

Companies such as 3Com and Novell first saw the possibilities of networking PCs. 3Com created Ethernet cards for connecting PCs together. Novell created NetWare file and print servers and marketed them along with Ethernet hardware to allow the computers in small businesses to communicate. IBM entered the fray with a different type of LAN called *Token Ring*. Other companies, such as AT&T with its StarLAN networking products, also created their own LAN protocols and devices.

Merging the LANs and the WANs

The convergence of massive corporate networks and small business or home networks was not an easy task. Suddenly small networks needed to protect themselves from viruses and hackers from the outside world. The LAN is still the small business's network of choice, but connectivity to the Internet, in some form, is becoming a requirement.

Check This Out

The distinction between public and private networks needs to be very clear. The rest of this book is organized in terms of public networks (such as the Internet) and private networks (such as an Ethernet LAN that you set up for your home or business).

The underlying premise of the Internet is that it is a network of networks. As that phrase implies, the Internet acts as an umbrella to uniquely identify every computer connected to it and to help determine the routes between those computers. In other words, the Internet is the public glue between lots of private networks.

A book on networking can go on about the hundreds of protocols and pieces of equipment that have ever sent bits of data across the room or across the globe. The truth is, however, that as computer networking has advanced, two key technologies now dominate how computers are interconnected:

➤ **Ethernet**   For local area networks (LANs), Ethernet is by far the technology that is most often used for transmitting data.

➤ **TCP/IP**   For the Internet and other wide-area networks, TCP/IP is the protocol that is used.

As for how you would go about building and connecting your own network, those two technologies align well with the way some of the discussions are organized in this book. Information is aligned according to

➤ **Private Networks**   If you are creating a network for your home or office, you control how your computers and other equipment are connected. You are also responsible for assigning names and addresses for each component on the network. Most likely, you would first create a LAN using Ethernet cards, hubs, and compatible wiring or cabling.

➤ **Public Networks**   If you wanted to connect your own computer (or the network of computers in your office) to a public network, chances are you would connect to the Internet. That requires using TCP/IP protocols.

For information to come and go between your network and the Internet, you need to configure a router to route information across that boundary between the private and public network. To be able to communicate across that boundary, you must use names and addresses that are assigned to you by authorities for the Internet.

Pieces of a Network

Every computer network includes *media*, *protocols*, and *applications*. Though we refine and expand on the components that make up a network later in this chapter (and throughout the book), nearly everything we discuss in this book falls into one of these three categories.

Network Media

Every network requires some physical medium for transporting information from one point to the next. Those media often consist of cables (made of copper or fiber optics), though they also can be the airwaves that carry satellite, microwave, or other wireless transmissions.

A lot of different equipment for transmitting data over the network media is described in this book. Common networking equipment that is connected to your computer includes *network interface cards (NICs)* and *modulator/demodulators (modems)*.

Modems are used to communicate greater distances over telephone lines or over direct cabling to connect to *Wide Area Networks (WANs)*. Standard dial-up modems provide slower transmission rates than are available with newer xDSL modems. To pass data between multiple networks, special pieces of equipment called *routers* are used.

NICs are often used with small networks referred to as *Local Area Networks (LANs)*. A NIC is the access point from your computer to the LAN. The NIC handles sending and receiving data and provides a place to plug in the network cable.

If you build your own LAN, you may use other equipment such as *hubs* and *switches*. A hub provides a central location for connecting together a group of computers on a LAN. A switch provides a means of connecting together multiple hubs and/or individual computers in a way that allows the network to still perform efficiently.

9

Network Protocols

You may wonder how networks know how to transmit data, manage the flow of information, and find destination computers that could be thousands of miles away. The answer is that networks use what are called *protocols*.

Protocols are sets of rules for managing data. They define when each side of a communication can send and receive data and how errors are dealt with. Protocols must also understand addresses, so they know whether to give the data they receive to an application program or to pass it on to the next destination on the network.

Groups of protocols typically work together to form different types of networks. For example, *Ethernet* protocols are used to define how information is transmitted on most LANs. *Transmission Control Protocol/Internet Protocol (TCP/IP)* protocols define how information is managed and transmitted on the Internet.

Network Applications

Once physical networks (wires, NICs, hubs, modems, etc.) are in place and protocols (Ethernet or TCP/IP) are configured, network applications are what use the networks to communicate. Applications can include *Web browsers* (for viewing Web pages), *email readers* (for reading and sending email), and *chat programs* (for chatting online).

Network applications work by requesting a *service* from another computer on the network. The application that requests a service is referred to as a *client*. The program on the other computer that receives the request is referred to as a *server*.

The terms client and server are used to refer both to the programs that request and provide services and to the computer hardware. For example, a *workstation* (a computer used by an individual) is considered to be a *client computer*. In contrast, a computer that is used by many people at once, storing and distributing large amounts of files, Web pages, or other data, is referred to as a *server computer*.

A *Really* Simple Network

To keep things from getting too technical right from the start, take a look at the following extraordinarily simple illustration. Figure 1.1 is not a computer network, but rather a simple communications network, consisting of a string connecting two tin cans.

This first network illustrates a few concepts that are similar to those of computer networks described in the rest of this book. The string represents the cables that information passes across on your network. The cans represent the endpoints where information is received, like modems or network interface cards (NICs) connected to a computer. (Modems are covered in Chapter 4 and NICs are discussed in Chapter 8, "Building Your Home Network.")

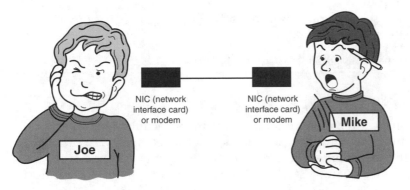

Figure 1.1

The simplest network I can think of: two kids, two cans, and a string.

In the illustration, the two kids can represent *computer systems* that send information back and forth. Imagine that one is talking while the other listens, and then the other will talk while the first one listens. If they had a signal, such as the word "stop," when each kid was done speaking, it could make communication smoother by preventing both kids from talking at the same time. The kids also might have rules for greetings so that Mike can verify that it is really Joe at the other end of the string. Those rules are similar to protocols used by computer networks.

Now let's take this example up to the next level, which is a little less obvious. For the moment, let's assume that the boys who are holding the cans are passing requests and information back and forth that they get from other people. With that in mind, you could add Sally and Susie to the illustration as clients and servers (see Figure 1.2). These clients and servers would operate at a higher layer than the boys holding the cans. (The concept of layers is described later in this chapter.)

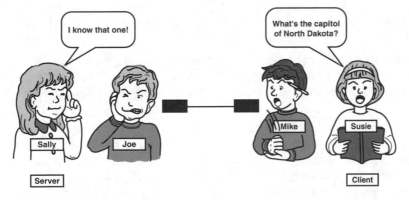

Figure 1.2

Adding clients and servers to a network.

Mike has a friend named Susie who wants to ask a friend of Joe's named Sally, "What's the capitol of North Dakota?" Susie could be said to be a client (requesting a service) and Sally could be a server (supplying the service). So, Susie asks Mike to send the question to Joe, and then pass it to Sally to have her answer it. Sally answers the

11

question (providing the service) and tells it to Joe. The message goes back to Mike who delivers it to Sally.

You have just seen an example of a client/server network!

How a Simple Network Can Grow

Running a wire or cable between two computers, writing a document on one computer, and sending it to a printer that is attached to another computer isn't too difficult. That is essentially the same process that happened with the cans-and-string example. You set up a wire, ask for a service from one computer, and provide it from another.

Because you bought a whole book on the subject of networking, however, you probably want to do a lot more with your computer network than connect two computers. So, let's drop the can and string and return to real computer networks to understand how those networks might grow.

A network consisting of one wire, or cable, and two computers (as represented by our tin can and string example) might be useful, but it's quite limited in the real world. Let's start with a simple computer network that consists of two computers, one of which has a printer that it can share over the network with the other computer, that are connected by a single wire. Here are some reasons you might want to add some complexity to this simple physical network:

➤ **Adding client computers**   What if, instead of having one computer that wants to share the printer, there are five? One solution is to purchase a *hub* (see Chapter 4) and plug all the computers and the printer into that hub. Another would be to connect them to a *bus* (see Chapter 6, "Take a Bus, Hitch a Star, Ring Around Network Topologies"), which essentially strings a wire or cable between each computer and terminates it at each end.

➤ **Connecting different kinds of networks**   Maybe one is a high-speed (100MB) LAN, whereas the other is a low-speed (10MB) LAN. You could connect the two networks using a *switch* (see Chapter 9, "Hooking Up Your Small Office Network").

➤ **Different kinds of logical networks**   What if you want the computers on your network to be able to communicate with computers on a network at another company? If both companies' networks were TCP/IP (in other words, part of the Internet or an intranet), you could add a *router* to your network and have the router use a *dial-up modem* or some high-speed connection to reach the remote network.

Using standard cabling, NICs, and hubs, you often can set up a simple network or configure an Internet connection in less than an hour. For larger networks, you can choose from a variety of network hardware vendors or network service providers. A decade or two ago, setting up computer networks was much tougher.

Network Layering and the OSI Reference Model

Networks are created in layers. To illustrate that fact, the Open System Interconnection Reference Model (OSI-RM) is often used. It is a seven-layer model that represents how networking protocols and services work together to form a computer network. The seven layers represent everything from the physical electrical transmission of bits on a wire (level 1) to the distributed network services available to user application programs (level 7).

OSI was designed to provide a framework for coordinating development of networking standards, while allowing existing protocols to fit into that framework. The International Organization for Standardization (ISO) developed this model and, along with organizations representing governments around the world, continues to develop and issue related standards.

Not every network needs to implement every standard, or even every layer, for the network to work. For example, network applications on similar computer systems may communicate directly to the transport layer. Even when all seven layers are represented on communication-end systems, there are usually communications nodes in between that only implement some of the lower layers.

OSI Illustration

The OSI reference model is easier to understand if you look at a picture. Figure 1.3 illustrates how the seven layers of the OSI Reference Model are organized. It shows two end systems, with the communication passing through a network-level node.

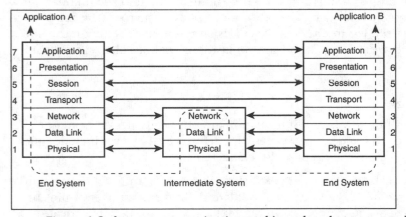

Figure 1.3

The OSI Reference Model divides networking services into seven layers.

Figure 1.3 shows communications taking place between application A and application B on two different computers. In this illustration, the communication crosses two different types of networks, with a network router managing the communication between the two networks. For example, the network level node could be a TCP/IP router that routes messages between one computer on a LAN and another computer that could be reached over a dial-up connection. The two computers can communicate, even though they are connected to two different networks. (If a single LAN connected the two computers, we would only show the two end systems.)

Here are some things about the illustration in Figure 1.3 that will help you understand the OSI Reference Model:

➤ The applications shown here are communicating over a full OSI protocol stack. This means each application can make requests for services, such as a file copy request or database query, without knowing anything about the location of that resource on the network.

➤ The applications request services from the application layer, which requests services from the presentation layer, which requests services from the session layer, and so on all the way down to the physical layer before leaving end system A.

➤ Each layer negotiates with its peer layer (the layer of the same name on the next adjacent system that implements that layer) to obtain the requested service.

➤ There are different protocols that could be used to represent each of the layers. This is particularly true from the network layer and below, which could consist of a variety of wide area and local area networks.

The Seven OSI Layers

Each of the seven layers has specific services it must offer to layers above as well as the means to request services from layers below. The following sections describe the characteristics of each of the seven layers.

Building a network is similar to building a house. You need to build the foundation (the wires and transmission protocols) before you can put on the roof (the applications to use the network). For that reason, layer 1 is represented as being on the bottom of the illustration while layer 7 (and the applications that use all seven layers) is shown at the top.

The Physical Layer

The physical layer defines how bits of information are physically passed from one communication device to the next. Characteristics defined at this layer include functional, electrical, mechanical, and procedural characteristics.

An example of a physical layer standard is *RS-232C*. The COM1 and COM2 ports on the back of your PC are RS-232C ports. This standard defines the number of pins on the connector, the size of the connector, and the type and meaning of electrical signals that go across the pins. Modems are the most common networking equipment to attach to an RS-232C port.

Data Link Layer

The job of the data link layer is to start the link between two communications devices, manage the link, and make the link inactive. Some amount of error correction is done by this layer to ensure that the raw stream of bits begin passed by the physical layer are reliable.

Besides providing error checking, the data link layer must handle flow control (to prevent more information flowing to the next device than the device can handle). A simple point-to-point link consists of managing data on a single wire between two devices, while multi-point links might consist of many peer stations broadcasting on the same line.

Network Layer

The network layer is by far the most complex of the seven layers. This layer must understand the underlying transmission technologies that connect network entities (end systems and routers). The network layer is designed to shield the transport layer from these complexities, so the transport layer can simply request communication from an end system.

Because OSI encompasses entities that are sometimes referred to networks on their own, OSI refers to those entities as *subnetworks*. To manage the different types of subnetworks, the network layer implements internetworking features that allow data to be routed over the different subnetworks.

The network layer supports both connectionless and connection-oriented subnetworks.

Transport Layer

The transport layer is responsible for providing end-to-end communication between communications end systems. This layer must be able to accept transport addresses, establish and terminate connections, and manage flow control of data.

The transport layer supports both connectionless and connection-oriented networks. There are five different transport protocols:

➤ TP0   Connection-oriented protocol that segments and reassembles transport layer data. This is the most basic transport protocol.

➤ TP1   Connection-oriented protocol that, on top of segmenting and reassembling data, can re-send unacknowledged data units. When many errors occur, this protocol can restart the connection.

➤ TP2   Connection-oriented protocol that can segment and reassemble data, plus it can handle *multiplexing* over a single virtual circuit. Multiplexing is when several streams of data can be sent simultaneously over the same communications channel.

➤ TP3   Connection-oriented protocol that does segmentation, re-assembly, and error recovery (like TP1). However, it also can multiplex data (like TP2).

➤ TP4   Can function as a connection-oriented or a connectionless protocol. This protocol can provide reliable transport, assuming an underlying network that does not do error detection.

The transport layer can be thought of as the top of the subnetwork services. All layers above transport provide services to applications, as opposed to managing the transmission of data between systems or devices.

Session Layer

The session layer lets applications control the interactions that occur during a communications session. For example, this layer can control which entity can send data at what times. The session layer is particularly useful when data entered during a session needs to be kept in sync.

During the course of a session transaction, a user may be able to go back to a major or minor sync point. For example, with a grocery checkout application a clerk might enter in the wrong price. The session layer could allow the clerk to back up to the previous item entered (minor sync point) or possibly back out all of the items from the customer (major sync point).

Presentation Layer

The presentation layer manages the presentation of data between application entities. Different computer systems can represent data in different ways. The presentation layer can, therefore, allow the two entities to agree on the type of data representation they will use and implement exchanges using the chosen data representation.

You could use a presentation protocol, for example, to encrypt data or to present data in a generic way that could then be translated into a form that could be used by a specific type of terminal.

The Abstract Syntax Notation (ISO ASN.1) is a way of representing different types of data in much the same way that programming languages do. A tag represents each data type, identifying the class of data as universal, application-wide, context-specific, or private. The tag also identifies the particular item of data within that class.

Application Layer

The application layer offers a variety of services to the application programs. This layer communicates directly with the user process that is engaging in the communication. Here are some of the application service elements that are supported at the application layer:

➤ File Transfer, Access, and Management (FTAM)   Defines how remote files are accessed and a means of transferring files.

➤ Common Management Information Protocol (CMIP)   Defines a management information base (MIB) and objects for managing data.

➤ Message Handling System (MHS)   Defines methods for delivering email among hosts. MHS is based on the CCITT X.400 protocol.

➤ Virtual Terminal (VT)   Defines how terminals can be emulated across networks.

➤ Directory Services (DS)   Defines methods for naming services, hosts and other network items. DS is based on CCITT X.500 protocol.

Unless you are developing networking protocols or applications, you do not need to know many details about the OSI reference model. On occasion, however, an OSI layer may be associated with a piece of network equipment (for example, a level-two switch or a level-three router). Understanding how equipment and protocols fit into this model can help you understand the functions they provide.

What Can You Get from This Book?

When you are done with this book, you should be able to

➤ Connect a network in your home or business (a LAN).

➤ Plug into a larger network (the Internet).

➤ Plan for and choose your network wiring and equipment.

➤ Share network resources, such as files, printers, Web pages, and CD-ROMs.

➤ Use your network to the max, for Web browsing, multi-user games, email, news-groups, application sharing, and other features.

➤ Understand how to secure your network.

➤ Prepare yourself for the incredible new content, network appliances, and huge increase in bandwidth coming to the Internet.

If you only want to read this book to find out how to use an existing network to browse the Web, read some email, and maybe play games, skip right to Chapter 10, "Taking Your Network for a Drive." That chapter will provide you with a survey of the coolest things you can do with your network. For the rest of you, full speed ahead.

Where To From Here?

From here, you might want to check out Chapters 2 and 3. Those chapters will give you a sense of what goes into building your own LAN (Chapter 2) and using the Internet (Chapter 3).

The Least You Need to Know

➤ A network can be as simple as two computers and one wire, or cable.

➤ Your private network can grow by adding hubs and switches to connect your computers.

➤ Connections to public networks, such as the Internet, rely on routers to reach remote computers.

➤ Computer internetworking arose from a mish-mosh of incompatible networking protocols, developed by computer vendors who were set on protecting their own businesses.

➤ The first PC computer networks relied on LAN technology (especially Ethernet) to connect. That trend continues today.

➤ Networks are built in layers. The OSI-RM is a common model used to represent how computer networks work.

➤ The rest of this book focuses on helping you create your own private, LAN-based network and connect it to the Internet.

Chapter 2

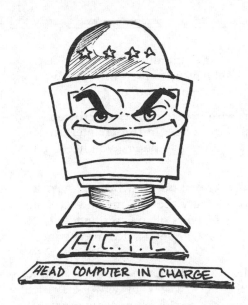

Having Your Own Network (LAN)

In this chapter

➤ Understand what a LAN is

➤ Learn how Ethernet LANs work

➤ Learn how to expand the capacity of a LAN

Before you worry about how computer networks direct data around the world, you should understand the most common small network technology: the local area network (LAN). If you want to connect the computers in your home or small business, a LAN is where you begin.

You don't need to know much about how a LAN works to use one. For that reason, this chapter introduces the most common equipment used to create your first LAN. Then it will direct you to other chapters for details on choosing equipment (Chapter 4, "Choosing Your Networking Hardware"), choosing networked workstations and servers (Chapter 5, "Network Servers and Clients at Your Service"), and designing network topologies (Chapter 6, "Take a Bus, Hitch a Star, Ring Around Network Topologies")

If you decide not to skip ahead after the chapter has introduced the basic building blocks of your LAN, you can stick around for descriptions of how the Ethernet LAN technologies work. Understanding how LANs work will give you better insight into the decisions you need to make later about how to purchase equipment, set up your LAN, and grow your network.

What Is a LAN?

A *local area network (LAN)* is a method of connecting a small number of computers within a limited geographical location. For example, you would create a LAN to connect the computers in your home or in a small office building. Although the distances, speeds, and numbers of computers on a LAN have increased with technology improvements, the LAN is still the most basic, useful type of computer network.

To have a LAN, you need at least two computers within a short distance (the distances are covered in the "Measuring Distances" section later in this chapter) that want to communicate with each other. To connect those computers, you need at least two types of equipment, and possibly three:

➤ **Network interface**   Typically each computer on your network will have a network interface card (NIC) that has as its sole duty the sending and receiving of data to and from the LAN. Although there are ways of connecting to a LAN using other ports on a computer (such as the parallel port), NICs are the most common way to connect.

➤ **Network medium**   Wires or cables are the most common network medium for carrying data between the computers and other devices on your network. Twisted pair (which looks like the wire you use to connect your telephone) and coaxial cable (which is like the cable used to connect your cable television) are the most common types of wiring for small LANs. Today, there are also wireless options and media such as *fiber-optic* (that allow longer distances) for connecting your LAN.

➤ **Hub**   The hub is the connecting point for the wire from your computer's NIC; it is the most common method of joining the wires that make up a small LAN. A hub is optional because you can skip the hub and just connect computers together in a chain using coaxial cable. Most LANs today, however, connect together using one or more hubs.

If you are purchasing new LAN equipment, make sure you get equipment that can work together. For example, you want to choose equipment that

➤ Uses the same LAN technology (such as Ethernet)

➤ Supports the same speed of data transmission (such as 10 or 100 million bits per second)

➤ Provides ports for the same types of connectors and cabling (such as RJ-45 on twisted pair cables or BNC on coaxial cables) See Chapter 4, "Choosing Your Networking Hardware," for descriptions of these cables and connectors.

Although it is possible to connect computers with network cards that run at different speeds and that use different kinds of cables, if you are starting from scratch, the best results come from matching the equipment. Before covering the details of how to choose and purchase different equipment, take a look at an example of a basic Ethernet LAN.

Connect a Basic Ethernet LAN

For the sake of simplicity, this chapter describes one type of LAN technology in detail: Ethernet. Ethernet is by far the most popular type of LAN technology, with constant improvements extending its lead over other LAN technologies. (See "Ethernet: The Killer LAN," later in this chapter for details.)

To put together the LAN, you need a NIC for each computer, the correct cabling, and a hub. Figure 2.1 shows an example of a LAN that uses this equipment.

The following sections contain basic information about these components.

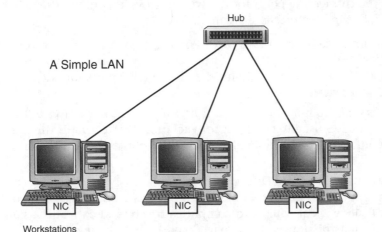

Figure 2.1

Build a simple LAN with a NIC in each computer, a hub, and a wire from each computer to the hub.

Install a NIC for each computer

The first thing you need to do is install an Ethernet NIC in each computer. Some computers today come with Ethernet cards already installed. A few years ago, computers rarely came with NICs. So, you might need to install a card yourself if your computer is NIC-less.

Ethernet NICs are defined by their transmission speeds and types of connectors/cabling. If you have a NIC already installed on your computer, you should see ports on the NIC from the back of your computer. Most likely, your NIC will have an RJ-45 port, although it might also (or instead) have AUI or BNC ports. Figure 2.2 shows examples of several NICs in the 3Com 3C509 series.

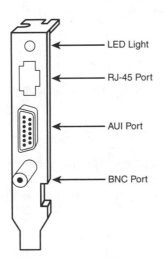

Figure 2.2

NICs can have RJ-45, AUI, or BNC ports, such as those shown for popular 3COM 3C509 cards.

21

The different types of NICs that are available are described in detail in Chapter 4.

A Hub for the LAN

Recall that the hub is the connecting point for the wire from your computer's NIC. A hub typically has the following features (see Figure 2.3):

➤ **Ports**   Typical hubs have from 2 to 24 ports. Ports are the outlets where you plug in your cables. Most ports for low-end hubs allow you to plug in twisted pair wiring with RJ-45 connectors. Some hubs will also have ports for one or more BNC or AUI connectors.

➤ **LEDs**   Little lights on the hub can tell you things about the condition of the hub. For example, there's usually one light for each port, indicating if the port is working, not connected, or faulty (which causes the port to be turned off or *partitioned*).

Depending on the model, other LEDs can indicate the activity on the LAN. For example, there might be an LED that blinks when packets are sent or when collisions occur. (Collisions occur when two computers try to send data at the same time, causing both transmissions to be damaged and have to be re-sent.)

➤ **Uplink button**   Some hubs include a button that changes one of the ports from a normal to a cross-over connection. This allows you to use a standard Ethernet cable to connect hubs together.

Figure 2.3

Hubs, such as this 3Com OfficeConnect Ethernet Hub, can have RJ-45, AUI, or BNC ports.

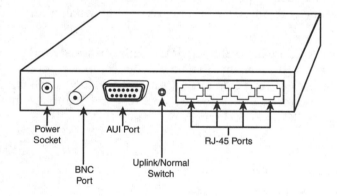

Power Socket

AUI Port

RJ-45 Ports

BNC Port

Uplink/Normal Switch

If you don't know what all these connectors are yet or how they work, don't worry. They are explained in detail later in this chapter.

Wires to Connect Them

With NICS installed and your hub ready, you next need to connect the ports from each NIC to the hub. To do this, you need cable that has connectors to match the ports supported by your NICs and your hub. Different cable types are described in Chapter 4.

Firing Up the LAN

To make your LAN operational, you need to plug in the power to your equipment and boot up the computers connected to the hub. At this point, from a purely theoretical, networking view, your LAN should be working. In a more practical sense, to get everything working, you might need to do a few other procedures for the computers on your LAN:

➤ **Install NIC drivers** Most computer operating systems will automatically detect common NICs and install the software (called *drivers*) needed to run the NIC. If that is the case, you probably won't need to do anything further related to the NIC's driver.

If the NIC cannot be detected, you will probably see an error message and be asked to install the driver. Your NIC might have come with a disk containing the driver or you might have to visit the manufacturer's Web site to get the latest driver.

➤ **Configure networking support** Although the computers on your LAN can communicate now, they might not be able to share files, printers, and other computing resources yet. You probably

Check This Out

If you are using a Microsoft operating system, check out the Microsoft Web site (http://www.microsoft.com) if you are having a problem getting your NIC to work. By typing the model number of your NIC into the search box, you can sometimes find solutions to problems that other people have had with the same NIC.

need to identify your NIC to each computer's operating system. This usually entails setting up network support, such as workstation support (for Windows file and print sharing) or TCP/IP support (for many other kinds of network services). See Chapters 7, "Making Those Internet Connections," or 8, "Building Your Home Network," for information on configuring networking for your operating system.

At this point, you should have a working LAN! Although the preceding information results in a working network, it just scratches the surface of all the choices you have for equipment, topologies, and expansion for your LAN. (And, security hasn't even been touched on yet!)

To go beyond this simple network, you should have a better understanding of how LANs work. For that, continue on with the description of Ethernet.

Ethernet: The Killer LAN

Although several different LAN technologies have been developed, Ethernet is by far the most popular LAN technology. Industry reports claim that Ethernet is being used by more than 80% of the world's interconnected computers. Other LAN technologies, such as Token Ring and Fiber Distributed Data Interface (FDDI), significantly trail Ethernet in market share.

Here are some of the reasons Ethernet is so popular:

➤ **Inexpensive**   The cost of an Ethernet starter kit (four-port hub, two Ethernet cards, and two cables) starts at around $100. Cheap 10Mbps NICs (which I don't particularly recommend) start at about $15. Extra computers and hubs can be added as you need them, typically without needing to upgrade your other equipment. (A bit is the smallest unit of data on a computer, consisting of a 0 or a 1. A 10Mbps NIC can transmit up to 10 million of these bits every second.)

➤ **Reliable**   With years of development behind it, the Ethernet technologies have evolved into a stable and reliable networking platform. Its success has also encouraged the development of new tools for troubleshooting and managing Ethernet networks. You can usually use the same tools as your increase the speed of your Ethernet to gigabyte speed (or higher).

➤ **Ready to Grow**   New technologies have been developed to allow Ethernet networks to grow dramatically beyond the small workgroups it was originally intended to serve. With technologies such as segmentation (that keep local traffic from clogging the whole LAN) and transmission rates growing from 10Mbps to 100Mbps to 1,000Mbps, Ethernet LANs can grow from small offices to entire campuses.

Standardization of Ethernet protocols has also ensured that products from different vendors can work together. Ethernet standards are handled by an organization called the IEEE.

Characteristics of the First Ethernet LANs

Ethernet is based on standards that are managed by the Institute of Electrical and Electronics Engineers, Inc. (IEEE), which is commonly referred to as "Eye-triple-E" by those in the electronics industry. The basic standard that aligns with the first Ethernet versions is 802.3. Most of the fundamental characteristics of 802.3 still apply to Ethernet today, although they have been enhanced to allow new types of cabling and higher transmission speeds. Here are some of the characteristics of the 802.3 specifications.

➤ **Carrier Sense Multiple Access with Collision Detection (CSMA/CD)** CSMA/CD describes the method by which information is transmitted on the LAN and how the network recovers from error conditions (such as when data collides because two computers tried to talk on the network at the same time).

➤ **10Mbps speed**   The original IEEE 802.3 specification defined operations at transmission rates of 10 million bits per second (10Mbps).

➤ **Coaxial cable**   Coaxial (coax) cables connect to the computer's network interface card through a transceiver that manages many of the physical functions, such as detection of collisions. Supported types of coax included thinnet and thicknet cables. Each *segment* (that is, the distance between each computer) could be 185 meters (thinnet) or 500 meters (thicknet).

➤ **Bus architecture** In a bus architecture, the computer connects to a wire coming from an adjacent computer. The connection then either continues to the next computer or caps off the network by adding a terminator (terminators are described in Chapter 4).

To improve connection speeds and distances allowed, higher speed transmission rates, different cabling alternatives, and other bus architectures have been added to 802.3 specifications. However, if a network is to be called an Ethernet network, it communicates by means of CSMA/CD.

Starting with the simple 10Mbps LAN where a few computers are connected in a hub, the next section describes how communication can take place between the computers on the LAN.

How an Ethernet Network Works

Ethernet LANs work by broadcasting bits of information on to the LAN's wire so that all stations on the LAN can see them. Those bits are organized into variable-length units known as *frames*. Making sure the frames are delivered properly to their destinations is the job of the CSMA/CD media-access process. Each frame contains information identifying the following components:

➤ **Preamble** Verifies that this is a frame.

➤ **Destination address** Indicates where the frame is going.

➤ **Source address** Indicates where the frame came from.

➤ **Type** Indicates what protocol will get the data after it arrives at its intended system.

The frame also contains the data that the frame is carrying and a frame checking sequence (FCS) that the computer receiving the data uses to check that the frame wasn't damaged in transmission. Figure 2.4 shows an example of an Ethernet Frame.

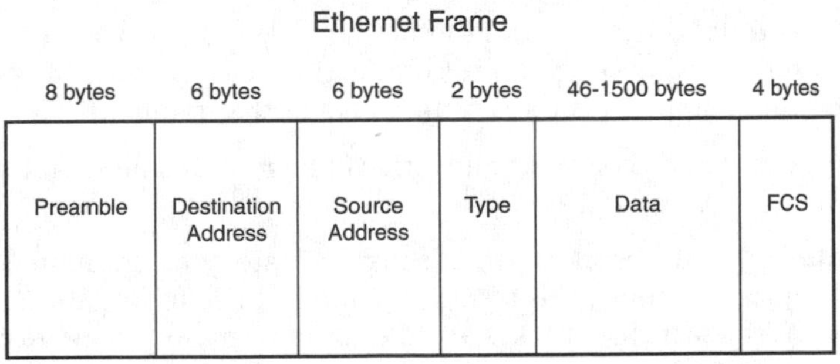

Ethernet Frame

Figure 2.4

Bits of data are organized together in frames on an Ethernet network.

8 bytes	6 bytes	6 bytes	2 bytes	46-1500 bytes	4 bytes
Preamble	Destination Address	Source Address	Type	Data	FCS

Every computer on the LAN sees every frame that is sent. If the frame is intended for a particular station, that station consumes that packet and passes its data to the higher-level protocol that will use the data.

25

The station that consumes the frame might or might not be the computer that ultimately uses the information the frame contains. For example, the frame might be intended for a router on the LAN that takes the data and routes it to another LAN or the Internet. Or the frame might be intended for a file transfer program that allows the data to be copied to the local computer. The frame gets to the next station and lets higher-level protocols decide what is to be done with the data it contains.

Techno Tip

A technique called *segmenting* can be used so that every station on a LAN doesn't have to see every frame. With segmenting, a switch is used as a boundary between LAN segments. As a result, frames intended for stations on the local segment never get sent to other segments. This can significantly improve total performance of the LAN. See Chapter 4 for descriptions of switches.

Directing Traffic: CSMA/CD

Whether on a 10Mbps LAN connected with copper wires or a 1,000Mbps LAN using fiber-optic cables, CSMA/CD makes the rules of how information is transmitted and errors are managed on an Ethernet LAN. To understand how Ethernet works, it helps to break down CSMA/CD and describe its component names: Carrier Sense, Multiple Access, and Collision Detection.

Carrier Sense: Is It Safe to Jump In?

Before a computer begins sending its data on an Ethernet network, its NIC uses a technique called *carrier sensing*. This means that the computer checks the state of the network to make sure no other computer is transmitting data at that moment.

There are three different states that a CSMA/CD network can be in: transmission, idle, or contention. Here is what your computer does, based on the state that it senses:

➤ **Transmission state**   If the network is in transmission state, your computer waits until the transmission is done, plus a *propagation* time. The propagation time takes into account the fact that it takes a while for information to get from one end of the network to the other. So, your computer will sense that the network is in an idle state when the propagation time has elapsed following the most recent transmission. (In other words, the network has been quiet for the waiting period after the most recent transmission.)

➤ **Idle state**   If your computer perceives that the network is in an idle state, it goes ahead and begins transmitting data.

➤ **Contention state**   When two computers have broadcast data at the same time, and data transmissions have been damaged, the network goes into a contention state.

This is not, by its nature, a perfect system. Especially on busy systems, it can happen that two computers both believe that it is safe to transmit at the same time and begin sending data. What happens then is a collision (discussed shortly), which puts the network in a state of contention.

Multiple Access: Sharing the Wealth

Ethernet is what is known as a *shared broadcast technology*. This means that all computers on the Ethernet LAN share the same wire (in other words, they can have *multiple access*) and broadcast information on the network so everyone can see it. All computers on your Ethernet segment recognize all data on the wire and take only the transmissions meant for them. There's no channel or wire that provides a dedicated path between your computer and the computer you exchange information with. (In other words, all computers are contending for space on the same wire so you are not guaranteed a clear path to send your data.)

Because the network is shared, everyone competes for access. It's rather like putting a big bowl of soup on the table, handing everyone a spoon, and saying "take as much as you like." With this arrangement, nobody's bowl is bigger than anyone else's bowl. However, there are two major issues that you must deal with:

➤ Because only one person can take a spoonful (that is, access the network) at a time, how do you determine when it's your turn?

➤ What do you do if, despite your best efforts, two people think it's their turn to take a spoonful and bash into each other's spoons (that is, transmissions have collided)?

Carrier sensing is used to figure out when it is safe to begin transmitting data on an Ethernet network. Collision detection is used to determine if transmissions have collided and deal with the problem.

Collision Detection: Who's Gonna Back Down?

Did you ever sit down to talk with a person, fall into a moment of silence, and then both talk at once? Typically, you would both stop talking, and then not be sure how to start up again. If you were an Ethernet network, you would have *collision detection* to deal with that problem.

When two computers start transmitting at the same moment because they didn't hear anything on the LAN for the required idle time, both transmissions become damaged. Therefore, both computers will need to retransmit their data at some time. When your computer detects a contention state, it goes into a back-off mechanism to figure out when data should be retransmitted.

Here's roughly how the back-off mechanism works. After sensing that a frame it sent was damaged, your computer stops transmitting the frame. After a short wait, it transmits the frame again. If there is another collision, it increases the back-off time by a fixed amount before trying to transmit again. The back-off time is increased with each subsequent failure until after about a half-dozen attempts, the network drops the packet. If a packet is dropped, that information is passed up to a higher level on your computer. If there is an excessive amount of dropped packets, you might see a message from your file transfer program or Web browser that your request failed because the network is congested.

Measuring Distances for Your LAN

The nature of Ethernet itself (that is, Ethernet data must reach the furthest point on the network in a set period of time) places limits on the distances between computers on your Ethernet network. It takes time for bits of information to traverse each meter of cable. Also some types of wire (such as twisted pair) take longer to transmit data than other types (such as fiber-optic fibers).

Although the time between a computer sending a packet and finding out that another computer has sent a packet that collided with it might seem miniscule, multiply that time over a long enough distance and you have a problem. The problem is that if there is a collision, the notice of that collision might not reach the farthest point on the network in time for the network to maintain its rate of speed.

To determine how far apart computers can be on a LAN, an administrator can do calculations to determine whether or not a bit can be transmitted between the farthest points on the LAN fast enough to maintain the rate of speed for the network (10Mbps, 100Mbps, or 1,000Mbps). This can entail measuring the delay caused by every length of cable and piece of equipment along the worst-case path of the network.

Figuring out bit transmission rates is all well and good if you are managing the growth of your own LAN. For a simple Ethernet LAN, however, there are some general rules that you can use to figure out how long the cables can be to connect your network.

These three cases determine maximum cable distances you could have on a 10Mbps network: The first is your simple Ethernet LAN where twisted-pair (RJ-45) cables connect each workstation to a hub, known as 10BaseT. The second is a bus-style Ethernet LAN where all computers are connected to a thinnet coaxial cable, known as 10Base2. The third is another bus-style LAN, but with computers connected to a thicknet coaxial cable, known as 10Base5.

To help keep the different Ethernet standards straight, fairly simple naming conventions are used with Ethernet standards. Names for these standards come in three parts:

➤ **LAN speed (in million bits per second)** Current LAN speeds are 10-, 100-, or 1,000 million bits per second.

➤ **Base (the method in which signals are carried)**   Most Ethernet proto-cols are *baseband,* meaning that only one signal (that is, one channel of infor-mation) is carried at any one time (as opposed to *broadband,* which can carry multiple signals at a time).

➤ **Type of physical medium**   One or two characters represent the physical medium type. For example, "T" is for twisted pair, "5" is for thicknet, "2" is for thinnet, and FL is for point-to-point fiber-optic cable. Table 2.1 shows some examples:

Table 2.1   Names of Ethernet Standards

Standard Name	Description
10BaseT	10Mbps on unshielded twisted-pair cable
100BaseFX	100Mbps on two-strand multimode fiber-optic cable
1000BaseT	1,000Mbps on Category 5 Unshielded Twisted Pair (UTP) wiring

Check This Out

Note that the distance estimates are just rule–of–thumb. The actual numbers can vary for equipment from different manufacturers. Also, for larger LANs containing multiple hubs, switches, and interconnecting cables, you need to take each leg of the journey between the most distant computers into account to accurately judge acceptable distance.

Cable Distances: Twisted Pair on a Hub (10BaseT)

To be able to maintain 10Mbps transmission rates on a LAN using twisted pair wires (RJ-45), the maximum length of each cable (from computer to hub) is 50 meters. This is because the maximum distance between any two end-systems on this network should not exceed 100 meters. This is referred to as a 10BaseT network, which is illus-trated in Figure 2.5.

Figure 2.5

For twisted pair 10Mbps Ethernet LANs, the maximum distance between end points shouldn't exceed 100 meters.

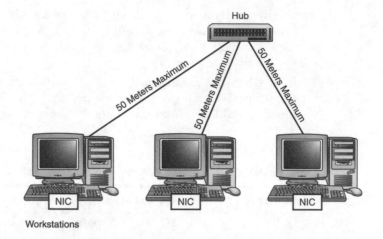

Cable Distances: Thinnet on a Bus (10Base2)

To maintain 10Mbps transmission rates on a LAN using thinnet coaxial cable, the total distance from one end of the network to the other should not exceed 185 meters. Because computers are connected to the bus from one computer to the next in a bus, to determine this distance you measure all cables from one end of the bus to the other. This is referred to as a 10Base2 network, which is illustrated in Figure 2.6.

Figure 2.6

Distances up to 185 meters are allowed on 10Mbps thinnet networks.

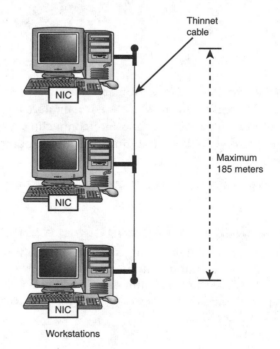

Cable Distances: Thicknet on a Bus (10Base5)

Because delays on thicknet cable are less than delays on thinnet cable, end-to-end thicknet LANs can be longer. Although thicknet cable can be more difficult to handle than thinnet or twisted pair, it can support a maximum distance of up to 500 meters. This is referred to as a 10Base5 network, which is shown in Figure 2.7.

Check This Out

See Chapter 4 for a description of different types of cabling and connectors that are available.

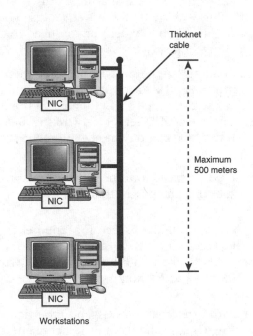

Thicknet cable

Maximum 500 meters

NIC

NIC

NIC

Workstations

Figure 2.7

For a 10Mbps thicknet network, a maximum length of 500 meters is allowed.

Expanding an Ethernet LAN

To this point, discussions have been mainly limited to 10Mbps networks with either twisted pair (on a single hub) or coax cables (on a single bus). Because of the great success of these 10Mbps Ethernet networks, organizations wanted to find ways to grow their overburdened LANs without throwing away their investments.

Here are some ways that a LAN can grow:

➤ **More speed**   Ethernet standards have advanced well beyond the 10Mbps speed of the early Ethernet networks. Today, there are Ethernet standards for 100Mbps speed (also called Fast Ethernet) and 1,000Mbps speed (also called Gigabit Ethernet). There are also standards efforts underway for 10 Gigabit Ethernet.

31

➤ **More Hubs and Switches**   To add more workstations to your LAN, you can chain together multiple hubs. This can work for a while, until too much demand for bandwidth (that is, the amount of data that can go through the medium) begins to slow the network. At that point, a technique called segmenting can be used to separate parts of the LAN using a LAN switch.

Multiplying the size of a LAN can also increase its complexity. With higher speeds, there are suddenly different cabling and equipment requirements.

Speeding Up an Ethernet LAN

Maybe your 10Mbps LAN was fine while you were just sharing a printer at home or connecting three computers at work. But, let's say that you want to use your network for more bandwidth-intensive applications (such as video) or you need to add a few more workstations. You might have a need for speed.

In some ways, increasing the speed of a LAN can be simple and convenient. Many of the same tools (NICs, monitoring software, and so on) can be used to build and manage faster Ethernet networks. They still use CSMA/CD to manage the network and still have the same frame sizes. The speed of Ethernet networks is measured in millions of bits per second (Mbps). Today, you can purchase equipment that transmits data at the following speeds:

➤ **10Mbps**   This has been the standard speed for Ethernet transmission for many years. It can still be used in homes or small offices that don't require high-volume traffic.

➤ **100Mbps**   This is becoming the new standard speed for Ethernet transmission. It is referred to as Fast Ethernet (discussed next). A Fast Ethernet connection can be used to handle data transmission between multiple 10Mbps networks. Many NICs and hubs support both 10Mbps and 100Mbps speeds, so they can communicate in either environment.

➤ **1,000Mbps**   This newer standard is referred to as Gigabit Ethernet. Gigabit Ethernet is popular for connecting large segments of Ethernet clients, in places such as university or corporate campuses.

100Mbps Fast Ethernet

The obvious advantage of Fast Ethernet over 10Mbps Ethernet is that it offers 10 times the bandwidth. The IEEE 802.3 committee adopted this 100Mbps Ethernet standard in June, 1995. So it has been well-defined and shaken out in the marketplace for several years now.

Many Ethernet NICs support both 10Mbps and 100Mbps connections, allowing you to use 10Mbps equipment today, while new equipment is ready to operate at the higher speeds. Fast Ethernet service is also compatible with 10Mbps service in other ways. For example, both standards use the same

➤ Frame format

➤ Frame size

➤ CSMA/CD for managing data transmission and error recovery

Check This Out

A new Ethernet standard is being developed called 10 Gigabit Ethernet Alliance (10GEA). Proponents of the new standard expect this technology to be used beyond small businesses and campuses and extend to network backbones. The IEEE task force is shooting for completion of the standard in March, 2002. For more information, see the 10GEA home page at http://www.10gea.org.

Using a feature called *fast link pulses (FLPs)*, a 10/100Mbps NIC can detect the speed being used by the hub and communicate with it at an appropriate speed. FLPs are compatible with 10Mbps normal-link pulses (NLPs).

Supported media for 100Mbps Ethernet LANs include 100BaseTX, 100BaseFX, and 100TaseT4 cables. The 100BaseTX standard can use Category 5 unshielded twisted pair wires or Type 1 or 2 shielded twisted pair with RJ-45 connectors (only two pairs are used). The 100BaseT4 standard relies on 4 twisted pair with Category 3, 4, or 5 unshielded twisted pair wiring. The 100BaseFX standard is used with two-strand fiber-optic cables.

With either 100BaseTX or 100BaseT4, only two hubs are allowed. Although the entire network diameter can only be 200 meters, you can connect two devices at up to 100 meters. With 100BaseFX networks, the entire distance can be 400 meters between DTE equipment, although if the devices are connected with a hub, only 300 meters total distance is allowed.

Check This Out

See Chapter 4 for a description of different types of cabling that is available.

1,000Mbps Gigabit Ethernet

With 1,000Mbps Gigabit Ethernet, network bandwidth increases 10 times again over Fast Ethernet. Gigabit Ethernet can be used over the following types of wiring:

➤ **1000BaseLX**   Uses laser technology on single-mode and multimode fiber.

➤ **1000BaseSX**   Uses short-wave laser technology over multimode fiber.

➤ **1000BaseCX**   Uses balanced shielded 150-ohm copper cable.

Today, Gigabit Ethernet servers are used most for providing backbone service between 100Mbps and 10Mbps networks, as well as connections to high-volume servers. This technology is well-suited for campuses and, like 100Mbps service, it uses the same frame format, frame size, and CSMA/CD management features.

Adding Hubs and Switches

Hubs and switches are two types of equipment you can use to expand the size of your LAN. Although both allow you to connect computers, as well as other hubs and switches, they serve different purposes:

➤ Hubs take data from one station and forward it to all the other stations connected to the hub. These units tend to be inexpensive, but functional for small networks.

➤ Switches, like hubs, can pass data from one station to other stations connected to the switch. However, switches have more intelligence built in. That intelligence allows switches to prevent data from going to segments where it isn't needed. Depending on how much intelligence is built in, a switch can be much more expensive than a hub.

Check This Out

See Chapter 4 for information on choosing hubs, switches, and related Ethernet hardware.

The primary difference between a hub and a switch is that a hub connects stations within the same collision domain, while a switch can segment parts of the LAN, creating multiple collision domains. In a nutshell, that means that a switch can

➤ Connect several hubs. Traffic that is then broadcast on one of those hubs would only cross through the switch if its traffic were intended for a station that is outside of that hub. This can significantly reduce the traffic on the entire LAN.

➤ Connect hubs running at different speeds. The switch could allow a 10Mbps segment connected to a hub to connect to a 100Mbps segment on another hub. The switch could manage the transmission rates between the two hubs.

Other management features are also built in to different models of switches. For example, some switches can monitor and analyze data that flows through the switch to troubleshoot problems or automatically detect and configure network devices. Although a hub can range in price from a few dollars to a few hundred dollars, switches can run into the thousands of dollars.

Where To From Here?

In this chapter, you learned about Ethernet LAN technology and how it works. In Chapter 4, you can see descriptions of networking hardware that you will need to actually build your network.

The Least You Need to Know

Right now, the least you need to know about LANs is this:

➤ Ethernet is the most popular technology by far for connecting workstations and servers together in private networks.

➤ A simple LAN can be built inexpensively, by purchasing a NIC for each computer, a few cables, and a hub.

➤ Although early Ethernet LANs ran at speeds of 10Mbps, today you can purchase LAN equipment to reach speeds of 100Mbps or even 1,000Mbps.

➤ Ethernet works by having stations broadcast frames of information on the network.

➤ Using Carrier Sense Multiple Access with Collision Detection (CSMA/CD), Ethernet has a method of detecting and correcting collisions of frames on the network.

➤ To increase the capacity of a LAN, you can add speed by upgrading your 10Mbps NICs and hubs to 10/100Mbps NICs and hubs. In that way, you can still use your existing equipment as you migrate to faster equipment.

➤ A hub lets you connect stations in the same collision domain (that is, all stations see all broadcasts on the LAN).

➤ Switches allow you to segment your LAN. In this way, hubs that connect to the switch can operate at different speeds and information that is intended for the local segment is never transmitted to the other segments. The result can be generally better performance of the LAN.

Chapter 3

Using a World-Wide Network (the Internet)

In This Chapter

➤ Understand how the Internet, intranets, and extranets are used

➤ Learn how domain name system naming and IP addressing identify computers to the network

➤ Find out what resources are available on the Internet

➤ Understand how intranets can be used in a corporate environment

➤ Learn how extranets can extend the boundaries of a corporate intranet

So, a little, private LAN isn't big enough for you? You want to be able to connect with people and computers all over the world? Well, if you haven't heard of the Internet before, then let me be the first to welcome you back from your decade-long shipwreck on a desert island. The Internet is here to stay and waiting for you to hop on.

Most people who have used the Internet have done it by dialing into an Internet service provider (ISP) from a PC at home or from some invisible hookup configured by a system administrator at work. Most people don't know where the Internet came from or how it works.

The Internet

The Internet is a massive computer network consisting of thousands of subnetworks and millions of computers worldwide. Although it began as a U.S. military project in the 1960s (used primarily by government agencies, universities, and government contractors), today it encompasses a vast range of commercial, educational, and recreational uses.

The World Wide Web

Although the number of computers and users on the Internet has grown since its inception, its greatest growth period began in the late 1980s with the creation of the World Wide Web. The Web placed a simplified framework over the Internet that enabled non-technical people to use the Internet for the first time.

Tim Berners-Lee invented the Web in 1989 as a project for organizing documents at the European Laboratory for Particle Physics (CERN). As Berners-Lee published information on the Web, organizations began adding Web servers. However, it is generally agreed that the release of Mosaic (a free, graphical Web browser from Marc Andreessen at the National Center for Supercomputing Applications) in 1993 spurred growth by making Web browsing available to a much wider audience. In 1993, NCSA and CERN formed the World Wide Web Consortium (`http://www.w3c.org`), which is still responsible for setting the course for the future development of the Web.

The Web made the Internet more accessible to the masses in the following ways:

➤ **Created Hypertext Markup Language (HTML)**   This enabled users to build graphical documents that contained images, formatted text, and links to other documents on the Web. Now HTML documents can include sound, video, and other content as well.

➤ **Created a simplified way of identifying Web resources**   Using uniform resource locators (URLs), a user can ask for a resource (such as a Web page or an FTP directory) directly from a server. Before, users had to log in to a computer, search for what they wanted, download a file, and then open it using an appropriate program.

The Web relies on the Internet's computer naming system, called the domain name system (DNS), as the basis for URLs. DNS is described later in this chapter. To specifically identify Web resources (documents, images, and so on), URLs add other information to host names. Figure 3.1 shows an example of a URL.

Figure 3.1

URLS identify the location of Web pages.

The first part of a URL identifies the protocol needed to display Web content. For Web pages, Hypertext Transfer Protocol (`http://`) appears in front of the address. For File Transfer Protocol, the prefix `ftp://` is used. The location of the resource on the server is placed at the end of the computer name. For example, a file, or resource, called swanhous.jpg in the /images directory on the Web server is added on as /images/swanhous.jpg.

Techno Tip

The *port number* is one piece of information that is implied, although usually not included, when you enter a URL. When your Web browser requests a service from the Web server, a particular port is requested to fulfill that service. For example, HTTP is port 80 and FTP is port 21 by default. To ask for the port specifically, you add a colon (:) followed by the port number to the end of the URL. For example:

```
http://www.handsonhistory.com:80
```

In this case, the :80 is not needed because port 80 is assumed. However, if Web service (or other service that you want) were available on a different port number, you would have to type that number instead of 80.

The *Web browser* is the program you use to access resources on the Web. Although browsers were first intended primarily to display Web pages (in HTML format), browsers have turned toward a one-program-fits-all approach.

How the Internet Works

Many of the design considerations that went into the early versions of ARPAnet, the predecessor to the Internet, are still apparent in the Internet of today. Because it began as a military project intending to ensure that computing resources had the capability to continue to respond during a nuclear attack (so the government could shoot back), the network had to have the following attributes:

➤ **Keep running no matter what**   There could be no single point of failure that caused the network to stop running. Even if whole areas of the network were destroyed, the remaining parts had to continue to communicate.

➤ **Join together incompatible equipment**   Communication needed to occur between computing systems of different agencies that were often incompatible. Usually they weren't even capable of sharing files, let alone communicating over networks in any meaningful way.

To meet the first criterion, the government decided to make the network a *packet-switching* network. Rather than have two communicating computers set up a connection and send data across that connection (like a telephone call), data is broken up into packets, with each packet labeled with the source and destination address of the data (like sending a letter at the post office).

The advantage of packet switching is as follows: Because each item of data knows where it is going, information can take any available route to reach the destination, and then be reassembled when the packets get there. If part of the network goes down, packets can take another route because communication doesn't rely on a particular connection staying up during the course of a communication.

As for the criterion of connecting incompatible computing systems, instead of replacing existing networks and computers, the Internet acted as an umbrella by placing new protocols over existing ones. As a result, the many types of networks available today can all be part of, and carry data for, the Internet by adding TCP/IP support to those networks.

The impact of this design on today's Internet is that the Internet can continue to grow by adding faster, higher-bandwidth backbones. A high-bandwidth backbone is like a superhighway—it allows a lot of data to be transported quickly over long distances. Older, less efficient networks can be retired. Internet traffic can be routed to networks that are less congested. Furthermore, even though it might be slower, the Internet itself can continue to work when parts of the network go down.

Resources on the Internet

The transformation of the Internet that was brought about by the Web marked a major change not only in who was using the Internet, but also in the way the Internet was used. Originally, users tended to be technical workers or students, as opposed to today's potential user—anyone with access to a PC and a modem. Furthermore, Internet programs were command-oriented instead of graphical.

With the transition to the Web, traditional technical and educational uses have given way to entertainment, shopping, and a wide range of business applications. The following sections describe both the traditional and current uses of the Internet.

Traditional Internet Uses

If you were using the Internet BW—Before Web—here are some of the things you were probably doing:

➤ **Email**   Mail messages were plain text (that is, letters you can type from the keyboard), with an occasional attachment containing a binary file (that is, special data files or programs). You probably needed to know how to use a command such as uudecode to decode any attached images or data.

➤ **Newsgroups**   This was, and remains today, a popular resource for exchanging ideas and information on topics of interest. Although improvements have been made, such as *threads* (to group responses by a particular newsgroup question) and HTML messages (which people with old newsreaders find annoying because HTML appears as junk in those readers), newsgroups continue to operate today much as they did before the Web was created.

➤ **FTP (file transfer protocol)**   To download software and documents from other computers, you can use the ftp command to access computers that are set up as FTP servers. After you log in, usually using an *anonymous* login, you can go up and down the directory structures to find and download the files you want. (With an anonymous login, you type anonymous at the FTP login prompt, and then your email address as the password. In this way, the FTP server can track you activities without requiring you to have a special user account on the computer.)

FTP servers are still supported today, although Web pages are often used to navigate documents and download sites to simplify the task of finding the right resources.

➤ **Gopher, WAIS (Wide Area Information Server), Archie**   Even before the Web, people realized that it was difficult to find documents by accessing one computer at a time and looking at filenames using the ftp command. To solve that problem, facilities for storing and indexing documents were created with programs such as Gopher, WAIS, Archie, and others.

Users did keyword searches to find documents of interest, and then selected a document from the resulting list to go to the site and get the document. Since the inception of the Web, however, with its tools that organize and search for documents much more effectively than facilities such as Gopher, WAIS, and Archie, the older programs are becoming obsolete.

Besides the services mentioned in the preceding list, there were also a variety of commands that were used with the Internet. For example, commands that can be run between two computers include telnet and rlogin (for remote login), rcp (for remote file copy), and rsh (to run commands remotely). These commands are used primarily between trusted computers on UNIX and Linux systems. A trusted computer is one that you believe to be secure (that is, you trust that users with malicious intent cannot gain access to it and cause a potential security risk to your computer).

Today's Internet Uses

In the United States, it's practically impossible to find a major corporation, educational institution, or government agency that doesn't have a presence on the Web. From these organizations' Web sites, there is a dizzying array of information, products, and services being offered.

As noted earlier in this chapter, the Web browser is the primary tool for using the Internet. Products such as Microsoft Internet Explorer and Netscape Communicator have become full Internet access suites. Besides browsing, these products also contain tools for using email, participating in newsgroups, conferencing, creating Web pages,

41

publishing Web content, and playing a variety of multimedia content (such as video and audio).

Although the space allotted here can't begin to cover all the resources available on the Internet, the paragraphs that follow describe several of the major uses of the Internet today. If you are about to make your first journey onto the Internet, know that you need a connection to the Internet, a PC, and a Web browser to start. Following are some of the things available to you on the Internet:

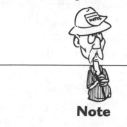

Note

For a description of features in Microsoft Internet Explorer, please see Chapter 10, "Taking Your Network for a Drive."

➤ **Shopping sites** Many expect online shopping and other types of commerce to become one of the major uses of the Internet. Online shopping offers convenience (it's open 24 hours a day), easy price comparisons, detailed product descriptions, and links to reviews and other supporting information.

Also, most anything you can think of can be purchased online—equipment, clothes, videos, food, automobiles, and so on. There are also auction sites such as eBay (http://www.ebay.com) where individuals auction almost every kind of item you can think of.

Methods for carrying out secure transactions have become quite good. Enter a credit card number, mailing address, and a few other pieces of information, and your order can appear at your door within a few days. Some sites offer access to many different online retailers. Those sites include the Yahoo! Shopping site (http://shopping.yahoo.com), Lycos Shop (http://shop.lycos.com), and AltaVista Shopping.com (http://shopping.altavista.com). Figure 3.2 is an example of the AltaVista Shopping.com site.

Figure 3.2

Search for products from multiple online retailers from AltaVista Shopping.com.

➤ **News and information**   All the major news services, newspapers, and other information media have Web sites where you can get the latest news, entertainment, and sports information. You can even tailor many of those sites to show you news on particular topics or regions of the country. Examples of these sites include `cnn.com`, `abc.com`, and `usatoday.com`.

➤ **Portals and Search engines**   Find information by searching the Web for sites containing certain keywords or sites that fall into specific categories. Portal and search engine sites include `yahoo.com`, `lycos.com`, `excite.com`, `hotbot.com`, `altavista.com`, and many others.

A portal is a Web site that can be used as a general jumping-off point to the Internet, usually allowing you to customize the type and amount of information that appears on the page. The intent is to encourage you to use the portal as your home page or at least as a page you visit often. A search engine is a program that lets you do keyword searches to find content on the Web.

➤ **Financial sites**   You can bank online, trade stocks, or apply for loans to name just a few of the financial services available on the Web. There are also tremendous (yet dangerous) resources for researching investment opportunities. Most online brokers (including `etrade.com`, `schwab.com`, and `ml.com`) offer some free financial research information, as well as premium fee-based services for their clients.

➤ **Education**   Most colleges, universities, and even K–12 schools have sites available on the Web. These sites can be resources for information about those institutions as well as a source for research information. You can even apply to some online colleges and universities and get a degree over the Internet. You can find educational institutions using keyword searches via a search engine or by finding categories of schools from portals such as Yahoo.com.

➤ **Entertainment**   Everything you might ever hope to know about movies, music, television, books, and other entertainment media can be found on the Web. Try Warner Brothers Online (`http://www.wb.com`), DreamWorks SKG (`http://www.dreamworks.com`), and Paramount Pictures (`http://www.paramount.com`) for recent movie clips and information.

➤ **Gaming**   You can download games and play them against online competitors right from your PC. There are traditional board games (such as chess), card games (such as bridge), and monster-killing games (such as Quake II and Doom).

➤ **Sports**   Major sports organizations (NBA, NFL, and MLB) have Web sites with tons of articles, pictures, and statistics. There are also many sports news organizations and plain old sports fanatics with Web sites.

➤ **Travel**   There are hundreds of Web sites that can help you find the perfect vacation spot, scope out its accommodations and tourist spots, and sometimes even book the travel arrangements.

➤ **Chat rooms**   These sites enable you to type messages or talk online to strangers all over the world. Chats associated with certain topics of interest can actually be quite useful. Sometimes you can join chat rooms where you can ask questions of entertainers, athletes, or politicians. One warning: Chat rooms are also magnets to Internet weirdos, so be careful what you divulge about yourself, and to whom.

These are just some of the general resources available on the Internet. To look into more resources on your own, go to one of the search engines that enable you to step through categories of topics (such as the Yahoo.com site). Then just start clicking topics that look interesting to you.

Figure 3.3 shows the Yahoo! home page (http://www.yahoo.com).

Figure 3.3

Find Internet resources from Yahoo! and other search sites.

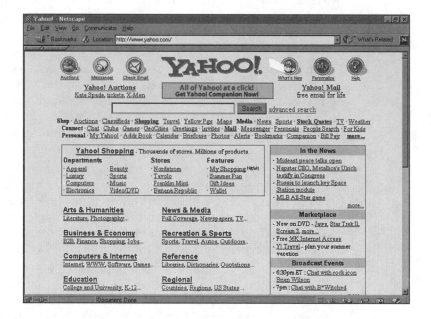

You might notice that the topics discussed here regarding the Internet are mostly those relating to organizations that want to make their resources available to the general public. By contrast, intranets want to limit network access to people within an organization and extranets want to limit network access to those who work closely with an organization.

Smaller than the Internet, Bigger than a LAN (Intranets and Extranets)

Intranets and *extranets* were created as a natural evolution from the public Internet. They reflect the desires of organizations to leverage the value of the widely accessible Internet with the need to communicate with employees and various associates in a secure way.

It helps to describe the features that are common to the Internet, intranets, and extranets. The most basic similarities between these networks are

➤ They are all built using TCP/IP protocols. These protocols define rules for such things as how messages are routed on the network and what types of services are supported.

➤ They use the same methods of identifying computers and users on the network. Names are organized in a hierarchy referred to as the *domain name system* (*DNS*) and numerical representations of those names are referred to as *IP addresses*. (DNS and IP addresses are discussed later in this chapter.)

➤ Because they use the same protocols and naming methods, the different types of networks can use the same network-ready applications (such as Web browsers and email), security methods, and system administration tools.

Differences Between the Internet, Intranets, and Extranets

If the Internet, intranets, and extranets sound similar, you might wonder what it is that makes them different. The truth is that from a technology standpoint, these types of networks are pretty much the same. The primary differences come from the way that the networks are used. Following is an explanation of how the Internet, intranets, and extranets differ:

➤ **The Internet**   The Internet is a "wide-open" network, made up of many public and private networks joined together. The vast majority of resources on the Internet are intended for public access. Users can view Web pages, send email, and access FTP sites associated with thousands of organizations all over the world.

➤ **Intranets**   An intranet is a private network that is controlled by a business or organization. It is intended for company business and is generally inaccessible to the outside world. Usually, people within the company communicate with each other using many of the same tools used on the Internet: Web browsers, network administration tools, and various collaborative programs.

➤ **Extranets**   An extranet is actually an intranet (privately maintained) that extends its network to remote users, suppliers, or other businesses or organizations with which it wants to collaborate. To extend outside of the company intranet, extranets often enable people from these outside organizations to connect to the intranet using secure connections over the public Internet. Extranet secure connections are accomplished with what are called *Virtual Private Networks (VPNs)*.

Note

Virtual private networks (VPN), for securely connecting to private networks over public networks, are described in Chapter 11, "Linking Your Home and Office Networks."

The Domain Name System

The domain name system (DNS) ensures that the computers on the Internet have unique names and IP (Internet Protocol) addresses. Domain names are organized in a hierarchy that is probably familiar to you by now; these days, it seems that every business has a .com (dot-com) Internet address that conforms to the DNS.

Well, that .com is just one of many top-level domain names. Each top-level domain name represents a category of domains under which many individual domain names exist. For example, following are some top-level domain names you might be familiar with:

➤ **.com** Includes commercial domains, such as large corporations, wholesalers, and small businesses.

➤ **.gov** Includes many U.S. government domains.

➤ **.org** Includes various kinds of organizations.

➤ **.edu** Includes educational institutions, particularly colleges and universities.

➤ **.net** Includes organizations associated with computer networks, such as Internet service providers.

Because the first top-level domains were created for companies, government agencies, and universities in the United States, as organizations from other countries joined the Internet, top-level domains were added for each country. Following are some examples of top-level country domains:

➤ jp for Japan

➤ uk for United Kingdom

➤ ca for Canada

➤ de for Germany

Network Solutions, Inc. (http://www.networksolutions.com) is where you can register for a domain name. That company allows registration of .com, .net, and .org domains (and it shares that responsibility with several other companies such as Register.com). Instead of contacting Network Solutions, you can often have the Internet service provider (ISP) you choose obtain a domain name for you. (Look in your local phone book to find ISPs that serve your area.) Before you can register the domain, you will need contact information from your ISP anyway.

Here are a few statistics about domain names (courtesy of Network Solutions):

➤ Of the .com, .net, and .org domains, 77% are .com, 15% are .net, and 8% are .org.

➤ Although there has been a lot of talk about people "squatting" on domain names (that is, registering them with the assumption that someone else will pay them for it), 80% of the people purchasing domain names purchase only one, while another 10% purchase only two.

➤ In the United States, California recorded the most domain name registrations as of April, 2000, followed by New York, Florida, Texas, and Illinois.

➤ For U.S. cities, New York has recorded the most domain name registrations, followed by Los Angeles, San Francisco, Chicago, and Miami as of April, 2000.

➤ Of the businesses registering for domain names in the first quarter of 2000, attorneys led the list, followed by computer software companies, Internet service companies, real estate companies, and advertising agencies and counselors.

➤ Of the countries outside the United States registering the most domain names, Canada leads the way, followed by the United Kingdom, Korea, France, Italy, and Japan.

Check This Out

To find out if a domain name is available, go to `http://www.networksolutions.com` and type the name you are interested in into the **Search for domain name** box, choose a domain (`.com`, `.net`, or `.org`), and click **Go**. Few common words or phrases are available any more in the `.com` domain.

Assigning Domain Names

After an organization is assigned a domain name under a top-level domain, it is within the organization's control to organize and name all its computers under that domain name. For example, for a commercial domain named `handsonhistory`, the domain name is

    handsonhistory.com

Any computers within that domain can either be added directly to the domain name or to additional subdomains. For example, computers named `decoys` and `baskets` might be called `decoys.handsonhistory.com` and `baskets.handsonhistory.com`. Or, you might add a subdomain of `crafts` and have the computers named `decoys.crafts.handsonhistory.com` and `baskets.crafts.handsonhistory.com`.

Assigning IP Addresses

The IP address is used to actually communicate with a computer on the Internet. Domain names are translated into IP addresses before requests to communicate with a computer are made (either a DNS server or a list of names/addresses on your computer usually does the actual translation).

The IP address is made up of four numbers (from 0 to 255), separated by dots. Each number is referred to as an *octet* because it consists of 8 bits. A bit is the smallest unit of information to a computer, with each bit representing either a 0 or a 1. So, if you understand binary numbers, you will know that all 8 bits set as 0 represent the number zero and all 8 bits set to 1 represents the number 255. Other combinations of 0s and 1s create other numbers between 0 and 255.

The following is an example of an IP address:

    123.45.67.89

Because any given organization usually has many computers, every organization is usually given a set of IP addresses to assign to its computers. Originally this set of numbers was associated with a Class of addresses (Class A, B, or C) each containing a different number of host (i.e. computer) addresses; address classes are discussed in the next section. Because IP addresses were running out, and the class system rarely resulted in the right number of addresses being assigned, a new method referred to as Classless Inter-Domain Routing (CIDR) is now being used. CIDR is discussed later in this chapter.

IP Address Classes

The four parts of each IP address actually represent two logical parts. The first logical part of each IP address represents a *subnetwork*, and the other part represents a particular computer on that subnetwork. The trick is that, depending on the network class, the parts of each address that represent the network and computer change.

A Class C network address contains up to 256 host addresses (the last of the four octets). A Class B network contains 65,536 host addresses (the last two of the four octets). A Class A network contains more than 16 million host addresses (the last three of the four octets). Remember, each octet represents numbers from 0 to 255, so you multiply 256 × 256 to get the number of Class B hosts and 256 × 256 × 256 to get the number of Class A hosts.

Needless to say, this was a fairly inefficient way of assigning addresses. In fact, whole Class A and Class B addresses are no longer assigned. Now you need to make a case for the number of IP addresses your organization gets.

IP addresses are running out, requiring that some tricks be used (such as assigning IP addresses dynamically as needed) until the next generation of the Internet is put in place. The next generation of the Internet (IPv6) has a virtually limitless number of IP addresses and uses six octets instead of the current four octets. (IPv6 is described in Chapter 16, "To the Internet and Beyond.")

Classless Inter-Domain Routing (CIDR)

Besides being wasteful for allocating addresses (a single class A, B, or C network number rarely fit an organization), IP classes were also inefficient when it came to handling Internet routing tables. Routing tables are lists of information that are stored on each router on the Internet so that it knows which networks to route packets to. The information that routers needed to do their job was getting to be too much. To improve this situation, Classless Inter-Domain Routing (CIDR) was adopted.

CIDR is similar to, but more flexible than assigning IP addresses. Using a different form of notation, IP address networks containing from 32 to about 524,000 host addresses can be assigned. A CIDR IP address uses a slash (/) followed by a number from 13 to 27 to indicate how many bits in the IP address reflect the network. Here is an example of a CIDR IP address:

```
123.45.67.89/16
```

Here, the first 16 bits (that is, first two dot-separated numbers, 123.45) represent the network number and the next 16 bits (that is, the last two dot-separated numbers, 67.89)reflect the host number. Wondering how many host computer could be in a network, based on the number following the slash? Here are the number of hosts you could have in each CIDR network:

/27	32 hosts
/26	64 hosts
/25	128 hosts
/24	256 hosts
/23	512 hosts
/22	1,024 hosts
/21	2,048 hosts
/20	4,096 hosts
/19	8,192 hosts
/18	16,382 hosts
/17	32,768 hosts
/16	65,536 hosts
/15	131,072 hosts
/14	262,144 hosts
/13	524,288 hosts

By assigning only the number of IP addresses to an ISP that the ISP needs, and having that ISP use the addresses in a single geographic area, routing becomes more efficient. Think of how zip codes work with the postal service. A zip code directs a letter to a particular post office that handles a particular geographic area. Imagine if letters sent to one zip code actually were destined for places all over the country. Each post office would require multiple routes within each zip code that routed letters again to distance places. That's how IP addressing often worked before CIDR. With CIDR, after a router knows how to locate the ISP's network, the ISP can manage the routing to all the computers on its nearby network.

Domain Names and IP Addresses in Intranets and Extranets

That was a quick description of how Internet names and addresses work, but you might wonder how that relates to intranets and extranets. In terms of host names, most intranets and extranets organize their computers under the company's domain name. However, if a computer from the Internet tries to contact a computer on the company intranet, in most cases the company's firewall will refuse that request (depending on how security is set up). A firewall is a specially configured computer that is there to monitor what information can travel in and out of the company's Intranet. (Firewalls are described in Chapter 14, "Securing Your Fortress.")

As for IP addresses, a special set of IP addresses is reserved to be used by any intranet. Because most or all the computers on the private part of a company's network might not be reachable from the Internet due to security constraints, this same set of IP addresses can be used by all intranets. Internet routers know that these addresses are never accessible from the Internet.

Check This Out

As with domain names, you can also obtain IP addresses through your ISP. If you would like to obtain your own IP addresses, however, you can do so by contacting the American Registry for Internet Numbers (http://www.arin.net).

Intranets

Opening up a company's network to the Internet can be dangerous (in terms of security) and can also hurt performance (if the whole world can access your network, it can slow network traffic within your company.) At the same time, however, Web browsers and Internet protocols can be great tools to include on a company's network. You can publish company manuals in HTML or use Web-based teleconferencing tools, for example.

Someone creating a network for a private company needs to consider the following:

➤ Security measures (discussed later in this chapter) are needed to protect company information, such as financial data and strategic planning information.

➤ For employees to get their jobs done, companies need to have the capability to manage and protect the performance and reliability of their networks.

An intranet is one way of allowing network connectivity within a company, at the same time protecting those resources from the outside world. In general, an intranet is a private network that uses the same software and hardware components as those involved in running the Internet. Although a small company, housed in the same location, can get by with one or two LANs connected together, a larger company might need to interconnect many separate networks from diverse locations. A well-planned intranet might be the answer.

With an intranet, a company can build its network using well-known, well-tested Internet protocols and tools. Employees don't need special knowledge to set up or use the network. Information can be shared using common applications, with a Web browser typically acting as the centerpiece of the user interface.

Security for Intranets

With an intranet, a company can manage network resources and determine the level of security with which it is comfortable. In many cases, this means secure local area networks (LANs) and wide area networks (WANs) connected to the outside world in a limited fashion through mechanisms known as firewalls.

For example, you might want to allow the engineering and human resources departments to have access to some company databases, but not allow the departments to access each other's LAN.

If more stringent security measures are required within the intranet, a variety of encryption techniques are available to keep particularly sensitive information from any

Watch Out!

Even if you have only a small LAN, it doesn't mean you are safe from hacker attacks and security breaches. If the information on your network is important to you, many of the same security techniques used in intranets might be useful for your LAN. See Chapter 14 for information on security techniques.

but the intended parties (examples are encryption techniques used to secure email messages). Basic levels of security can be enforced using standard password protection— requiring that a user log in to establish identity before gaining access to services that are restricted.

51

Intranet Uses

Using an intranet, relevant and timely company data can be distributed to employees quickly and efficiently. The network can also serve as a means for collaboration on projects through file sharing, for example. The following are some ways of effectively using an intranet within a company:

➤ **Employee services**   Intranets can be used for online company phone directories, bulletin boards, company policy documents, and information on corporate locations and internal services.

➤ **Conferencing**   Intranets can offer software that supports video conferencing, audio conferencing, online chats, whiteboards (a window that appears on everyone's screen in the conference that everyone can draw on), and application sharing. These features can be used together so employees at different locations can hear and see the same information.

➤ **Project management tools**   Scheduling tools, workflow software, project timelines and a variety of other tools that chart the productivity of a project can be shared on an intranet.

➤ **Libraries**   Online libraries can be maintained so that documents that are relevant to engineers, marketers, sales, and management are easily accessible within the intranet.

➤ **Databases**   Databases of sales data, financial information, inventory, and various kinds of analysis can be selectively made available to employees on the intranet.

➤ **Web pages**   Instead of just sending memos, employees can publish appropriate information on Web pages in HTML format. This might include technical discussions of a project, company activities, or just something personal that an employee may want to share with others.

Anything that can be done on the Internet can also be done on a company intranet. One big difference in how you set up services, however, is that Internet servers will be outside your firewall, although intranet servers will be behind it. You want critical company data to be behind the firewall and public data to be outside of it. It is up to each company to implement the policies to decide how the intranet is to be used and to allocate the computing and network resources to support those policies.

Extranets

An extranet extends the concept of intranets outside of a single company to other companies, agencies, or individuals that need to collaborate with the company on an ongoing basis.

One factor that typically characterizes an extranet is the way in which it extends the company intranet. Those who are connecting from outside the intranet are usually doing so over a public network (in particular, the Internet). Although this can result in some performance hits, it can be a cost-effective solution because inexpensive Internet connections are widely available.

The extranet requires some special security considerations. To ensure that corporate computing assets are safe, off-site users typically use such techniques as encryption or tunneling (discussed at the end of this chapter) to keep their communications secure. In general, extranets are less expensive than creating and maintaining leased lines. A company has to pay extra for lines that are leased from local phone companies to carry its data, while it only has to pay for a connection to the Internet to use the Internet to carry its data. However, a major drawback of extranets is that the performance of the network is out of the hands of the local company. For that reason, applications that require real-time response, such as banking and airline reservation applications, might not get the performance they need by communicating over the Internet.

Extranet Uses

For many applications, an Internet connection from a high-speed modem is quite acceptable for extranets. These are applications that, in case the network is temporarily congested, can wait a few extra seconds for a response. The following are some items a company might want to offer its partners on an extranet but not make available to the general public:

➤ Wholesale pricing lists

➤ Project plans and milestones

➤ Inventory availability information

➤ Special partner/dealer programs, including discounts, sales incentives, and promotions

➤ Company internal contact information

➤ Product specifications

➤ Marketing reports and studies

➤ Product support literature, including technical support databases

Building Security into an Extranet

Because important company assets are being exposed outside the boundaries of the corporate intranet, special attention needs to be paid to security issues. That attention will be focused on the following factors:

➤ Remote users are who they say they are.

➤ Connections between the remote users and the intranet are secure.

➤ The scope of the information and resources available to the remote user are limited.

To verify the identity of a remote user, the first line of defense is still a username and password. When a system administrator sets up a company's computer network, users are typically given individual user accounts with passwords. When a more rigorous identification is necessary, *digital certificates* can be required. A digital certificate more stringently establishes the identity of the user. A digital certificate can also satisfy the second item listed previously by enabling the two parties in the communication to establish an encrypted communication session.

Establishing certificates was once an expensive and complicated job. Now there are ways for a company to be its own *certificate authority (CA)* and issue digital certificates. Companies such as VeriSign (`http://www.verisign.com`) can help you manage your own digital certificates.

When it comes to the third item listed previously, a company can use the same measures to secure its resources against unauthorized access from its extranet partners as it does against unauthorized access from employees within the company. Access to secure LANs can be blocked using firewalls and password protection can be used to protect sensitive data.

As with access to resources by employees within an intranet, a company needs to set up security standards and performance requirements for its extranet. By doing this properly, a company can provide the information its partners need in a timely manner and still protect other computing resources.

Where To From Here?

After reading this chapter, you understand how the Internet, intranets, and extranets are used. In particular, you understand the types of resources best suited to each type of network and different security considerations associated with each network type.

To learn more about topics related to the Internet, intranets, and extranets, you can refer to the discussion of virtual private networks in Chapter 11. If you are getting tired of theory and want to set something up, skip to Chapter 9, "Hooking Up Your Small Office Network" or Chapter 8, "Building Your Home Network" to set up an office or home network.

The Least You Need to Know

Right now, the least you need to know about the Internet, intranets, and extranets is this:

➤ All three types of networks (the Internet, intranets, and extranets) are based on TCP/IP protocols and naming conventions.

➤ The domain name system (DNS) and IP addresses are used to identify host computers and other network resources in each type of network.

➤ The World Wide Web made the Internet accessible to the general population.

➤ Some older Internet applications, such as email and newsgroups, are still popular today. Older document search and storage methods, such as Gopher, Archie, and WAIS, are becoming obsolete.

➤ The uses of the Internet are too numerous to describe; some popular uses include online shopping, online gaming, Internet searching, news access, and online chats.

➤ Intranets are closed networks that use the same protocols and addressing style used by the Internet.

➤ Extranets are networks that are maintained by a company, but extend beyond the physical boundaries of the private network so partners and suppliers can access some level of information from that network.

Part 2
Gathering Your Network Gear

A network is a lot like plumbing: You just connect some pipes and attach them to your favorite appliances. Pretty soon, everything will flow in the right direction to the right places.

Okay, so a network might be a bit different from plumbing. With networks, there are topologies, architectures, and protocols representing how they are constructed. Instead of pipes and valves, you have cables, routers, and hubs connecting everything. And instead of sinks and tubs, you have desktop computers, server computers, printers, and other devices sending and receiving stuff on the network.

Chapters in this part describe the different components that fit together to form computer networks.

Chapter 4

Choosing Your Networking Hardware

In This Chapter

➤ Choose computers that meet your network needs

➤ Select cables and connectors

➤ Understand communications hardware (hubs, bridges, routers, switches, and gateways)

To most computer users, information magically comes and goes from their computers. They don't think about *network interface cards (NICs)*, cables, or *routers*. To the uninitiated network administrator, that "magic" can look like a puzzle of wires and black boxes.

To help you unravel the puzzle of computer networks, this chapter describes the kinds of hardware you can use to connect your network, as well as the types of computers and other devices you can connect to it. If you are nervous, you can start with something as simple as a wire connecting two personal computers. If you are adventurous, you'll want to know about equipment used to connect local area networks (LANs) and to route messages to other networks.

Choosing Types of Computers

If you are creating your first network, you will probably be connecting the existing computers in your organization. That usually means connecting Windows PCs, Macs, and possibly UNIX workstations. You might even have a file or print server around. So the job of choosing computers might already be done for you.

If you are starting from scratch, however, there are a variety of hybrid computers that are specifically designed for use on a network. Remember that with a network, every computer doesn't need to have every piece of hardware directly connected to it. Instead of all the computers being the same, you can have a few very powerful computers and many that are less powerful.

For the purposes of discussing the different types of computers you can have on your network, the next sections divide computers into three categories:

➤ **Standalone computers**   Those computers that can work without being connected to a network (although, of course, they can be connected).

➤ **Network computers**   Network computers might lack key hardware or software components, allowing them to work only when connected to a network.

➤ **Servers**   Servers are computers that offer services (such as printing or applications) to other computers on the network.

Techno Tip

The more powerful computers typically act as *servers*. This means that the computer offers a service to *client* computers on the network. The client computer (such as a desktop Windows PC) might need servers to provide a service that isn't available on the client computer. There are a few different types of servers:

➤ *Print servers* manage document printing.

➤ *File servers* centrally store files.

➤ *Application servers* launch applications that appear on the client computers.

➤ *Management servers* manage a group of personal computers.

Standalone Computers

Personal computers were not originally designed to connect to a computer network. In fact, the first homes and even many small offices that owned computers rarely had more than one computer, making the idea of a network rather silly.

Today, with many multi-computer locations, most computers either come network-ready (with a NIC installed) or enable you to add a card later. The following are some of the most common types of computers you might encounter when you connect your first network:

➤ Personal computers (PCs)

➤ Laptop computers

➤ Macintosh computers

➤ UNIX workstations

Personal Computers (PCs)

PCs are by far the most common type of computer around today. Typical configurations have everything needed to run applications and save data locally. Hardware usually includes a hard disk (for permanent storage), CD-ROM drive, floppy disk drive, monitor, keyboard, and mouse. The CPU is usually from the Intel Pentium family (or is compatible). Built-in modems are included in most new PCs, and NICs (usually Ethernet) are almost always available. The operating system tends to be Windows 9x or Windows NT or Windows 2000 Professional.

Laptop Computers

It's convenient to have the capability to go on the road and take your computer with you. It's even more convenient if you can connect that laptop into a network so you have access to the information you need. Most laptop PCs come with a PCMCIA card slot that is about the size of a credit card and enables you to add NICs (or other types of cards) so you can connect to the network while you are at the office. From the road, you typically use the laptop's built-in modem to dial in to the network. The operating system is typically the same as PCs.

Macintosh Computers

Apple Macintosh computers have been popular for multimedia applications such as graphic arts and audio/video applications. Some Apple Macintosh computers have built-in Ethernet ports, including the Macintosh Centris 650, Power Macintosh, and most Quadra computers. The new iMac computer includes a 10/100BaseTX Ethernet card. Apple Workgroup Servers also contain Ethernet cards. If your Macintosh doesn't have an Ethernet port, you can purchase several different Ethernet cards from Apple.

UNIX Workstations

For CPU-intensive applications, UNIX workstations have always been popular. For example, UNIX workstations are often used by scientists, special-effects and graphics artists, architects (using CAD/CAM), and stock brokers. Imaging and modeling are excellent applications for UNIX workstations.

Although it's true that some of the most popular versions of UNIX, such as Solaris, SCO Open Desktop, and Linux, do run on PCs, UNIX can also run on many other types of hardware (such as mainframes or super computers). UNIX workstations tend to mean higher-priced computers with large disk capacities, a powerful processor (or

Check This Out

See Chapter 7, "Making Those Internet Connections," for a more complete description of the UNIX operating system.

possibly several), a lot of random access memory (RAM), and probably built-in Ethernet hardware. Sparc processors are very popular for use on UNIX workstations that need to run applications that require lots of calculations (for example, weather tracking, film special effects, or stock trading).

Although typical UNIX workstations operate just fine on their own, they almost always include NICs so they can connect to a network. This is because UNIX workstations are most often used in businesses where people need to work together on projects.

Network Computers

When huge mainframe computers ruled the world, many people used the same computer from multiple dumb terminals (that is, a keyboard and screen with no graphics, just letters and numbers). Using simple text and function keys, users performed repetitive tasks such as data entry, reservations, or telemarketing.

These days, network computers are available to replace dumb terminals with hardware that can run today's more sophisticated applications. Network computers are typically scaled-down PCs or workstations that offer a few advantages over dumb terminals:

➤ Applications can be graphical instead of text oriented.

➤ Much of the processing can take place on the network computer, avoiding bottlenecks from slow networks or overburdened servers.

Network computers also are intended to offer the following advantages over full-blown PCs or workstations:

➤ By including less hardware, the initial cost of the network computer can be lower.

➤ Maintenance costs can be lower because each network computer can be managed from a server. Therefore, users are not responsible for maintaining their own computers.

➤ By centrally distributing software, a company makes sure each client runs the latest applications.

➤ Because these computers might have no floppy disk drives, CD-ROM drives, expansion slots, or even hard disks in some cases, the risk of corruption or computer viruses is greatly reduced.

The client network computer might be a mere shell of a computer (a monitor, CPU, a network interface card, and not much else). In fact, the popular term used to describe one of these computers is *thin client.* In essence, the use of thin clients offers a way for an organization to more tightly control computer costs and usage but still offer sophisticated applications.

The previous edition of this book described entries into the network computer market that included Javastations from Sun Microsystems and Net PCs from Intel (and other manufacturers). Both of those products have died off. New devices that are hoping to take the world by storm include a variety of wireless and hand-held devices. See Chapter 18, "Networking Your Kitchen Appliances," for descriptions of some of these devices.

Watch Out!

Because network computers often lack either hard disks or full operating systems, users might not have the capability to run certain high-end applications that expect a full PC operating environment.

Server Computers

From a hardware standpoint, a server computer doesn't need to be much different from a client computer. Servers often run on the same computer architectures—PCs and Sparc workstations—as client computers. However, because many users rely on servers, servers usually are much more loaded with hardware than the typical client.

A server computer generally has more RAM, larger hard disks, and a higher-speed processor (or multiple processors) than a client computer. For example, it's not unusual for a small workgroup server to start at 256MB of RAM, whereas client processors might have only 64- or 128MB. A client might have a 1GB hard disk, whereas a server might have several 9GB, 18GB, or 36GB hard disks.

Larger server systems, such as the Dell PowerEdge 6400, can carry up to four 700MHz processors and 8GB of RAM. That server can also hold up to eight 73GB disk drives. As for its capacity to handle traffic from the network, this server can manage several NICs at the same time. Server computers do tend to run different operating systems and management software than clients. For example, file servers tend to run on NetWare, Windows NT, Windows 2000, Linux, or UNIX operating systems. Software such as Compaq's Intelligent Manageability can be used to manage PCs, provide fault management (to minimize downtime), and handle security management to prevent unauthorized access.

Computer Networking Components

To connect to a network, most computers rely on either a modem (for phone line or other serial connections) or a NIC (for a LAN connection). Modems come with nearly every computer made these days. NICs are most often used to communicate on Ethernet LANs; see Chapter 2, "Having Your Own Network (LAN)," for a discussion of this topic.

In the scramble to control what is expected to become a huge market for home and small business networks, a variety of new methods for connecting networks has begun to appear. These include network hardware that enables you to connect computers using existing telephone or electrical wiring in the home.

Check This Out

For more information on network operating systems and server management software, see Chapter 5, "Network Servers and Clients at Your Service."

Techno Tip

COM ports are the connectors on your computer that you can plug "serial" devices to. The word serial comes from the style of data transmission, where each bit of data is sent in order in a stream. On PCs, a COM port is typically a 9-pin connector, although older computers also have 25-pin connectors. The electrical standard that defines the number of pins, pin assignments, and data transmission for these COM ports is RS-232C. The RS-232 standard was originally adopted in 1960 by the Electronic Industries Association.

Modems

Modems enable you to connect your computer to a computer network over standard telephone lines. Although the first modems were painfully slow, improvements in technology have made them viable even for applications—such as Web browsing—that are graphics-intensive.

Contributing to the popularity of modems is the fact that most modems adhere to a common set of standards. This means that any modem that transmits data at a particular speed (such as 28.8Kbps) can connect to any other modem over phone lines that can communicate at the same speed. Hardware standards dictate that modems be connected to RS-232C ports (COM ports on PCs), and a standard control language is used (modems using that language are referred to as Hayes-compatible).

Modem Features

Although most modems sold today sport similar features, performance can vary greatly—especially among those modems that are rated at higher speeds. Here are a few things to know about the modems you use:

➤ **Speed**   The speed at which modems transmit and receive data is rated in bits per second (bps). When communicating over telephone lines, speeds can range from 300bps to 57,600bps. Achieving higher speeds not only requires clean phone lines but also requires that both sides of the communication support the transmissions rate (also called the *baud rate*).

➤ **Compatibility**   Not only do both sides communicating by modem need to support higher speeds for data to be transported at those speeds, there are different standards supported by modem manufacturers to achieve those speeds. Eventually, all 56Kbps modems will operate using the V.90 standard. In the mean time, your ISP might support k53flex technology for 56Kbps speeds. 3Com used x2 technology to achieve 56Kbps, but is moving toward the V.90 standard. If you are purchasing 56Kbps modem, the important issue is that it be V.90 compliant.

Check This Out

Don't always believe the numbers on the box when it comes to how fast a modem really performs. Significantly different speeds are realized depending on line conditions, the type of data being sent, and whether compression is used. Read some modem reviews before you make a purchase. Visit the C|Net computers.com site, and then select Modems for modem reviews.

➤ **Fax/voice support** Most modems today can support fax transmissions and voice communications, as well as data transmissions. If you have an older modem, make sure those features are included if they are important to you.

➤ **Flash memory** Some modems today come with flash memory for storing supported protocols. This means that if the manufacturer corrects or updates the software that runs the modem, you can install those changes. If you have a modem from 3Com, you can visit 3Com's Web site (http://www.3Com.com) to download the latest software to your modem.

Using Modems with Your Network

Although most of the traffic in networks used by small businesses probably occurs on the LAN in the office, modems can serve an important role in your network. Modems connected to your network can be used to

➤ Provide a method for employees on the road to dial in to the network to check email, download documents, or run applications. For users who work at home or in another location, this might be their only way to reach your network.

➤ Offer access to outside networks (such as the Internet or other wide area networks, or *WANs*) for your network's users.

If there is a lot of traffic between your network and outside networks, you might want to consider getting a higher speed communications line. Special modems are available to handle higher-speed lines. For example, many homes and small offices are turning to DSL and cable modems (from slower dial-up connections) for high-speed connections to the Internet. For businesses, Integrated Services Digital Network (ISDN) has been a popular medium for higher-speed Internet connections. (See Chapter 7 for details on using ISDN media for high-speed connections.)

DSL

Digital Subscriber Line (DSL) technology is an extremely popular way to get high-speed Internet access using your existing phone lines. With DSL, you can share the same line with your telephone and DSL Internet service...at the same time! DSL is most often offered through your local telephone company, although you can usually ask your Internet service provider (ISP) to order the service for you.

Before you purchase a DSL modem, you need to do some research. First, you need to make sure that DSL is available in your area. Next you need to match your DSL modem with the same type of DSL service offered by your DSL provider. This process is described in more detail in Chapter 7.

Unfortunately, there are different implementations of DSL technology. Usually the easiest way to go about solving the problem is to purchase the DSL device from your service provider. ISPs often offer them at a discount anyway for buying their service. Here are the different DSL options:

➤ **HDSL**　High bit-rate DSL. HDSL is an early version of DSL that is used for wideband symmetrical transmission (that is, same transmission rates in both directions).

➤ **SDSL**　Symmetric DSL. SDSL is similar to HDSL, except that it allows for higher rates of transmission.

➤ **VDSL**　Very high bit-rate DSL. VDSL is a newer DSL technology that is expected to support much higher transmission rates than other DSL technologies, although it will require shorter distances.

➤ **ADSL**　Asymmetric DSL. With ADSL, a larger portion of bandwidth is available for downstream rather than upstream communications.

➤ **IDSL**　ISDN DSL. IDSL offers slower data rates than ADSL (only 128Kbps). This service is more like ISDN than DSL in its transmission rates.

Speeds of your DSL modem range from 256Kbps to 1,500Kbps (or 1.5Mbps). You will pay more to your DSL provider for higher speeds. DSL modems plug right into your regular plain old telephone service (POTS) telephone jack in the wall on one end and into an Ethernet interface on the other end. So, if you use DSL to connect your workstation to the Internet, you can plug its Ethernet interface into your NIC or if you have a LAN you can connect that interface into your hub.

By getting a DSL modem that is packed with features, you can save yourself some money and trouble. For example, the Cisco 675 DSL unit combines several different features, including

➤ **Routing**   The DSL unit can route messages from your LAN to your DSL service provider, effectively having interfaces on both networks to provide that service.

➤ **Dynamic Host Configuration Protocol (DHCP)**   The DSL unit can assign Internet Protocol (IP) addresses (and related information) automatically to each workstation on your LAN.

➤ **Network Address Translation (NAT)**   The DSL unit can perform NAT services, so the computers on your LAN can use the Internet without having public IP addresses. (See Chapter 3, "Using a World-Wide Network (the Internet)," for descriptions of public and private IP addresses.)

Cable Modems

If you have cable television at your home or business, chances are that your cable provider is offering Internet service (or will be soon). The equipment that you use to access the Internet from the cable that comes into your house is a cable modem.

Like cable television, cable modems are designed to allow a lot of data to be pumped into your house. A cable modem can receive data downstream (from the Internet) at rates as high as 3Mbps. Upstream rates (to the Internet) can be up to 1Mbps.

You can get both internal and external cable modems. Like DSL, the cable modem requires an Ethernet interface for you to plug into. That could be a workstation's NIC or a port on your hub. Instead of plugging into the telephone outlet, however, the cable modem plugs into the cable outlet you use to plug in your cable television.

In general, cable modems are easy to install and offer a big improvement in speed to regular analog modems. However, there are differences in performance among cable modems from different vendors, so do some homework before you buy. In reality, throughput rates might be closer to 1Mbps than 3Mbps, with some models coming in even slower.

NICs

A NIC fits into the expansion slot on your computer to provide an access point to the network. A cable plugs into the back of the NIC to connect to your local area network hub. Or it might use a T-connector to connect to a LAN bus.

The type of NIC you use depends on several issues:

Check This Out

Some of the pros and cons of using cable modem service as opposed to DSL are described in Chapter 7.

➤ **The type of network you are connecting to**   Ethernet is the most popular type of LAN, followed by token-ring networks. With Ethernet, you can connect up to 1,024 nodes and communicate at speeds of 10Mbps. Fast Ethernet (100Mbps) and Gigabit Ethernet (1,000Mbps) are also available these days. Token ring can connect up to 255 nodes at 4– and 16Mbps. (Chapter 2 describes different types of Ethernet networks.)

➤ **The type of bus used in your computer**   The bus consists of the wiring inside the computer that connects the internal parts—central processing unit (CPU), memory, and so on. The expansion bus allows expansion boards (such as NICs) to be added to the computer. Most bus types are ISA (for 8- and 16-bit cards), EISA (for faster 32-bit cards), PCMCIA (for notebook computers), or PCI (for 32- and 64-bit cards). (Different bus architectures are described in Chapter 8, "Building Your Home Network.")

➤ **The type of connectors used on the NIC**   Popular types of connectors include BNC and RJ-45. By far, RJ-45 connectors are the more popular choice for home and small business networks. (See the descriptions of cables and connectors later in this chapter.)

All the NICs used on your network must support the same network protocol (that is, Ethernet or token ring). However, the computers can have different bus types and connectors (if you use adapters or hubs that support different types of connectors).

The speed at which your equipment operates must also match, with a few exceptions. If the computers on your LAN have some Ethernet cards that run at 10Mbps and others that support both 10Mbps and 100Mbps, the cards can automatically adjust to work at the lower speeds. If you add a network switch to your LAN, you can have different segments of the LAN operating at different speeds.

Techno Tip

Instead of buying NICs, hubs, and cables separately, you can buy LAN connection kits that include everything you need. Typically, these kits enable you to start with two PCs and add hardware for additional PCs. Examples of these kits include 3Com OfficeConnect Networking Kit (`http://www.3Com.com`) and D–Link DE-905 Network Kit for Small Workgroups (`http://www.dlink.com`).

New Networking Hardware

Studies on home and small-office computer use have determined that users are ready for the power that can be gained by networking their computers. However, many people shy away from the idea of running new cables through their house. Several relatively new network technologies have been developed to deal with that issue.

Some of the new technologies aimed at small networks enable people to create computer networks without adding new wiring to their homes. Although not yet widely used, many of these technologies are available today:

➤ **Phone lines**   A product called HomeRun from Tut Systems (http://www.tutsystems.com/products) enables computers in a building to connect to a network through the standard copper wires and phone jacks already in the building. These wires can be shared simultaneously without disturbing telephone traffic. The advantage is that you don't have to run any special wires to connect your network.

➤ **Power outlets**   A product called PassPort for connecting computers over the power lines that run through a house has been developed by Intelogis, Inc. (http://www.intelogis.com/products). One feature that makes this approach attractive is that there are usually many more power outlets than phone outlets in a house. This makes it more convenient to connect computers almost anywhere in the house.

➤ **Radio frequency**   RadioLAN, WebGear, and Proxim are products that use radio wave technology to create LANs. Although this type of technology has been around for a while, it is still prohibitively expensive for most small networks. Its big advantage is that you don't need wires between the computers.

RadioLAN (http://www.radiolan.com) offers both indoor and outdoor wireless products that operate at 10Mbps. WebGear (http://www.webgear.com) offers a product called Aviator that lets you connect devices that are up to 75–125 feet apart. Proxim (http://www.proxim.com) offers the Symphony wirefree solution for homes and small businesses.

➤ **Infrared**   Another type of wireless networking relies on infrared technology. Add an infrared adapter card to a computer at one end of the room. Connect an infrared sensor to the hub or daisy chain network, and point it toward the computer. The computer can then log on to the network. Infrared offers the advantage of not needing wires, but doesn't support distances as great as those supported by radio frequency.

In the coming years, some network technology will probably arise as the leader in the home and small business market. As of today, however, the jury is still out.

Hardware for Joining Computers

Even though there is a wide range of networking hardware available today, relatively few components are needed by an administrator of a small network.

If you are connecting a LAN (with no connections to outside networks), you probably only need cables to connect each computer's NIC and optionally a hub to connect the computers. Other networking hardware described in this section will help you if your network routes data to other networks or must extend beyond the physical limits of a LAN (for example, to extend a LAN to another building).

Cabling and Connectors

Each of the different types of wiring or cabling you can use with your LAN has different characteristics. In particular, cabling (along with required transmission speeds) affects how far apart the computers can be and how quickly data can travel between them. Popular types of cable are

➤ Coaxial

➤ Twisted pair

➤ Fiber optic

Coaxial Cable

A *coaxial cable* is similar to the type of cable that is probably already in your home, connecting your cable television. A center wire is inside the coaxial cable and is wrapped in insulation and a grounded shield of braided wire. Coaxial cable can carry more data than telephone wires and protects better against interference.

Standard coaxial cables used with Ethernet LANs are often referred to as *thicknet* and *thinnet*. Each type has different characteristics:

➤ **Thicknet**   This was the original type of cable specified for Ethernet. Because the cable is thick (about 1cm), it is fairly difficult to install. Supported cables include Belden numbers 9880 (PVC) and 89880 (plenum cable, which is made of Teflon and is more expensive than ordinary cable). Thicknet uses male N type connectors.

With thicknet, an AUI (Attachment Unit Interface) cable is also needed to connect the NIC to an external transceiver before connecting to the thicknet cable. On one end of the AUI is a female 15-pin connector (with a sliding latch). The other end of the AUI has a male 15-pin connector.

➤ **Thinnet**   This type of cable is more flexible than thicknet cable. The cable is about .5cm thick. Coax thinnet cables can be of type RG 58 A/U or RG 58 C/U. Each end of the cable must have a male BNC connector. (See Figure 4.1 for an example of a BNC connector.)

Coaxial cable is more difficult to string through a building than twisted pair (telephone-style), discussed next. Coax is thicker, heavier, and more expensive that twisted pair. Often, workstations are connected using twisted pair, whereas coaxial might be used to connect Ethernet hubs or switches.

Twisted Pair Cable

Twisted pair cables consist of two pairs of wires that are connected on each end to an eight-pin RJ-45 connector. The name is derived from the fact that the two wires in each pair are twisted together from one end to the other. (Wires are twisted to help reduce interference.)

Unshielded twisted pair (UTP) and *shielded twisted pair (STP)* are the two basic cable designs that are available. In STP cables, the wires are covered in a conducting shield. In UTP cables, balancing and filtering techniques are used instead of shielding.

All twisted pair cabling is made of copper wire. With more demands on copper wire coming from higher speed Ethernet networks (100Mbps and 1,000Mbps), higher quality copper cabling has been developed. Here are some of the latest choices:

➤ **Category 3**   This cable is suitable for 10Mbps networks. It contains 4-pair of UTP wire.

➤ **Category 5**   Standard Cat 5 wiring consists of 4-pair of UTP wires. It can be used to connect Ethernet networks from 10Mbps to 100Mbps. Some enhanced Cat 5 wiring can support 1,000Mbps Gigabit Ethernet. This cable is commonly used for wiring offices.

➤ **Category 6**   Like Cat 5 wiring, Cat 6 contains 4-pair of UTP wires. It can operate at higher frequencies (up to 400MHz) than Cat 5. This wiring is suited for Gigabit Ethernet.

Note

Standard Ethernet cables are used to connect computers to a hub. To connect a hub to another hub, however, you need what is called a *crossover* cable. A crossover cable switches the wires used to send and receive data, so that both hubs don't try to send and receive data on the same wires. Some hubs come with a special button that changes a port to a crossover port, allowing you to use a standard cable to connect the hubs.

Fiber Optic Cable

A *fiber-optic* cable consists of a bundle of glass or plastic threads that transmit data in the form of modulated light waves. *Bandwidth* (that is, the amount of data that can pass through) is much higher with fiber-optic cables than with traditional copper cables.

Although fiber optic is more expensive and more difficult to install than copper cables, it has become more popular in recent years. The tremendous performance gains can outweigh the initial setup costs in a short time.

Ethernet Connection Standards

A variety of standards are used to determine the equipment you need to connect computers in an Ethernet network. Each standard defines the types of cable and connectors to be used and the speed supported by the network, which in turn defines the distances between computers that are allowed. Your options include 10Base2, 10Base5, 10BaseT, and 100BaseT. (See later sections for descriptions of each type of cable and connector used.)

Ethernet 10Base2

This connection type uses thinnet coaxial cables to achieve speeds of 10Mbps. With thinnet, you can string your computers together in a *daisy chain* (that is, in a line from one computer to the next instead of joining together in a central hub).

To create a daisy chain, you use a T connector on each 10Mbps NIC to connect the computer from one neighbor to the next. A BNC 50-ohm terminator is used at both ends of the chain. A terminator is a small piece of metal that caps off the end of the T connector.

Figure 4.1 shows the hardware used in connecting a 10Base2 Ethernet network.

Figure 4.1

10Base2 thinnet Ethernet networks enable you to daisy-chain computers.

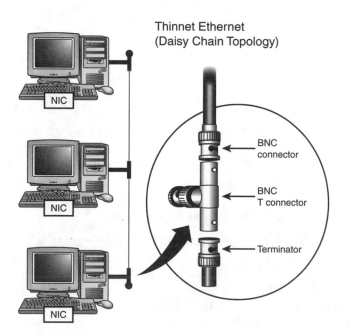

Thinnet Ethernet
(Daisy Chain Topology)

BNC connector

BNC T connector

Terminator

Thinnet wires carry signals at 10Mbps. Each segment can be up to 185 meters. Up to 30 connections can be supported (each workstation and repeater connection point represents a connection).

Ethernet 10Base5

The 10Base5 standard is older than the 10Base2 method, and uses thicknet coaxial cabling (discussed earlier in this chapter). Although the cabling is thicker and more difficult to handle than either thinnet or twisted-pair wiring, it does support greater distances between computers and more computers on each segment.

Extra cabling is required with 10Base5 because the transceiver is external to the NIC. Here, an AUI connector on the NIC is connected by an AUI cable to an external transceiver. The transceiver then connects to the thicknet coaxial cable via an AMP tap. The thicknet cable itself is terminated with type N connectors. A thicknet cable tap is also called a *vampire tap*.

A 10Base5 thicknet wire carries signals at 10Mbps. The AUI cable can be up to 50 meters long, whereas the thicknet cable can be up to 500 meters. Up to 100 connections can be supported.

Ethernet 10BaseT

The 10BaseT method relies on twisted pair wiring (either shielded or unshielded) to connect computers. This wiring is similar to the wire you use to plug in your telephone, except that it uses 8-pin RJ-45 jacks instead of the smaller 4-pin RJ-11 jacks. This is the most popular method of connecting computers in a LAN.

Most often, wires are plugged into a 10Mbps NIC on one end and a hub on the other. You can purchase hubs with different numbers of ports, depending on how many computers you need to connect.

Watch Out!

With all that said, avoid this connection method if you can help it, unless you need longer distances between computers. Thicknet is expensive, heavy, and difficult to work with.

Figure 4.2 shows an example of hardware used in connecting a 10BaseT twisted pair Ethernet network, also known as a *star topology*.

RJ-45 twisted-pair wires carry signals at 10Mbps. Distance from the NIC to the hub should not be more than 100 meters.

Figure 4.2

Simple jacks and hubs connect computers on a 10BaseT LAN.

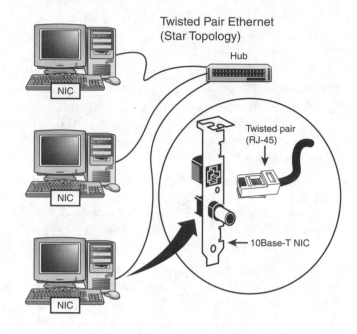

Twisted Pair Ethernet (Star Topology)

Hub

Twisted pair (RJ-45)

10Base-T NIC

Ethernet 100BaseT

To support the new Fast Ethernet, new cabling standards have been developed. These new transmission and cabling schemes can support data transfer rates of 100Mbps.

Check This Out

You can connect two computers using twisted pair cable. However, that cable must be a *crossover cable*. On this cable, the pins are crossed over (pin 1 to pin 3; pin 2 to pin 6) so that both sides transmit and receive on different wires. This method of connecting makes it unnecessary for you to have a hub, if you are only connecting two computers.

There are several different cabling methods associated with Fast Ethernet:

➤ **100BaseTX**   This type of cabling consists of two pairs of twisted pair wiring (high quality).

➤ **100BaseT4**   This type of cabling consists of four pairs of twisted pair wiring (normal quality).

➤ **100BaseFX**   This type of cabling consists of fiber-optic cables.

Other Network Equipment

Networks that consist of more than a few computers around the office usually require more equipment in addition to NIC cards and cables. The following sections define some of the other networking equipment you might encounter in a computer network.

Hubs

Hubs are used to connect multiple computers to an Ethernet LAN. A hub can have different kinds of ports to support different media types (thinnet, thicknet, twisted pair, and so on). However, a single hub can only support one speed at a time. In other words, all NICs connected to the hub must communicate at 10Mbps or 100Mbps.

The hub acts as a repeater by taking incoming data sent by computers on the LAN and repeating that data out of all the ports to other computers. Hubs also amplify the signals to improve signals that can be weakened from traveling great distances. Most 10BaseT networks use hubs to connect computers on a LAN. However, if you were only connecting two computers, you could get by without using a hub if you connected the two using a crossover cable.

Switches

A *switch* is a piece of networking equipment that can connect multiple segments of a LAN together. In effect, the switch can act as a boundary so that groups of computers on different hubs can each run at different speeds or even, possibly, using different protocols. The switch can do two things:

➤ Reduce total LAN traffic by preventing data intended for communication between computers on a segment from being broadcast to other segments for which the information is not intended.

➤ Allow one hub to operate at one speed (such as 10Mbps) and another hub to operate at another speed (such as 100Mbps).

The features just described are referred to a *bridging*. In fact, a switch is sometimes referred to a *bridge*.

Routers

Routers are used to route messages among sub-networks on a computer network. For example, a router might be connected to a company's LAN that contains a Web server. That router is also connected to a line to the Internet. Both incoming and outgoing messages between the company's LAN and the Internet pass through the router.

Check This Out

When you plan your network, you must take into account bandwidth and other limitations that determine how many computers you can connect on a LAN. For a discussion of network planning issues, please see Chapter 9, "Hooking Up Your Small Office Network."

Techno Tip

Collisions occur on an Ethernet network because of its design. Ethernet is a CSMA-CD (Carrier Sense Multiple Access with Collision Detection) type of network, as discussed in Chapter 2. Because computers on an Ethernet LAN sometimes broadcast on the network at the same time without knowing that another computer has begun transmitting, messages sometimes run into each other. Ethernet is designed to correct for that, but if there are too many computers on the network, collisions can slow down network performance.

Techno Tip

The Internet is made up of multiple subnetworks. A LAN can be made up of multiple segments. In the OSI Reference model (described in Chapter 1, "What Is a Network"), LANs operate at level 2 and subnetworks operate at levels 3 and 4. For that reason, different kinds of equipment are needed to direct data between segments and subnetworks. A network switch can connect multiple LAN segments while a router connects multiple subnetworks.

There are dedicated routers designed to route messages from one network to another as their main job. Some computers have routing protocols built in, so instead of purchasing a separate router, you can use that computer to do routing between various networks. The UNIX operating system is an example of a system that has built-in routing capabilities. DSL modems also often have routing capabilities.

Gateways

A *gateway* is similar to a router, except that a gateway routes messages from one type of network architecture to a completely different type of network architecture. For example, a gateway might route messages between the Internet (a TCP/IP network)

76

and an IBM Systems Network Architecture (SNA) network. In this case, the two networks are different all the way to the top of the seven-layer OSI reference model.

Communicating between two completely different network architectures would be like trying to send a letter to someone who could only be reached by phone. For the letter to reach its destination, you would have to translate both the addressing data (name, address, and zip code) into a phone number. Then it would have to translate the written words from the letter into spoken words on the telephone. Although what I just mentioned is a metaphor, it represents the kind of actions that a gateway must take. All addresses and data must be translated when they cross the gateway between networks of different architectures.

Note

In recent years, the term *gateway* has been used less strictly than it was originally intended. Sometimes gateway is used to describe routing functions within the same type of network.

Where To From Here?

This chapter described the different networking hardware items you can use to put together your network. Managing the networking hardware (and software, for that matter) requires an understanding of the operating systems running on the network. To learn next about these systems, see Chapter 5.

The Least You Need to Know

Right now, the least you need to know about networking hardware is this:

➤ A variety of computer workstations and servers can be connected to your network. These can include workstations, servers, and special network computers.

➤ NICs and modems can be used to connect to a network. Modems are used to dial remote networks whereas NICs are used on local area networks.

➤ Most LANs communicate over coaxial or twisted pair cables. However, some newer technologies allow computer LANs to connect using a building's electrical wiring, telephone lines in the building, or wireless radio frequencies. Also, fiber-optic cable is becoming more popular for greater speeds and distances.

➤ Hubs act as a connection point for the computers on a LAN. Switches are used to connect segments of a LAN to improve overall performance of the network. Routers deliver messages acress network boundaries, among networks of the same type.

Chapter 5

Network Servers and Clients at Your Service

In This Chapter

➤ Learn to set up network services in peer-to-peer or client/server arrangements

➤ Understand file servers, Web servers, and other types of network servers

➤ Read about workstations, thin clients, and other clients for accessing servers

➤ Find out what networking features are available in Windows, NetWare, and Linux/UNIX operating systems

---

It is all about caring and sharing. Well, at least it's about sharing. The only reason to have a computer network is to be able to share stuff: documents, printers, video clips, images, or just an open chat. So every computer on a network will either offer communications services, use those services, or do both. There's no reason to connect a computer to a network that doesn't do those things.

This chapter describes the kinds of computing systems that you might want to have connected to your network. I begin with a bit of networking theory to explain peer-to-peer and client/server networks. Then I describe the kinds of computer operating systems you can choose from and the kinds of *client* (service user) and *server* (service provider) systems that are available.

Peer-to-Peer Versus Client/Server Networks

➤ **Peer-to-Peer Networks** In this type of setup, the computers are all considered equals. (See "We Are All Equal: Peer-to-Peer Networks," later in this chapter, for details.) So, if you want to open a file or send a document to a printer, you would make a request that goes directly to the computer of the owner of that file or printer. For example, a request might consist of clicking the Print button on your word processor, selecting your friend's printer from a list, and clicking OK.

➤ **Client/Server Networks**   In this type of network, shared files, printers, newsgroups, applications, and other stuff are connected to central server computers and accessed by client computers. A client is typically a single-user workstation (a Macintosh or Windows PC); a server tends to be a beefed-up multi-user computer (such as Linux, Windows NT, UNIX, or NetWare).

Check This Out

A server computer must have special software to be a server. A server may or may not have special hardware. What makes it a server is that it provides a service to other computers on a network.

That said, often a server that needs to provides critical files to a company or Web pages to people around the world will rely on more powerful hardware. That is more because of the demand on the server than on the fact that it is a server. In a small office, for example, an old 486 computer might do well as a print server for a couple of low-volume printers.

Many networks use a combination of these approaches, treating some computers as servers and others as peers. The key points that you want to consider are whether to

➤ Centralize the services on your network (that is, have expensive hardware and file storage managed from a few server computers)

➤ Spread the services around (that is, have every person store his own files on his own workstation and attach hardware willy-nilly to different workstations).

Before I get into the details about peer-to-peer and client/server networks, take a look at the following side-by-side comparison of the two network types. This should help give you an idea of the attributes of each type of network. In Table 5.1, I list the most important characteristics of both network types.

Table 5.1 Peer–to–Peer and Client/Server Networks Contrasted

Issue	Peer-to-Peer	Client/Server
Cost	Inexpensive	Can be expensive
File Sharing	Yes	Yes
Geek Factor	Low	High
Growth	Very limited	Potentially unlimited
Logging	Virtually none	Advanced logging
Maintenance	Moderate	Significant
Management	Little or none	Advanced management
Location of Services	Spread out	Centralized
Remote Printing	Yes	Yes
Remote Sessions	Not generally	Yes
Scalability	So-so	Excellent
Security	Little or none	Advanced security
Setup	Quick and painless	Complex
Shared peripherals	Yes	Yes

The next section describes the different approaches.

We Are All Equal: Peer-to-Peer Networks

Small office or home networks are often set up in a peer-to-peer arrangement. Peer-to-peer networks are typically small (10 workstations or fewer) and are nearly always local area networks (LANs). Their chief characteristic is this: They have no centralized server and, therefore, no centralized control.

In peer-to-peer networks, each workstation has roughly the same capabilities as its peers. In this respect, peer-to-peer networks offer you the bare minimum: the ability to share files, peripherals, and other resources.

Advantages of Peer-to-Peer Networks

The principal advantages of peer-to-peer networks are *simplicity* and *economy*—simplicity because peer-to-peer networks take only minutes to establish, and economy because the requisite hardware and software are inexpensive. Buy a few PCs running some version of Microsoft Windows and a network kit—typically one Ethernet card per computer and a hub—and you're good to go.

In a peer-to-peer network, printers, scanners, and fax machines can be shared, as shown in Figure 5.1. Thus, any connected peer can access remote peripherals. For example, this allows a user at Workstation 3 (see Figure 5.1) to print from a printer connected to Workstation 1.

Figure 5.1

All workstations can share the same printer.

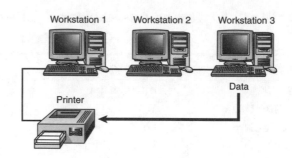

Likewise, all workstations can share directories and files. Therefore, a user at Workstation 3 can transfer files from Workstation 1, as shown in Figure 5.2.

Figure 5.2

Moving files on a peer-to-peer network is easy, because all machines can share their files and directories.

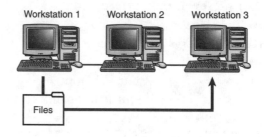

Note

To learn more about networking hardware (such as hubs and network cards), see Chapter 4, "Choosing Your Networking Hardware."

In these respects, peer-to-peer networks give you the most networking bang for your buck in small, trusted workgroups. To set up such a network takes less than an hour. To learn how, see Chapter 8, "Building Your Home Network."

Disadvantages of Peer-to-Peer Networks

The principal disadvantage of peer-to-peer networking is the lack of centralized control. Here are problems with peer-to-peer networks that could be better addressed with a client/server arrangement (discussed in the next section):

➤ **Inconsistent Availability**   If you need a file right now, and the file's owner is not available, you may be out of luck. For example, if Judy goes on vacation for two weeks and you absolutely need the legal brief she was working on, if her office is locked, her computer shut off, or her password unknown, you may not get that file.

➤ **Lack of Central Control**   One person might protect your proprietary documents on a computer that's locked in a closet and protected with passwords and guard dogs. Another person might leave for lunch with his computer on and all your company's secret strategy papers in his My Documents folder. Without central control, your company documents are as safe as the weakest peer.

➤ **Uneven Performance**   Today, your documents might print on Joe's computer just fine. Tomorrow, he might need to attach a scanner to his parallel port for a few hours (and disconnect the printer you need). Likewise, that CAD/CAM program that Betty runs may slow down her computer's capability to act as a router between you and another LAN in your building.

Techno Tip

Trusted computers are ones that are under your control and are considered safe from outside attacks. As a result, the computers can be set up to freely exchange information without causing a serious threat to the information on them.

If you have more than a handful of people on your network, you probably want to think about moving from a peer-to-peer to a client/server arrangement. By adding file, print, and other kinds of servers, you can offload those jobs from individual workstations. Besides computer performance, people performance should improve as well. In the long run, it is better to allow your people to do their work and let dedicated administrators manage document storage and refill paper trays. That's what dedicated servers and administrators are for.

Check This Out

I might have given you the impression that peer-to-peer networks cannot be networked with the world at large. That's not entirely true. In fact, it's possible to tie several peer-to-peer networks together using remote communication. Thus, one peer-to-peer network in one building can send information to a similar network in another.

The key here is not that you can't; it's just that you might not want to. Imagine a business in which everyone keeps her own petty cash, buys her own office supplies, and files every document she works on in a personal filing cabinet. After an organization grows to a certain size, it becomes as economical to centralize computing resources as it does other functions of the business.

Serving Up a Client/Server Network

In client/server networks, workstations rely on data and services from one or more centralized servers. These servers can control various systems including applications, printing, communication, and administration.

Check This Out

The term *client/server* actually originated in the programming community. It refers to a programming model in which a single server—typically an application server—can distribute data to many clients (for example, the relationship between a Web server and Web clients or *browsers*). Many network applications and protocols are based on the client/server model. However, in recent years, the terms *client* and *server* have been more generally applied to machines that run either client or server software. The distinction is now minor (because the more recent interpretation is in wide use).

Advantages of Client/Server Networks

The principal advantages of client/server networks are centralization, security, and logging capabilities. Let's talk about these for a moment.

Centralization

Centralization is a powerful advantage for several reasons. First, it allows easier and more efficient file management. This is especially true in reference to file storage. By enforcing centralized file storage, you proof your system against even the most disorganized employees.

The truth is, even folks who are exceptionally organized in other areas of their lives might lack organization in their computing. I would estimate that 80% of all computer users have useless files cluttering their computers. Worse still, most users have such files scattered across their hard disk drives. (You know the drill. They install a game, find that it doesn't work, and forget to uninstall it. Or worse, they give their directories ambiguous names, names that don't even remotely reflect their purpose.)

In a centralized file-management environment, *you* control file and directory names, locations, sizes, and so on. The drawback to this, of course, is that you're responsible for organization.

Security

Another key advantage of client/server networks is increased security. Most client/server environments have discretionary access control, which allows you to incisively grant or deny access to files, directories, and resources based on user, host, time, or date. For example, you can specify that Joe User can access the SYS:ETC directory on a NetWare server only from his own workstation (and then only between the hours of 8:00 a.m. and 5:00 p.m.). In peer-to-peer networking, this type of stringent security policy cannot be enforced (or at least, not without purchasing and installing third-party security suites).

Also, the operating system that you use on your server computer can be inherently more secure than most desktop systems. For example, UNIX, Linux, and NetWare servers were designed from the ground up to handle stringent access methods that are not available in Microsoft Windows operating systems.

Logging

Finally, client/server networks typically have excellent logging facilities, allowing you to debug your network sessions. This is in contrast to most peer-to-peer configurations, which by default keep few or even no logs.

Note

To learn more about network security (and how client/server networks help implement it), see Chapter 14, "Securing Your Fortress."

Disadvantages of Client/Server Networks

There are also some disadvantages to client/server networks, as listed here:

➤ **Centralization**   Although centralized resources and management are definite advantages, if your servers go down, so does your productivity. Clients rely on the server for data. In most cases, if the server dies, your clients die with it. For this reason, you should always have several, full-featured workstations on hand. With critical data, you should also consider techniques such as *mirroring,* where identical copies of data files are stored on multiple computers or hard disks.

➤ **Complexity**   Client/server networks are more difficult to configure and administer than peer networks. This can add to your cost (for example, you might have to train your staff).

➤ **Expense**   Server operating systems, software, and hardware are more expensive than their peer-to-peer counterparts. However, the cost-per-user can be much lower if many people use the server.

The next section describes the different types of network servers that are available, followed by the types of client computers that can take advantage of these servers. After that, some of the most popular operating systems that you can use on a network are described.

Some Shall Serve and Others Shall Be Clients

If you decide to move your network from peer-to-peer workstations toward a client/server model, you can begin to see how cost savings can improve. As your servers get fatter and more powerful, your client workstations or other devices can get thinner. In other words, as you move services onto a server, you can get by with less expensive clients.

The following sections describe what kinds of services can be moved from workstations on to server computers. After that, you'll see what kinds of client computers and devices are available to use these services.

Serving Files, Web Content, and Other Stuff

Do many people in your organization need to access the same files, run the same application programs, or quickly turn out printed documents? If so, you can potentially save time, money, and effort by setting up a server to handle these services.

The following sections run down some of the most popular types of servers that you might want to set up on your network:

➤ Application servers

➤ Web servers

➤ File servers

➤ Mail servers

➤ Print servers

➤ Directory services servers

➤ Fax servers

In most cases, you can use a computer running the Linux or other UNIX-like operating system as the base for configuring these servers. (Operating systems are described later in this chapter.)

Application Servers

Application servers house applications such as ledgers, databases, word-processors, or other office-oriented programs. In an application server-based network, clients rarely store information locally. Instead, clients make inquiries and send updates to the server.

A typical application server environment is where the server houses a contact database and its accompanying application. In contrast, clients run a scaled-down version of the application that allows users to view records from (or transmit new information to) the server. Many mainstream software firms have developed complex packages for application server environments. Good examples are Lotus Notes and Microsoft Access.

The principal advantage of application servers is centralized management of data. Also, application servers obviate the need to install full-blown applications on client workstations. This saves space and money.

Depending on how the application server is configured and how the applications are launched, the applications might be drawing on processing power from either the server or the client computers. If the server is handling the processing, the server might require multiple central processor units (CPUs) and extra random access memory (RAM) to handle the load. The client computers, on the other hand, could potentially be thin, inexpensive devices that might only need enough processing power to handle the graphical user interface (GUI).

Web Servers

Web servers are used to publish Web pages and related content on the Internet. Every time you ask for an address beginning with "http://" from your Web browser, that content is delivered to you from a Web server.

Here are just a few of the kinds of content that a Web server can serve up:

➤ **e-Commerce**   Web servers can deliver forms and scripts (small programs) that allow people to choose products, select delivery methods, and enter credit card information to make purchases.

➤ **Audio**   Music and speech can be stored on a Web server and delivered to the Web browser where that content can be played or stored.

➤ **Video**   Clips from movies or television shows can be downloaded and played from Web servers.

➤ **Documents**   A variety of document formats can be obtained from Web servers and displayed in a Web browser.

If you or your company want a presence on the Web, you either need your own Web server or you need to sign on with a Web-hosting company that can provide that service for you. For many people and small businesses, it is more economical (both in time and money) to hire out all or some of that service to a hosting service.

Because so much information is being placed into hypertext markup language (HTML) format (the language of Web pages), you might want to consider setting up a Web server that is used internally in your office. Many companies today have such an arrangement to allow employees to access Web pages detailing company policies, benefit programs, or company events.

File Servers

File servers centralize data storage. The server stores files, and the client requests them. Commonly used for development in software design and other "sharing-type" work, file servers are excellent for use in collaborative work environments.

One popular type of file server on the Internet is called a File Transfer Protocol (FTP) server. FTP servers are designed to be fairly secure mechanisms for offering documents to users on the Web. Often these servers allow visitors to copy files from a defined set of documents and folders, while preventing (or restricting) the user's ability to copy files to the server.

Mail Servers

Mail servers act as gathering places for email destined for the users who have accounts on those mail servers. Although the function of mail servers is quite simple in theory (someone sends an email message and the server holds it in a file until the user asks to read it), managing mail servers has actually become quite a complex job.

Today, email servers need to be configured to deal with such things as *viruses* (files containing sneaky, harmful content) and *spamming* (an onslaught of email messages sent to massive numbers of users). Likewise, the tools for managing mail servers are quite complex and all seem to be written in geek. In many mail servers, there are massive plain-text configuration files that an administrator can set up to define how mail is forwarded, who is denied service, and how messages are queued.

The most popular types of email servers are Internet Mail Access Protocol (IMAP) and Post Office Protocol (POP) servers. From a user's email reader (such as Microsoft Outlook), requests to send or receive mail go directly to one of these mail servers. If the account and password are correct, the mail server handles the request.

Print Servers

Print servers manage networked printer peripherals and allow authorized individuals to print from their workstations. Today, folks use print servers less than they used to because many software companies have integrated printer management into their software, eliminating the need for a dedicated server.

One advantage to using print servers is that they distribute documents to printers that are not busy at the moment. They can also add a measure of security to printing; for example, certain high-end color printers might need to be restricted to certain users.

Directory Services Servers

Directory services servers contain indexes of users, workstations, applications, network servers, and other information associated with a network. Their chief function is to enable easy administration of large networks (more than 100 computers). Often, directory service servers provide an index of absolutely everything on the network. This index can include the exact types of computer hardware on the network, the types of operating system each is running, and even the applications (and versions of those applications) that are installed on each.

Fax Servers

Fax servers manage network fax traffic through one or more fax/modem cards. Users request faxes that have been sent or received with software on their client or workstation. In turn, the server reports (and can deliver) those faxes to the user.

Although fax servers are a relatively new phenomenon, many manufacturers have created fax server software. For more information, check out `http://www.3com.com` or `http://www.panasonic.com`.

As you can see, client/server computing is complex. There are servers for nearly everything. Indeed, some network operating systems (most notably Linux and other UNIX systems) ship with all the aforementioned servers. Offloading server features from workstations has given rise to a variety of client computing devices. The next section describes some of these devices.

Signing Up a New Client

By now you know that clients are PCs, workstations, or other devices on which users run applications. Clients rely on servers for resources, such as files, devices, and even processing power. Many times, a client is nothing more than an application or machine designed specifically to access data that is centrally housed on a server. In other words, a client might be not much more than a screen and a keyboard.

There are several types of clients, including

➤ Workstations
➤ Thin clients
➤ Diskless clients
➤ Fat clients

Let's take a look at each one now.

Workstations

The term *workstation* has two meanings, one traditional and one contemporary.

The traditional definition of a *workstation* is a microcomputer that's designed expressly to run the UNIX operating system. Workstations were used by people who needed a lot of processing power (such as engineers, architects, computer scientists, and stockbrokers).

In today's networking world, the term *workstation* has a more general, relaxed meaning. For our purposes, a workstation is any full-fledged computer attached to a local area network. That is, a workstation is any computer that has client and application software, advanced storage facilities, and essential extras such as a hard disk, a CD-ROM drive, a floppy disk drive, a monitor, a mouse, and a keyboard.

Another way to classify a workstation is this: any computer that can operate effectively as a standalone system, without network connectivity. For our purposes, let's say that any desktop computer (Windows PC, Mac, or desktop UNIX system) is a workstation.

I assume that most of you will be using a PC or a Macintosh computer as a workstation to access any servers that are available. As your servers become more powerful, you could have the opportunity to save some money by purchasing scaled-down client computers, such as thin clients and diskless workstations, discussed in the next two sections.

Thin Clients

Thin clients are machines or processes that have only the bare minimum in localized software. Localized software is software that runs on the thin client's own processor, as opposed to a program that runs on another processor and is sent to the client. The thin client's express purpose is to interact with a centralized server.

Whenever thin client users need to run a program, they download that program from the server. Such thin clients are used in networks where servers perform all the data processing. In this respect, thin clients are a throwback to the dawn of networking.

Until recently, thin clients have only been practical for large enterprises and here's why: Small businesses typically use commercial-off-the-shelf (COTS) applications such as Microsoft Word and Excel. Thin clients are most useful for networking proprietary systems, such as those used in retail or in production environments.

Simplified tools for developing Web applications and Web-ready thin clients are making thin client computers more practical for small business. To learn about tools for developing and deploying Web-based thin client programs, visit the products page for Citrix System on the Web (http://www.citrix.com/products).

Diskless Clients

Diskless clients are machines that have neither software nor networking firmware installed. Instead, they rely on floppy boot disks or erasable programmable read-only memory (EPROM) boot chips. These load tiny software modules into memory that establish a connection between the diskless client and the server. Such configurations are rare these days.

Diskless clients reached their heyday in the early 1990s, particularly on the Novell NetWare platform. If anything, the major advantage of diskless clients is that they're incredibly inexpensive. For example, you can establish a diskless client using a 386 PC with 8MB of RAM. So long as you're accessing NetWare only (and running DOS-based applications on the server), your 386 PC would fly. However, the disadvantage of diskless clients is pretty fundamental: They have no storage and rely exclusively on the server. When the server is down, the diskless client is down.

Diskless clients also exist in the UNIX world. However, these don't rely on boot floppy disks. Instead, older UNIX workstations (SPARCstations in particular) house firmware that can communicate with a boot server over the network. In other words, when the diskless client starts up, it gets all its network address, name, and basic start-up information from a network server.

Fat Client Scenarios

Fat clients are machines that have infinitely more local software than thin clients but still not as much as PCs. You can technically refer to any PC or workstation as a fat client. However, there are several firms that actually manufacture *bona fide* fat clients. In the fat client scenario, data might still be stored on a server, but applications that manipulate that data reside on the local machine. Fat clients, therefore, move users away from centralized computing.

Your Network Brain Centers: the Operating Systems

An *operating system (OS)* is the combination of software programs that work together to manage your computer. It stands between the application programs (such as word processors and spreadsheets) and the hardware. In essence, the OS allows your programs to use the hard disk, CPU, CD-ROM, serial ports, printer, and so on.

A *network operating system (NOS)* is dedicated to managing network resources. It can be a server—handling file storage, printer sharing, application sharing, or Web publishing—or it can act as a central place for managing network traffic, users, or computers.

With the exception of NetWare (which is a pure network operating system), most of the operating systems described in this chapter can act as regular workstations. However, each system contains enough networking features to allow it to be configured to provide dedicated network services.

This section describes several different operating systems that you could use on your network. However, most of the examples in this book focus on two different operating systems:

➤ **Windows 95/98/2000**　On the client side, most people have at least one PC running some Windows operating system. If that is all you have, you can share those computer systems in a peer-to-peer network.

➤ **Linux**　If you want to expand your network to include a server operating system, I recommend using Linux. Linux is a freeware version of UNIX that is available everywhere and very well documented. (You can purchase a Linux book that includes the entire operating system for just a few dollars.) To tell the truth, it's a bit tough at first to learn Linux. But, if you have an old PC you are not using, Linux is an inexpensive way to learn about setting up networking services.

Check This Out

Although most people think of Microsoft Windows when they think of PCs, PCs can support many different types of operating systems. In fact, most popular operating systems, including UNIX, Linux, and NetWare, all can run on PC hardware. For example, with a Red Hat Linux CD and about an hour of time, you could completely replace Windows on your hard disk with Linux. Also with Linux and UNIX, as your needs grow, you can purchase more powerful workstation or mainframe computers to run those systems.

Although most operating systems provide many of the same services, they often do so with different levels of complexity and power. You can expect to find some or all of the following features in the systems described in this chapter:

➤ **Network hardware support**   With most systems you can connect modems (for dial-up networks) and Ethernet cards (for local area networks) to your computer. Some systems support hardware that allows connections to wide area networks as well.

➤ **File sharing**   Most systems enable you to share file folders or whole disk drives with clients on the network.

➤ **Printer sharing**   Most systems enable you to share printers with client computers over the network.

➤ **Device sharing**   Most systems let you share other hardware devices, such as CD-ROM drives and removable storage drives, on the network.

➤ **Web services**   Most systems enable you to add software that allows the computer to act as a Web server (to publish Web pages on the Internet).

➤ **Network administration**   Most systems include features for monitoring the network and managing other computers on the network. Advanced systems might offer directory services, which enable you to store and disseminate information about computer resources on the network.

➤ **Security services**   Most systems provide some level of network security. This can be as simple as providing passwords for users to protect their files or as complex as a firewall for screening traffic between multiple networks.

This chapter describes several operating systems that are available to use on your network.

Microsoft Windows Operating Systems

All the Microsoft Windows operating systems contain some level of networking support. Although Windows 95/98 systems are primarily desktop computers, they offer most basic client networking features. Windows NT, however, was designed for working in networked environments. The latest Windows 2000 operating system, however, has both desktop (Windows 2000 Professional) and server (Windows 2000 Server) versions.

Microsoft Windows 95/98

If you have Windows 95 or 98 computers connected to your network, you might already have all the support you need for basic networking. To expand the networking capabilities of Windows, you can add a variety of software enhancements (such as NetWare client support).

Figure 5.3

Microsoft Windows 95/98 are the most popular client desktop operating system.

Features available in Windows systems can be divided into connectivity features, protocol features, and services. Here is a list of connectivity features built into Windows 95/98/2000:

➤ **Dial-up connection**s   Most popular modems are supported by Windows 95/98/2000. Modems enable you to dial up remote computer networks.

➤ **LAN connection**   A variety of network adapter cards are supported to allow you to connect to Ethernet, Token Ring, and a variety of other types of networks. Also, any specialized driver that is available for a PC will come with its own driver to install in Windows.

Network protocols that are supported by Windows operating systems include at least the following:

➤ **TCP/IP (Internet)**   The TCP/IP protocols that allow you to connect to the Internet are available with all Windows systems.

➤ **IPX/SPX (NetWare)**   Protocols, such as IPX and SPX, are available for connecting to NetWare file and print servers.

➤ **NetBEUI**   The NetBEUI protocol, which allows you to do file and printer sharing among Windows peer workstations, is built into every Windows system.

After you are wired and configured to use the network, there are several basic networking services that are built into Windows operating systems. Along with those, there are many more network applications that come with Windows or can be purchased for your network. Here are some of the most basic network services that are already in Windows:

➤ **Remote login**   With user accounts set up properly, you can log in from another computer on a network and have access to the user's desktop and applications.

➤ **File and Printer Sharing**   The printer and file sharing features in Windows operating systems allow networked computers to share each other's printers and files. With file sharing, you can share individual folders or entire drives. Files and folders can be shared freely or be password protected.

Many different network applications are also available with Windows. Today, the centerpiece of network applications is the Web browser. Windows comes with Internet Explorer, although Netscape Communicator can be added instead. The Web browser lets you display Web pages (HTML) and file server contents (FTP), as well as a variety of audio, video, image, form, and document content.

Other applications within the Internet Explorer and Netscape Communicator suites allow you to send and receive email, participate in newsgroups, do conferencing, and compose Web pages (to name a few features). If you want your Web browser to be able to play or display other kinds of Web content, there are ways of configuring it to launch specific applications when it encounters data of a specific type. For example, you could launch your favorite music player when your browser encounters any MP3 files.

Microsoft Windows 2000

Windows 2000 is Microsoft's latest operating system offering. Unlike earlier versions of Windows that had limited networking support, Windows 2000 has many new networking features. Products are divided into the following two categories:

➤ **Windows 2000 Professional**   This operating system is aimed at the business desktop and laptop markets. Microsoft calls it the "desktop operating system for the Business Internet." It contains many new networking clients and administration. These include utilities for administering and monitoring the network, such as:

Net Watcher (to monitor clients and shared resources)

System Monitor (to allow remote monitoring of a system)

Remote Registry Service (to enable a remote administrator to change a computer's Registry)

➤ **Windows 2000 Server Family** This is actually a family of products, aimed at different types of network server markets. Features in Windows 2000 Server products include

Web and Application services (to serve a variety of Web and multimedia content)

Directory services (to manage hardware and software across large networks)

Security services (to provide security protocols and functions, such as encryption and public key infrastructure)

Note

Internet Explorer was added to some versions of Windows 95 and comes automatically with all later Windows versions. If you have Windows 95, but do not have Internet Explorer, you can download Internet Explorer free from Microsoft. Go to `http://www.microsoft.com/ie` and select the **Download** link.

Communications and Networking (to provide secure network communications, routing, virtual private networks, and DNS name service)

Management services (to configure, boot, and install software to groups of client computers)

Cross-platform integration (to interoperate with a variety of client computers)

Terminal services (to remotely access servers from terminal devices)

File and Print services (to hierarchically manage distributed file servers and storage media across the network)

An advantage of Windows 2000 over other network operating systems is that it offers an easy migration path from both Windows 95/98 (client) systems as well as Windows NT (server) systems. Many of the same applications can be run on both platforms.

Novell NetWare

A decade ago, NetWare was the leading product for providing file and print services to networked PCs. Although the rise of the Internet has shifted the focus of networking, NetWare and other Novell products are still used by millions of network users all over the world.

Figure 5.4

Windows 2000 features advanced networking services in both its Professional and Server editions.

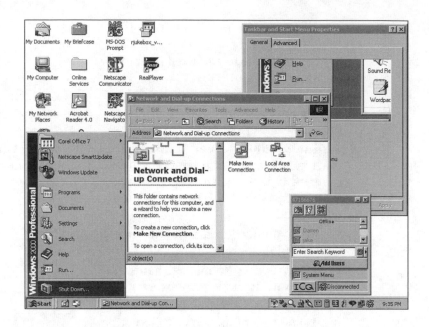

NetWare is, by all definitions, a network operating system. Its main job is to act as a server for file and print services. Along with those features, NetWare offers a complex set of security and management features to determine who has access to which services from the network.

Although NetWare began as a network operating system that was used primarily on IPX/SPX protocols (over Ethernet LANs), today NetWare servers can also be used in pure TCP/IP network environments. NetWare has also added to its traditional strength in file sharing and printer sharing by offering many Web-based services.

NetWare is not particularly appropriate for a home network, where you don't usually need high-volume printing or file sharing. However, here are some reasons that you might want to add a NetWare server to your small office network:

➤ **Speed**   Because NetWare is dedicated to serving up files and printing, it doesn't have the overhead of other general-purpose operating systems (such as Windows or UNIX). If high-volume file storage and retrieval is needed by your business, NetWare could be an excellent addition to your office.

➤ **Security**   You can configure access to files and folders down to the smallest details on a NetWare server. Security can also be managed remotely from different computers on your network.

➤ **Management**   If your office network grows to hundreds of computers, there is a really great feature in NetWare called ZENworks. With ZENworks, you can centrally manage all the computers on your network. You can keep track of all the hardware and software on every workstation from one location.

➤ **Application Launcher**   This feature of ZENworks enables administrators to gather and distribute even the most complex applications. The administrator captures applications by scanning the workstation before and after an application is installed. The resulting files, folders, configuration files, and Registry entries are gathered and distributed automatically to user workstations with Novell Directory Services (NDS). The point is that everything that is associated with an application can be copied from one computer and distributed to another computer on the network.

Linux and Other UNIX Systems

Networking features were being built into the UNIX operating system before PCs even existed. From the beginning of the Internet, UNIX has been the predominant Internet operating system. Today's UNIX systems are rich in networking features and are still the systems most often used to develop cutting-edge networking technology.

There are many different versions of UNIX available today, but Linux has experienced the most recent spurt of popularity. For the sake of simplicity, this book focuses on Linux as the preferred version of UNIX for people who want to learn how to set up their own servers. Most of the feature descriptions in this section, however, apply to most UNIX systems.

Strictly speaking, Linux is not a network operating system in the same way that NetWare is. Whereas NetWare is dedicated to managing network resources, Linux offers a full range of features that allow it to act as a workstation, a peer, a server, or a client. By design, Linux is also not limited by PC hardware. There are versions of Linux running on more powerful workstations, and versions of UNIX that run on everything from PCs to super computers. Figure 5.7 shows an example of Red Hat Linux, with the GNOME desktop environment providing the user interface.

Although Linux and UNIX were once used primarily from dumb character terminals (screens that showed only letters and no graphics), *graphical user interfaces (GUIs)* are now available on every version of UNIX. In fact, even the GUIs are network ready.

What Is Linux?

Linux is a free, UNIX-like operating system that was created in 1991 by Linus Torvalds when he was a student at the University of Helsinki. He posted it to the Internet and soon received code fixes and new programs. Today, nearly 10,000 programmers contribute to the coding, testing, and discussion groups that continuously improve the Linux operating system.

Although Linux code was written from scratch, the operating system didn't exactly come from thin air. Published standards that drove the development of the UNIX system, POSIX in particular, made Linux about as much like UNIX as possible without actually owning the trademark. In many ways, however, Linux has developed beyond UNIX because there are so many people contributing to its features and improvements.

Figure 5.5

In the past few years, Linux has become a powerful server operating system in the UNIX system market.

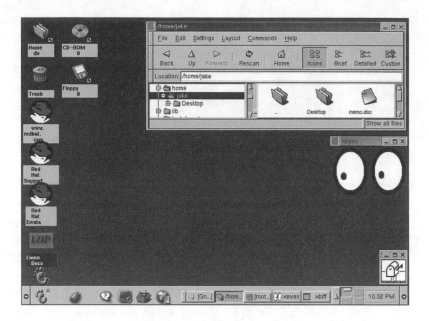

There is no shortage of networking standards for Linux to adhere to. Linux contains a full complement of networking features, particularly related to the Internet. Linux programmers tend to be especially savvy about the Internet—they used the Internet as the primary tool for communicating and distributing information about Linux.

Distributions of Linux

Currently, there are Linux versions that run on Intel-compatible PCs, Digital Alpha computers, and Sun SPARC computers. Although the source code of Linux is available free on the Internet, there are ready-to-run (binary) versions of Linux available from commercial vendors for a fee. These include

➤ Red Hat Linux (`http://www.redhat.com`)

➤ Caldera OpenLinux (`http://www.calderasystems.com`)

➤ Debian Linux (`http://www.linuxpress.com`)

➤ S.u.S.E. Linux (`http://www.suse.com`)

➤ Slackware (`ftp://ftp.cdrom.com/pub/linux/slackware`)

These commercial versions of Linux tend to be fairly inexpensive (starting under $30). With the addition of installation procedures and often some form of technical support, many users find the benefits of a commercial distribution worth the small price. These distributions are also available free if you download them from the Internet.

Advantages of Linux

Using Linux offers many advantages, including the following:

➤ It's free to anyone who wants to download it and is inexpensive in packaged CD-ROM forms.

➤ Corrections and enhancements are continuously being made by thousands of developers around the world. (Some say Linux developers outnumber the developers on any other operating system 10 to 1.)

➤ Because the source code is readily available, those who are so inclined can modify it to suit their own needs.

➤ There are thousands of free or inexpensive add-on packages available to run on Linux.

Linux also contains a rich set of networking features that rival any commercial operating system today. These features include the following:

➤ **Networking features**   Programs for using networks (email, browsers, ftp, and so on) and tools for administering the network (routing, logging, and management tools) are built into the basic Linux system. Even advanced features (such as firewalls and Web servers) come with the basic distributions.

➤ **Multi user cost economies**   Besides being built to network, Linux was also built to accommodate multiple users and multitasking. This means that many users can be using the computer at the same time and that each user can be running many programs at once.

➤ **Centralized administration**   From a central Linux system, an administrator can manage many users, workstations, and even multiple networks. Applications, disk space, printers, and a variety of devices can be shared in a way that makes life easier for end users.

Disadvantages of Linux

Of course, using Linux has its disadvantages, too:

➤ **Not ready for prime time?**   Some people feel that Linux has not yet proven itself as being reliable enough for a company's mission-critical applications.

➤ **Made for geeks**   Although UNIX was designed for networking from the ground up, it was not designed for ease of use. It's nearly impossible to do everything required to manage a network without an understanding of the UNIX shell, editing system files, and compiling programs.

Many of the most powerful UNIX tools (especially those for managing networks) still require you to run text-based commands. With menus or icons for some tools, you need to remember command names and options to do your job. The bottom line is that you probably won't want to take on UNIX to manage your network without some training first.

➤ **Applications still missing**   Many business applications, especially those you can purchase off the shelf, don't run on UNIX. Because of the economics of developing applications for the PC marketplace, many software vendors and companies that create their own applications run only on Windows operating systems.

➤ **UNIX systems are different**   Even though most UNIX systems began from source code originally delivered from AT&T, the UNIX systems that have made it to market all contain some subtle— and some not so subtle—differences. In particular, many vendors have added their own simplified methods for administering the systems. As a result, even if you learn how to set up one type of UNIX system, chances are you can't use the exact same sequence of commands, options, or configuration files to do it on another UNIX version. That's why administering a UNIX system doesn't mean learning an exact set of procedures—it means fiddling with it until it works.

On the whole, Linux is a good way to create your first server systems. However, if you feel more secure trusting your business to commercial operating systems, there are commercial versions of UNIX available. These include Solaris from Sun Microsystems (http://www.sun.com) and SCO UNIX and UnixWare from Santa Cruz Operation (http://www.sco.com).

Where To From Here?

With some background on network hardware (Chapter 4) and computing systems and services (this chapter), you can proceed to Chapter 6, "Take a Bus, Hitch a Star, Ring Around Network Topologies." In Chapter 6, you can learn how networking equipment can be arranged in different topologies (that is, ways of connecting computers), depending on your needs.

The Least You Need to Know

Right now, the least you need to know about network clients, servers, and operating systems is this:

➤ Peer-to-peer networking arrangements are useful for small office and home networks. They are easy and inexpensive to start, but lack central security and management features.

➤ Client/server networking is useful in larger networks, in which it is more efficient for such features as document storage and network management to be handled on a centralized computer.

➤ Basic networking, such as file and printer sharing, can be done from even the least-sophisticated network operating systems (such as Windows 95).

➤ With the addition of Internet Explorer and dial-up networking, Microsoft Windows operating systems have become more powerful tools for connecting to networks (particularly the Internet).

➤ NetWare offers advanced networking features, including Novell Directory Services (NDS). By using ZENworks with NDS, administrators can centrally administer user configurations, software distribution, and computer hardware setups.

➤ Linux and other UNIX operating systems have the richest set of networking features. Along with its excellent set of features, Linux has the advantage of being available free. UNIX-like systems can be difficult for non technical people to administer and work with, however.

Chapter 6

Take a Bus, Hitch a Star, Ring Around Network Topologies

> **In this chapter**
>
> ➤ Learn about topology
>
> ➤ Discover different topologies and their purposes
>
> ➤ Choose a topology for your network

Maybe you start off with a network that connects a few computers in your office. In time, your office grows to include hundreds of computers. Later, your business adds two branch offices that each has ten or more computers. How do you lay out your computer network to accommodate the present, while still keeping an eye to the future?

Network topology refers to the physical layout of your computer network. This includes the way in which each computer is wired into the network, as well as how equipment (such as hubs and switches) is used to join together different parts of the network.

In this chapter, you'll learn the advantages and disadvantages of each topology type and which one is best for you. You will then learn how your topology can expand as new computers need to be added to your network.

Topology Types

Much like different network types, each topology type has its advantages and disadvantages. These qualities in many instances run parallel to the advantages and disadvantages of networks. For example, various topologies will render you varying performance in the following areas:

➤ Centralization

➤ Cost

➤ Maintenance and troubleshooting

➤ Scalability

➤ Security

➤ Speed

➤ Stability

Note

Your choice of network topology will be also influenced by other considerations, including distance. Network cable types (and other transport hardware, such as hubs, routers, and switches) have widely varying limitations on distance. Some can transmit only a few hundred feet, although others can transmit well over a thousand. Newer technology, such as Fiber Distributed Data Interface (FDDI), can support distances of two kilometers or more between stations. To learn more about wire, hardware, and distance, see Chapter 4, "Choosing Your Networking Hardware."

In addition to these factors, you'll also need to consider a special issue called the *single point of failure (SPF)*. This is a physical or logical location (a server, hub, wire, or router) where one or more network device connects. When this connection fails, one or more workstations will be unable to transmit data.

Every network has at least one single point of failure. In networks that perform mission-critical tasks, the trick is to minimize the damage that occurs when that single point finally fails. As you'll see, different topologies pose different limitations in this regard.

Let's start with the simple topologies:

➤ Bus

➤ Star

➤ Ring

The Magic Bus: Bus Topology

Bus topology (sometimes called *linear bus topology*) is simple and works like this: The network is supported by a long, uninterrupted cable called a *backbone*. This backbone is the root of all connectivity. Network devices (workstations, terminals, and peripherals) draw their network feed from the backbone, as shown in Figure 6.1.

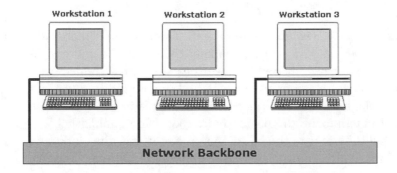

Figure 6.1

All workstations tap their connectivity from the backbone. In this respect, a backbone is much like a river. It flows through the valley (your network), supporting life on its banks.

Bus topology is typically used in smaller networks. A common scenario is where 10 users (or fewer) need to share data and peripherals. In such environments, not only are workstations usually within close proximity to each other, but users rarely send data very far.

Advantages of Bus Topology

For many years, bus topology was exceedingly popular, due largely to its simplicity. Implementing bus topology is very straightforward: You simply string a backbone and plug in your workstations. Moreover, bus topology is inexpensive because it requires neither hubs nor routers.

If you implement a bus topology in a small office environment, it's not necessary to house all workstations in the same space. You can still achieve a widespread office LAN by winding your backbone through the building. (So long as the wire is continuous, it doesn't matter how many twists and turns it takes.)

Check This Out

Hubs are hardware devices that centralize network activity. Network cables run from workstations to the hub. The hub then repeats the signals it receives, and these are routed out again to other network devices. *Routers*, on the other hand, are more complex, and route packets in and out of networks. Read more about these devices in Chapter 4 and packets (and packet switching networks) in Chapter 3, "Using a Worldwide Network (the Internet)".

Techno Tip

The backbone cable must be *terminated* at both ends. This is accomplished with a T (sometimes called a *T-pin*), a device that terminates the signal at either end. T-pins are so named because they're shaped like a letter T with three connectors. Two of these connectors ensure a continued signal, and one is used to splice in a workstation. When T-pins are used for termination, a small plastic or metal cap is placed on the end. This terminates the signal. (Note that if you establish a bus-based network and fail to terminate the backbone on either end, the workstations probably won't recognize one another.) You'll find more on termination in Chapter 4.

Disadvantages of Bus Topology

There are three chief disadvantages to bus topology:

➤ **Bus topology–based networks are difficult to troubleshoot**   If you experience problems at the network level, you might find it difficult to isolate the source. (Problems of this nature include traffic jams, where, for a variety of reasons, packet delivery might slow to a crawl.)

➤ **Bus topology lacks central administration**   Because most bus topology–based networks have no hubs, routers, or switches, they're difficult to manage. For example, you can't perform network segmentation. (*Network segmentation* is where hardware devices segregate some workstations from others. Such segmentation increases your security and ease of management.)

➤ **Bus topology is subject to speed and performance constraints**   In bus topology, only one workstation at a time can send data. Thus, each additional workstation eats substantial network resources. Bus topology is therefore undesirable for use in client/server networks because clients often make multiple requests. A large population of clients attached via bus topology will slow your network considerably.

Additionally, bus topology–based networks have a high-profile single point of failure. That is, if your network backbone fails, the entire network is effectively knocked out.

Finally, bus topology is undesirable from a security standpoint. Data sent from one workstation is transmitted to all remaining workstations. Under normal conditions, only the intended recipient captures that transmission. However, with simple modification, any connected workstation could capture all transmissions (even though that workstation is not "entitled" to the information). This is a minor point, however. Bus topology is rarely used in secure network environments.

Techno Tip

To network my home computers for the first time, I used a bus topology. I had two PCs and two Ethernet cards (with BNC connectors). I put T-connectors on each card with a terminator on one side. Then I connected a thinnet cable between them. (See Chapter 4 for a description of thinnet cables.) Later, to add a third computer, I removed a terminator, and then connected another thinnet cable to the third computer (adding a terminator to the end).

For me, the bus topology was a cheap way to get started because I had BNC hardware lying around and didn't have to buy a hub. Eventually, I changed over to a Star topology (covered next) because I added several new computers and a DSL modem that all had RJ-45 connectors.

Thank Your Lucky Stars: Star Topology

Star topology is significantly more structured than bus topology, and focuses on centralization. In a typical star network, each computer or peripheral is connected to a central point, as shown in Figure 6.2. Thus, the failure of one connection will not usually affect the others.

Note

This is not always true. Certainly, if the main connection houses a mail server and it fails, other workstations will not be able to retrieve mail. However, in star networks, if one cable connection goes down, the others remain unaffected.

Figure 6.2

In star networks, each network device attaches separately to a centralized hub.

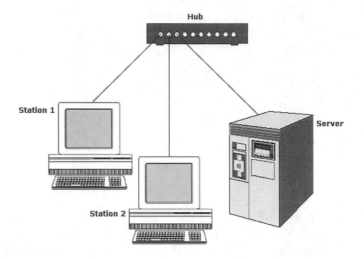

Advantages of Star Topology

The chief advantages of star topology are

- ➤ **Star topology offers centralization**   Thus, star networks are more easily managed and secured.
- ➤ **Star networks are usually faster than bus networks**   Because each workstation is independently wired directly to the hub, data is transmitted directly, allowing greater speed and organization.
- ➤ **Star networks are stable**   If one workstation fails, the rest continue to operate unhindered. Damage control is therefore much easier. (Compare this to the total single point of failure in bus topology.)

Another major advantage of star topology is that reconfiguration is a snap. For example, you can instantly add or subtract workstations and peripherals by plugging them into the hub.

Additionally, star networks free you from many limitations common to bus-based networks. For example, star topology allows you to break your network into segments. (These are small groups of workstations in close physical proximity to one another.) You needn't necessarily house all workstations in close physical proximity. Instead, you can create departmental islands and later connect these to other LANs or LAN segments of varying topologies.

Disadvantages of Star Networks

The chief disadvantage of star networks is that they have a single point of failure at the hub level. Hence, if a hub cable breaks (or the hub fails for other reasons), all workstations on that segment will lose connectivity.

Finally, star networks can represent a greater initial investment because even inexpensive hubs start at about $90, although bus topologies don't require hubs. Additionally, the average hub has between 8 and 20 ports (*ports* are what your workstations get plugged into). Although some low-end ports can have as few as 4 ports. If the number of workstations you have exceeds the number of available ports, you'll need to buy another hub. (Frankly, if your network is of any size, you might end up stringing several stars together.)

Ring Topology

Ring topology features a single cable to which all workstations and peripherals are connected. In this respect, ring topology marginally resembles bus topology. The difference is that a ring network's backbone is a closed loop (hence the term *ring*), as shown in Figure 6.3.

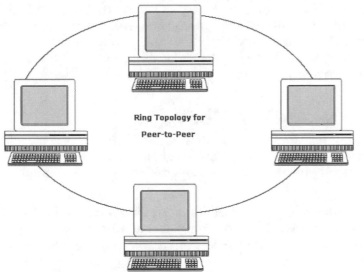

Ring Topology for

Peer-to-Peer

Figure 6.3

Ring networks rely on a single backbone, much like bus-based networks

In a ring configuration, data travels around the ring from one workstation to the next. Each workstation or network device acts as a repeater, regenerating the signal and passing it on. Each workstation also has two neighbors, forming a closed ring or circuit system as illustrated in the previous Figure 6.3.

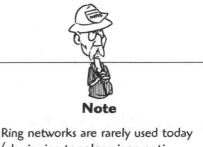

Note

Ring networks are rarely used today (classic ring topology is an antiquated technology). However, when used, such networks are almost always peer-to-peer.

109

Advantages of Ring Topology

Ring topology has the same basic advantages as bus topology:

➤ Ring networks can be easier to establish.

➤ Ring networks represent low initial overhead (that is, no need to purchase a hub, and each wire only has to connect to the next workstation instead of having all wires come back to the hub).

Disadvantages of Ring Topology

The chief disadvantage of ring networks is that they have not just one point of failure, but many. (That number is equal to the number of connected network devices.) This is a pretty critical issue.

To appreciate the difference, imagine this: Suppose you had a star network with six workstations and one file server. If the file server died, all six workstations would be unable to download files. However, all six workstations could still function and communicate with one another. In a ring setting, that isn't true. If even one network device fails, or the cable between any two workstations is disconnected, the entire network is temporarily incapacitated.

Growing Your Network Topology

So far, I have described three network topologies (bus, star, and ring) that you could use to create a local network containing from two to perhaps two dozen computers. The next step is to understand how that topology can grow to add more computers to your network.

Just to back up a bit, I want to remind you of what I mean by "your network." As you will recall, the Internet is a network of networks. Your local network (the one connecting the computers controlled by your organization) is connected to other networks (such as the Internet or another network in your company) through what are called *routers*. Within your own network, however, additional segments of your network can be connected using *hubs* and *switches*.

The example in this section describes a situation in which you are beginning with a simple star topology, with three computers connected to a four-port hub. Figure 6.4 shows an example of this network.

Expanding the Topology with Hubs

You have a four-port hub and you get three more workstations, a network printer, and a server computer, bringing the total to seven nodes (in other words pieces of

110

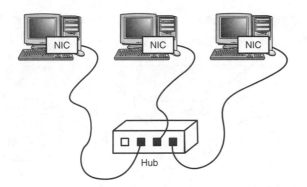

Figure 6.4

A simple example of a star topology begins with a four-port hub.

equipment connected to a network). The easiest way to connect these computers to your network is to add another hub. You can do this with a technique known as *daisy chaining*.

Daisy chaining involves connecting a port on one hub to a port on another hub. This topology is also sometimes called a *star-bus* topology. With daisy chaining, the cable connecting the two ports either has to be a *cross-over cable* or one of the hubs must have a special port that automatically (or perhaps by pressing a button) does the cross-over.

The result of this example, shown in Figure 6.5, is that all seven nodes on our LAN can communicate together. If you purchase hubs from the same manufacturer, the hubs will probably also stack together and interlock in some way (so you can keep them together neatly in a contained area).

Note

This example represents an Ethernet LAN using TCP/IP addressing. Right now, all addresses could easily be on the same network (for example, 192.168.4). To connect to other networks, you will have to use a router, as described later in this chapter. To learn more about IP addresses, see Chapter 3, "Using a World-wide Network (the Internet)."

The potential downside to daisy chaining is performance. Daisy-chained hubs broadcast all information on the network to all computers on all hubs. There is no intelligence built into hubs that prevents data meant for a computer on the local hub from being sent to all the other hubs as well.

You might also find that communications on your network slows by connecting too many hubs. So your next step might be to use some means of limiting the information that is passed across the hubs. One way to do that is with a *switch*.

111

Figure 6.5

Daisy chaining hubs is a quick way to add to your network.

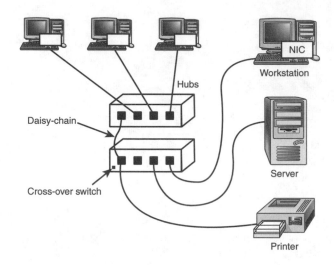

Techno Tip

Bridging involves connecting two low-level (OSI level 2) networks by a device so data can pass between the boundaries of low-level networks of different types or be filtered (to prevent certain kinds of traffic from passing between the two networks). For example, bridging can be used to connect a 10BaseT network to a 100BaseT network. Because those two types of networks can't communicate together at the same speed, the bridge smooths the transition between the two networks.

Although the word "bridge" is sometimes used to refer to hardware that does bridging, more often the bridging product is called a *switch*. A switch does what bridges originally did (lets you connect multiple hubs), but include additional features. Switches also operate at the hardware level, making them much faster than software-based bridges.

To learn more about switches and bridges see Chapter 4.

Expanding the Topology with Switches

Our little example network is about to grow from 7 nodes to 400 nodes. (We just did a hostile takeover of a competitor who went bankrupt from buying too many computers.) So, our new topology has a couple of problems to solve:

➤ If we were to daisy-chain hubs, the network would become too congested. Every file transfer, print job, or other network use would be broadcast to all hubs.

➤ Some computers on the network have 10Mbps (10BaseT) Ethernet Network cards, although others have 100Mbps cards (100BaseT). The 100BaseT computers need to communicate with each other at high speeds (they are transferring video), although the other computers can get by with lower-speed 10Mbps communications (they mostly send email and transfer documents).

The solution is to divide the LAN into *segments*. Each segment consists of a set of computers that contain Ethernet connections of the same speed. Preferably, these computers are ones that need to communicate most frequently. The computers are connected to the same hub, and then each hub is connected to a *LAN switch*. The Figure 6.6 is an example of this configuration.

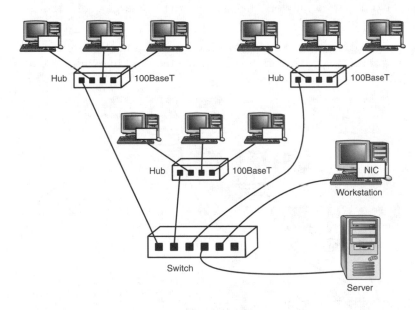

Figure 6.6

When a LAN becomes congested, connecting hubs to a switch reduces unnecessary traffic.

In Figure 6.6, there are two 10BaseT segments and one 100BaseT segment. Also, one workstation and one server, each requiring a lot of bandwidth, are connected directly to the switch. Despite the fact that there are different segments, only one TCP/IP network is involved (for example, if the network number were 192.168.4, IP addresses could be 192.168.4.10, 192.168.4.11, 192.168.4.12, and so on). See Chapter 3 for details on IP addresses.

When the switch sees data that is intended for a computer on another hub, it directs that data to the correct hub. If the data is intended for the current hub, then that data never gets beyond the switch. You can see how huge data transfers to your co-worker in the next office (on the same segment) can be done much more efficiently with a switch.

Although switches are more expensive than hubs, they are much less expensive than they were 10 years ago. Although you can find a four-port hub for under $100, an inexpensive four-port switch will start at more than $200. This switch, however, allows you to connect several thousand computers and other nodes to your LAN. Switches with special management features, or that can connect different LAN protocols (AppleTalk, DECNet, Ethernet, and so on) and entire companies or campuses, can easily run in the thousands of dollars.

Expanding the Topology with Routers

If you need your network to connect to the Internet or to different locations of a business that have different TCP/IP network numbers (see Chapter 3 for details on TCP/IP), you need to add a router to your topology. Before LAN segmentation was available, routing was the only way a network that was getting too large could be segmented (that is, you would split the LAN into different networks).

Figure 6.7 takes our growing LAN example and shows it connecting to the Internet. Our example has grown from a single network to an inter networked network.

Figure 6.7

Adding a router to your network allows it to connect to the Internet or other wide-area network.

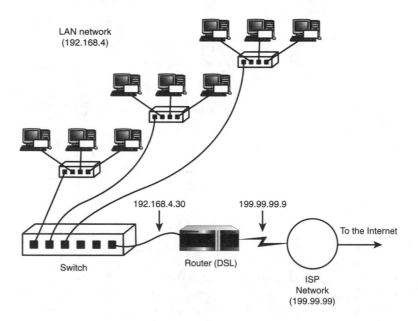

114

Here are a few points that you should notice about Figure 6.7:

➤ The equipment providing the routing function is a DSL modem. This could also have been a cable modem, a dial-up modem, or a variety of other equipment.

➤ The router is connected directly to the LAN switch. This gives it its own dedicated LAN segment.

➤ Notice that one side of the modem has a network number that is on the local LAN (192.168.4.30), although the other side of the modem has a network number that is associated with the ISP's network (a fictitious 199.99.99.9 network). Here's the point: to be a router, the DSL modem must be part of both networks (in other words, have IP addresses on each).

➤ The ISP's network is then connected to a high-speed connection to the Internet backbone.

A Comparison of Bus, Star, and Switched Topologies

Chances are you'll be erecting a local area network supported by bus, star, or switched topology. In Table 6.1, the advantages and disadvantages of these topologies are contrasted side by side.

Table 6.1 Comparison of Bus, Star, and Switched Networks

Issue	Bus	Star	Switched
Bandwidth	Shared	Shared	Dedicated
Cost	Inexpensive	Moderate	Expensive
SPF*	Critical	Less Severe	Less Severe
Growth	Limited	Good	Good
Management	Little or none	Considerable	More Advanced
Scalability	Poor	Good	Excellent
Setup	Easy	More difficult	Complex
Speed	Variable	Can be variable	Static
Stability	Low	Moderate	High
Suitable for...	Peer-to-peer	LAN/Client/server	LAN/Client/server
Troubleshooting	Difficult	Manageable	Easy

* This information represents single point of failure factor (or, how devastating an actual failure is).

115

The Least You Need to Know

Your choice of topology will be based on many factors, including

➤ What you're using the network for

➤ Your network type

➤ The layout of your office or home

When building a local area network, choose your topology carefully. Try to factor in cost, bandwidth, scalability, growth, stability, and management (remember, too, that your network topology has great bearing on your network's security). The following checklist is a good yardstick:

➤ If you're building a very small peer-to-peer network (10 nodes or fewer), bus topology might suffice. Such networks are easy to configure, expand on, and connect to. Typically, you can establish a bus topology–based network with little more than your workstations, some cable, and a few network interface cards (NICs). This makes your installation and administration costs quite low. Bus networks are cheap, quick, painless, and suitable for home or small business environments.

➤ If you're building a small to medium-sized LAN for more serious business settings, choose star topology. It offers speed, increased security, reliability, and a less critical single point of failure. It also allows you to more incisively segment your network. Star networks are relatively easy to establish, only moderately expensive, and exceptionally versatile. Star topology is most often employed in Ethernet LANs (see Chapter 2, "Having Your Own Network (LAN)," for details on Ethernet).

➤ Ring networks are relatively easily established, inexpensive, and suitable for close-quarters.

➤ If you are using a star topology, you can easily grow your network by adding more hubs and connecting them together in a daisy chain. If performance begins to slow, you can add a switch to effectively segment your LAN to reduce network congestion.

➤ To reach the Internet or other wide-area network from you LAN, you need to add a router. A variety of equipment can be used as a router, including DSL modems, cable modems, or standard dial-up modems.

Part 3
Building Your Network Base

You've gathered the pieces you need to build your network, so now it's time to put it together and use it. Putting together your network means installing your equipment and wiring, configuring the network, and choosing that connection to the Internet.

Chapters in this part take you through the process of connecting to the Internet (Chapter 7, "Making Those Internet Connections"), building a home network (Chapter 8, "Building Your Home Network"), and hooking up a small office network (Chapter 9, "Hooking Up Your Small Office Network"). Chapter 10, "Taking Your Network for a Drive," describes programs for using your network. Chapter 11, "Linking Your Home and Office Networks," helps bridge the gap between your home and office networks.

Chapter 7

Making Those Internet Connections

In This Chapter

➤ Find out about high-speed DSL and cable services for accessing the Internet from your home

➤ Learn about satellite and wireless services for providing Internet access

➤ Understand how ISDN and Frame Relay services can be used effectively in small businesses

➤ Find out how LAN switching service can help connect branch offices and campuses

---

Internet network backbones can transmit tons of data around the world in the blink of an eye. Home and office networks can commonly deliver data among local computers at speeds from 10 to 100 million bits per second. So, why would you connect your speedy LAN to the Internet using a modem that is hundreds of times slower than your LAN?

For many people today, your bottleneck from home to the Internet is the dial-up line that connects you to your ISP. The good news is that you can significantly improve that bottleneck today (in most areas) for not much more than you are already paying. DSL and cable modems are the two most dominant technologies for upping that speed.

On the business side, more options for connecting to the Internet, and other wide area networks, are appearing every day. With your business Internet connections you also have challenges that the home surfer doesn't have. Support and reliability are much more of a factor if your business needs to send critical data to customers and others, or maintain a presence on the Web.

Although anyone can get any of the services described in this chapter provided the service is available in their area and they are prepared to plunk down enough money, some Internet connections are more geared toward home than business use. So this chapter divides discussions on Internet access into home and business Internet access offerings.

Connecting Your Home to the Internet

A few years ago, if you wanted to dial up to the Internet from home, you would contact an Internet service provider (ISP). That ISP would give you a phone number of a modem pool at the ISP. Then, you would set up your computer modem to dial into that modem pool to get connected to the Internet.

Although you can still use this method of getting on the Internet today, and in fact, you might have to if there are no other choices in your area, it does have its drawbacks. Here are some of them:

➤ **Slow speed**   Maximum speed that you could achieve using a dial-up telephone line is 56Kbps (and in reality, 56Kbps modems don't even transmit that fast, as described later). When the Internet first became popular a few years back, 14.4Kbps and 28.8Kbps modems were the top speeds available.

➤ **Slow to connect**   If you just want to check your email, you have to wait for the modem to dial out and connect to the ISP before you can start getting data.

➤ **Uses a phone line**   While you are on the phone, you are tying up the phone line. Nobody else can dial in or out. Some people basically double the cost of their Internet service by getting an additional phone line that is used primarily for Internet access.

➤ **Busy signals**   No ISP maintains one dial-in modem for everyone that might possibly connect to it. So, at peak access time (often early-evening), you might get a busy signal when you try to dial in. Low-cost ISPs often sell too many subscriptions. Customers pay the price by not being able to get on, sometimes for hours or days.

➤ **Possible long-distance**   If you don't have an ISP in your local calling area (which is getting more rare), you have to add long-distance charges to your Internet connection cost.

Despite these disadvantages, dial-up is still a very popular (perhaps the most popular) way to get on the Internet from home or on the road. If you are an occasional Internet user—some Web surfing, the occasional email—it might still be the most economical.

Today, however, the better value comes from the high-speed Internet services that are offered by local phone companies and cable television providers. These companies are the first to enter the home high-speed-Internet contest because they have something that other companies don't: Wires that already run into your home.

If you are just now considering which way to go with your home Internet connection, read the following sections regarding Dial-up modems, DSL, and cable modems. If DSL and cable aren't available in your area, and dial-up just isn't doing it for you, I describe some wireless, satellite, and other services you might want to consider.

Note

It is difficult to make exact speed comparisons between different types of Internet connection services. Not all equipment performs at the speeds for which it is rated. Existing line conditions can reduce the rates you get. Likewise, if you are using a shared connection, your performance might vary from one moment to the next based on the demands by others in your neighborhood.

Reading this chapter should give you a sense of how each type of service is meant to perform and how it can vary. Armed with that information, you can evaluate your Internet access options on a case–by–case basis.

Dial-up Connections

If you have a phone line, you can always connect your computer to the Internet using a dial-up modem connection. As described earlier, there are disadvantages to dial-up connections. However, their main advantage is that they're available everywhere there is a telephone jack to plug into.

Choosing a Modem

Your computer might already have a built-in modem. One way to find out is to see if there is a port that supports a regular RJ-11 telephone connector. Another way is to go ahead and begin configuring a dial-up connection (in Windows 95/98, open **My Computer**, **Dial-Up Networking**, **Make New Connection**). During that process, Windows should detect your modem and let you choose it to set up a connection.

If you need to get a new modem, the primary way of differentiating modems is by their speeds. In general, you should go for a modem with the highest speed. Modem transmission rates have topped out at 56Kbps, so you want a modem that supports that rate.

If you are buying a new 56Kbps modem, make sure that it is compliant with the V.90 transmission standard. Originally there were different standards for 56Kbps modems, but the future is V.90. If cost is an issue, you can pick up used 28.8Kbps and 33.6Kbps modems for a lot less. In all cases, make sure that your ISP supports the speed and, with 56Kbps, the transmission standard of your modem.

Checking Out the ISP's Dial-up Service

Before you sign on for dial-up service with an ISP, there are a few pieces of information you should find out first:

➤ **Price** When you do price comparisons, make sure you know what is built into each package price. Although most ISPs offer unlimited connect time with dial-up accounts, some will offer lower rates for a limited number of minutes per month.

➤ **Modem ratio** Although no ISP has a modem for every customer, some have fewer modems available than others. A reasonable subscriber-to-modem ratio was originally about 10:1. With more people online now for longer periods of time, a ratio of 7:1 or 6:1 is more reasonable.

Find an ISP with a 4:1 ratio and you might never get a busy signal—although you might get an ISP that is losing money at $19.95 per month. (Reports were that when AOL subscribers were having trouble getting connected in 1997; AOL's ratio went as high as 35:1.) In any case, you want an ISP that strives for no busy signals.

➤ **Setup software** Check whether the ISP has a CD or floppy disk containing software that will help get you configured. Although you can set up dial-up communication manually, it's much easier if the ISP has software to do it for you. Usually the ISP also gives you software you need to use the Internet, such as a Web browser, file transfer programs, and mail readers. Some ISPs will just give you a dial-up number, login ID, and password and leave you on your own.

➤ **Extras** The extras that you get with the service can sometimes help you separate two ISPs. Ask whether you get any of the following extras with your account:

➤ **email** You should have one or more email accounts.

➤ **newsgroups** Does the ISP have a news server? If so, does it support all the groups you might be interested in?

➤ **Web page** Can you have a personal Web page? If so, how much storage space are you allowed with it? Also, are you allowed to use scripts on the pages, so they can include forms, special content, or e-commerce features?

➤ **FTP area**   Are you given disk space where you can store files on the ISP's site?

If you start adding it all up, you begin to see that the $19.95 per month doesn't mean the same thing with all ISPs. The same ISP that offers your dial-up connection might offer DSL or cable connections as well. To get those higher-speed services, however, you can also go directly to your local phone company or cable television provider. Those services are described next.

DSL connections

DSL is the low-cost choice for high-speed Internet connections using the standard copper wires that are already in your home for telephone service. Not surprisingly, the easiest way to get this service is through your local telephone company.

Advantages of DSL

DSL stands for Digital Subscriber Line. With DSL service, you can be connected to the Internet all the time and still use the same line for your telephone service (at the same time). Subscribing to DSL service has several major advantages over dial-up connections for home subscribers:

Note

Although the local telephone companies control telephone wires and cable television companies control cable wires coming into homes and business, there are ongoing discussions about access to these lines. As you might guess, ISPs want to use these lines for their own customers, with DSL and cable providers typically competing by offering their own ISP services. This matter is still being worked on.

➤ **Much faster**   Although the maximum modem speed is 56Kbps, a typical DSL unit can receive data at 7Mbps and send data at 1Mbps. (Actual real-life services are much slower in both cases, however.)

➤ **Up all the time**   You don't need to dial up to connect to the Internet. The DSL connection is always live, so you just open your Web browser or email program and start using it. (There are some less expensive DSL services that let you share a connection to the DSL provider. In that case, you typically click an icon when you are ready and you are almost instantaneously connected to the DSL provider.)

➤ **Dedicated service**   DSL offers a dedicated line from your location to the DSL provider. That has several positive attributes, such as: service quality isn't reduced when a lot of people in your neighborhood are using the service, and the connection to the Internet is more secure.

Techno Tip

Kbps stands for kilobits per second, and Mbps stands for megabits per second. A 1-kilobit transmission moves 1,024 bits across a line in 1 second. A megabit transmission moves about 1 million bits in 1 second. Compare the fastest modem (56Kbps) to DSL's highest receiving rate (7Mbps):

➤ 56Kbps =   57,344 bits per second

➤ 7Mbps = 7,000,000 bits per second

Neither type of unit actually operates at that speed, although DSL will edge closer to that number as infrastructure improves. By comparison, however, you can begin to see the gap between the two services.

➤ **Other cool features**   Depending on the DSL unit you get, there are usually other features built in to allow you to manage your LAN as well. For example, the Cisco 675 DSL unit acts as a router (to route messages between your LAN and the Internet), DHCP server (to automatically assign addresses to the computers on your LAN), and NAT server (to allow your LAN to use private IP addresses and still communicate on the Internet). These services provide simple ways of connecting multiple PCs in your home or office to the Internet over a single high-speed connection.

Disadvantages of DSL

There are a few items on the downside with DSL service. Here are some of them:

➤ **Lack of standard**   Often you see DSL preceded by an "x" or other letter. That's because there are different techniques for DSL transmission. So, xDSL is the generic term to describe DSL service. ADSL is Asynchronous DSL and SDSL is Synchronous DSL service. VDSL is Very high bit-rate DSL.

Before you get a DSL unit, you should make sure of the type of service being offered by the DSL service provider. Better yet, see what deals the provider will offer on the unit for signing on with its service. (See Chapter 4 for details on different types of DSL service.)

➤ **No roaming**   The DSL service comes right to your home or business. If you are on the road a lot, or even down the street with your laptop, you might need to sign up for a separate dial-up service just to read your email. Other providers offer limited dial-up service with your DSL subscription.

➤ **Not available everywhere**   The telephone companies need to install special equipment to support DSL connections. It's more cost-effective to put this equipment in metropolitan areas where it can be shared by many customers that are in close proximity. Prices can also be higher outside of cities because there is less competition.

Choosing a DSL service

If you do have DSL service in your area, you probably don't have a choice of which company you get it from. You get the service from the local telephone company. That is why I try to make the distinction between the DSL provider (your phone company) and your ISP (which might or might not be a different company).

With DSL in high demand in many areas, you can sometimes do better signing up with an outside ISP than by going directly to the telephone company. Because the ISP is probably a bigger customer than you are, it can sometimes exert more pressure to get your service turned on.

Some DSL providers offer different levels of DSL service at different rates. You should choose the service that suits your needs. In other words, if you have a big family that all loves to play Quake on the Internet at once, you might want to sign up for higher transmission rates.

Just to give you an example, Table 7.1 shows the DSL rates available in Salt Lake City, UT from Qwest Communications (formerly U.S. West). I show you these just as a means of comparison. The rates will surely change as soon as this book hits the bookstores. Rates in your area will probably differ as well.

Table 7.1   Price/Performance Comparisons for DSL Service

Transmission Rates	Cost
256Kbps (both directions)	$19.95 per month, plus you must click to get on
256Kbps (both directions)	$29.95 per month, always on
512Kbps (both directions)	$65 per month, always on
768Kpbs (both directions)	$80 per month, always on
1Mbps (upstream); 1Mbps (downstream)	$120 per month, always on
1Mbps (upstream); 4Mbps (downstream)	$480 per month, always on
1Mbps (upstream); 7Mbps (downstream)	$840 per month, always on

On top of these costs, you need to purchase a DSL unit (which the company offers at a discount, but often range between $99 and $199 depending on features) and an ISP service. Your DSL service basically gets you to the telephone company central office. From there you need to pay for the actual Internet connection. In this case, Qwest can provide ISP service as well, and package it with the cost of DSL service. The equipment is not difficult to install, but if you would rather have the DSL provider do it, there will probably be an extra fee involved.

Cable Modem Connections

A cable modem allows you to use the cable coming into your house for cable TV and share it for television and Internet access. The thickness of the coaxial cable used in this type of connection can accommodate a lot of data being pumped through it.

Advantages of Cable Modems

If you already have cable television service to your home, a cable modem can be an inexpensive addition to the service. Cable modems have a lot of advantages over dial-up connections and a few over DSL:

➤ **Really Fast Downstream Transmission**   Cable television service was designed to pump high-quality video into your home. Likewise, it can send Internet content into your home at very high speeds. Information traveling from the Internet to you is referred to as flowing *downstream*.

➤ **Easy installation**   There isn't much more to getting cable Internet service than connecting the cable modem and doing some simple configuration.

➤ **Up all the time**   Like DSL, but unlike dial-up connections, cable Internet service is up all the time. You don't have to wait for the modem to dial and connect.

➤ **No additional resources**   The cable modem shares the wire with your cable television at the same time. No need for an additional phone line or any additional wiring.

Disadvantages of Cable Modems

There are three main disadvantages of cable modem Internet service. All are based on the nature of cable Internet access and might be a problem for you as someone just surfing the Web.

➤ **Shared access**   Unlike DSL, which typically provides a dedicated circuit between your location and the DSL service provider, cable subscribers share their Internet connections. As a result, high demand during peak hours could theoretically result in lower performance.

Shared access only applies to the connection between your location and the cable service provider. After your data hits your ISP's network or the Internet backbone, it's no different than DSL. Some studies have shown that there are no noticeable performance delays from shared access. Perhaps that will change, however, as many more people sign on to cable Internet access.

➤ **Slower upload speeds** Although you can have speeds of 1Mbps or 2Mbps when you download files from the Internet, upload speeds (where you send files to the Internet) might be limited to 128Kbps or 256Kbps. Of course, 256Kbps is still pretty fast (about five times faster than a 56Kbps modem). It's just nowhere near as fast as the download speeds.

➤ **Security** The fact that many customers share the same access connection could theoretically pose some security risk. Although another customer on the same access line could possibly see data sent from other users with the right kind of equipment, it would be very difficult to decrypt that data.

DSL gets around this problem by provisioning a circuit from the customer to the DSL provider's central office. This makes it easier for the DSL service provider to individually protect each individual customer's security, as well as each customer's bandwidth.

Cable companies will also point out that you might not always get fast performance because other factors in the network might result in bottlenecks. For example, you might have a slow computer processor or you might be accessing a Web server that is overloaded.

Choosing a Cable Modem Service

Some cable companies are offering very compelling prices for their Internet services. In some cases, that service comes with a lot of nice extras as well, including enhanced content.

In general, cable providers offer fewer choices of packages for their Internet service. Just to compare cable Internet services to DSL service in the same market, look at information on cable Internet service in Salt Lake City, UT. Here is what the cable Internet service from AT&T@Home includes and costs. (Again, the prices might be different by the time you read this, but it can give you an idea of how to compare services to DSL and other cable services.)

The basic AT&T@Home service supports download speeds of 1Mbps to 2Mbps. Supported upload speed is 128Mbps. The cost of the service (at the time this was written) was $39.95 per month. However, that includes a $10 fee per month for renting the cable modem. If you were to buy your own cable modem (for about $200–$250) you could would pay only $29.95 per month. The service also includes ISP services, which saves you another $10–$30 per month.

AT&T@Home is also more of an entertainment package than you would typically get with DSL service. Special content that is suitable for high-speed connections is offered with the service. This includes the ability to participate in online games and chats. It also includes content for downloading video and audio files that would be slow with a regular modem.

Here are a few other features that come with the package that could possibly tip the scale when comparing cable to other high-speed Internet services:

➤ **IP addresses**   You get one IP address, with additional IP addresses available at $4.95 per month.

➤ **email**   You can have up to seven email accounts.

➤ **Web page**   Each email account can have its own Web page. You are allowed to consume up to 10MB of disk space for each of the seven email accounts' Web page (that's up to 70MB total).

➤ **Newsgroups**   You have access to a news server to participate in thousands of newsgroups.

As you can see, the services offered by cable and DSL Internet providers can be quite compelling. However, if you don't happen to have support for either of these two services in your area, there are some other possibilities.

Satellite and Wireless

Some new types of Internet services are on the way soon. For areas where running cable wires or adding extra DSL central office equipment just isn't practical, there are several wireless technologies that are, or will soon become, available.

Although these new satellite and wireless services might become competition to DSL or cable, it is more likely that they will migrate to locations that can't offer DSL or cable in cost-effective ways. Their markets will be to offer speeds greater than 56Kpbs modems could offer in remote locations.

Satellites that broadcast television content can likewise broadcast Internet content to people who prefer a dish to a cable. Current offerings download Internet content from the satellite, but require a modem to upload data. Services that are expected out soon will offer two-way communications.

Various kinds of wireless technologies are being deployed to offer Internet services. Like satellite, these services save the cost of putting wires into the ground to get customers. Challenges to both these types of services include

➤ **Cost of equipment**   Satellite and wireless dishes tend to be more expensive than other high-speed access equipment.

➤ **Line-of-sight considerations**   Some wireless technologies require that there be a direct line of sight between the provider and the customer. For that reason, it helps to have big buildings or mountains around that can support tall antennas.

➤ **Limited frequencies**   Frequencies that can carry wireless data are controlled and licensed by the Federal Communications Commission (FCC). There is a limited amount of these licenses because of the limited amount of bandwidth in the sky.

How Home and Business Internet Services Differ

The level of Internet service required by home users can be drastically different than the service required by businesses. Although DSL and cable Internet access packages might be fine for home use or a small business, they are tuned primarily for Web surfing. Here are some drawbacks to most DSL and cable access that might make them inappropriate for business use:

➤ **No server support**   Often DSL and cable Internet access doesn't allow you to add a Web server or other type of server to the network.

➤ **Limited upload support**   This goes along with the lack of server support. If your business is to distribute video content on the Web, DSL or cable probably won't work for you.

➤ **No level-of-service guarantee** To keep costs low and gain the greatest number of customers, critical service is not typically offered with DSL and cable Internet access. If your connection goes down, you might have to wait as anyone would to get phone or cable television service repaired.

> **Check This Out**
>
> See Chapter 16, "To the Internet and Beyond," for more information on companies offering new technologies in satellite and wireless Internet access to compete with DSL and cable.

➤ **No special monitoring**   If something goes wrong with your Internet service, it's up to you to figure that out and report it (while your customers are failing to get through). Some business Internet services can monitor your Internet connection, 24-hours a day and 7-days a week.

For the reasons just mentioned, and other reasons you see in the next section, there are many specialized Internet access services available to business customers. Although some of these services focus on providing more bandwidth between the business and the Internet, other services focus on providing services that make a business's Internet service reliable and secure.

Choosing a Business Internet Connection

Although a business can certainly purchase DSL or cable Internet service (if it is available), other types of Internet service are designed specifically for businesses. Some examples of Internet services geared toward business include Integrated Services Digital Network (ISDN), Frame Relay, Asynchronous Transfer Mode (ATM), and LAN Switching.

Whereas a few years ago you would typically just purchase data lines from your local telephone company, many new players have entered into the arena in recent years. One type of vendor, referred to as Competitive Local Exchange Carrier (CLEC), purchases data communications services in bulk and resells them to smaller businesses.

With the entry of new companies in the data communications field, you need to be sure of data communications products you are getting before you sign on. Besides looking for the best price for the highest speed, check for features such as reliability and serviceability.

Sometimes lower prices can be the result of over subscription to a service. Try talking to current customers of the service you are considering to see if the vendor is coming through on its promises. Most customers are happy to talk (or vent) about how well a vendor has delivered its services.

ISDN Service

Integrated Services Digital Network (ISDN) has long been a popular technology for small business communications, telecommuting, and remote branch office access. Because it has been around longer, ISDN has been deployed in many more places than DSL (in the United States and around the world).

Although ISDN connection speeds are comparable to DSL, and ISDN is more expensive than DSL, ISDN has proven to be a reliable and cost-effective network service. Many businesses that are set up to allow access to their offices from employee's homes use ISDN because they are set up for high-speed, dial-in access.

With ISDN, instead of just carrying one voice conversation over the phone line that enters a location, ISDN allows there to be three separate communication paths at the same time. This can be useful for a business that might require several network activities at once: someone on the phone, a credit card authorization, and data transmission, for example.

ISDN supports 128Kbps transmission rates that can be increased to 256Kpbs or even 632Kbps using different types of compression. ISDN also integrates easily with other network technologies, such as X.25 (a network protocol that is popular in Europe) or Frame Relay (discussed next).

Of the three communication channels, two of the channels (called B-channels) can be used for 128Kbps transmission of both data and image. The third channel is called a *D-channel,* which can be used to manage calls and send packet data. Improved service can be gained by adding more B-channels together, to result in speeds up to 1.5Mpbs.

Some believe that DSL might replace ISDN one day, because it can be offered at a lower cost. However, because of distance restrictions that make DSL unpractical in some places, ISDN will probably continue to be around for a long time.

Frame Relay

Frame Relay is. a packet-switching protocol that operates over wide-area networks (WANs). With packet-switching protocols, each group of data (referred to as a packet) contains its own address information so that each packet in a sequence can take a different route to its destination. At the destination, packets are reassembled in the correct order and presented to the application receiving the information.

Frame Relay transmission speeds are available from 56Kbps to 1.544Mbps (T-1) and sometimes 45Mbps (on T-3 lines, discussed later in this chapter). Although originally designed to operate over ISDN networks, Frame Relay is now available over a variety of network media.

For businesses that need high-quality and reliable communications services, Frame Relay can be a good choice. Frame Relay service often is monitored to guarantee that a specific level of data transport is maintained. A typical business that subscribes to Frame Relay service might offer email and general Internet access to its employees.

Frame Relay can offer high-quality service in part because it relies on virtual circuits to provide a dedicated path between the Frame Relay devices. High speeds can be guaranteed and monitored. However, for companies that are operating Web servers or otherwise large amounts of inbound traffic, Frame Relay might not be a good fit. During peak usage, the provider might limit service to the committed information rate (CIR) that the customer signed up for.

Some Frame Relay services are being replaced today with services that can provide faster throughput. One example of such a technology is Asynchronous Transfer Mode.

Asynchronous Transfer Mode (ATM)

Like Frame Relay, Asynchronous Transfer Mode (ATM) transfers data in packets. ATM is an excellent choice for transmitting audio and video because it is able to manage such data in small chunks, preventing any single data type from taking over too much of the available line.

ATM is fast. Data transfer rates range from 25Mbps to 622Mbps. Also, ATM uses fixed channels to transfer data. In that way, data cannot take different paths, as it can with TCP/IP protocols. As a result, managing data can be done more consistently.

However, ATM networks cannot adapt as well to bursts of traffic that can be better served by taking different routes.

There are different types of ATM service available:

➤ **Available Bit Rate (ABR)** If the network is not busy, and a burst of traffic goes above the guaranteed minimum capacity, the network can allow the higher rate of traffic.

➤ **Constant Bit Rate (CBR)** With CBR, ATM sends data in a steady stream.

➤ **Variable Bit Rate (VBR)** Allows for a defined capacity for throughput in which data can be sent unevenly. Often this type of service is used for video conferencing, voice, and integrated data.

➤ **Unspecified Bit Rate (UBR)** Provides no guaranteed level of service. For that reason, this type of service is not good for streaming video (which requires steady throughput), but can be used for applications such as file transfer.

Dedicated T-1 or T-3 Lines

For businesses that have a large amount of incoming or outgoing traffic, a dedicated T-1 or T-3 line is often the best solution. T-1 and T-3 lines are often used by ISPs to connect to the Internet backbone. Here are some of the attributes of T-1 and T-3 connections:

➤ **T-1** Supported data rate for T-1 lines is 1.544Mbps. A T-1 line consists of 24 channels. Each channel can support 64Kpbs of data transfer. If you don't need an entire T-1 line, most carriers will allow you to lease part of a T-1 line (called fractional T-1).

➤ **T-3** Data rates of approximately 43Mbps are supported by T-3 lines. A T-3 line is made up of 672 separate channels. Each channel supports transmissions of 64Kbps. Again, ISPs often use T-3 lines to get to the Internet backbone. T-3 lines are also used on the Internet backbone itself. (DS3 is another term used to describe T-3 lines.)

To use a T-1 or T-3 line for your own business, your ISP must support these connection types. Because T-1 and T-3 are dedicated lines, they might not be as useful to businesses that need to communicate with multiple ISPs. These are excellent line types for businesses that want to manage their own Web servers, FTP servers, or email servers.

If you are going to order your own T-1 or T-3 line, you should consider the type of service agreement you want. In the service agreements you can specify such things as

➤ Acceptable down time

➤ Service availability

➤ Repair response times

If your traffic begins to exceed the service you have ordered, you can usually add bandwidth incrementally. For example, you could add additional bandwidth in 1MB, 3MB, and 15MB increments.

LAN Switching Service (LSS)

Some data service providers offer high-speed Ethernet service between customer sites. Some providers refer to this product as LAN Switching Service (LSS). LSS is one way of connecting offices in a campus environment. The telephone company or other vendor supplies the infrastructure and the customer uses it to interconnect its locations.

Connection options for LSS can range from 10Mbps to 100Mbps service. Because this service has only a few, well known components (commonly used with Ethernet networks), the service is easy to connect and maintain. No WAN equipment needs to be added to the Ethernet LAN equipment that is already in place.

Where To From Here?

By now, you should have already sized up the hardware and software needs of your networks, thought about the topologies you wanted to use to connect equipment, and evaluated your Internet connection needs. From here, you can continue on to Chapter 9, "Hooking Up Your Small Office Network," or 8, "Building Your Home Network," to start setting up your own office network or home network.

The Least You Need to Know

Right now, the least you need to know about getting an Internet connection is this:

➤ Dial-up connections are a popular way of getting on to the Internet from home, but have speed limitations and tie up your phone line.

➤ DSL is a popular high-speed Internet connection type offered by many telephone companies. It allows for connection speeds of up to 7Mbps downstream and 1Mpbs upstream for DSL customers. DSL also offers "always up" service.

➤ The same wire that brings cable television into your home can provide Internet access as well. Cable Internet service provides upload speeds that are similar to DSL, however it can provide significantly higher download speeds.

➤ For remote locations, wireless and satellite Internet service can offer high-speed Internet access. Currently, however, two-way Internet satellite service is not yet available.

➤ Businesses can have more demanding service and reliability needs for their Internet access. For that reason, getting guarantees for levels of service and support are important.

➤ ISDN is a well-tested service for cost-effective data transmission services for small businesses. Although it is deployed more widely than DSL today, some expect DSL to replace ISDN some day because of lower costs and higher transmission rates.

➤ Frame Relay can provide a higher-quality of Internet service than ISDN. Higher-speeds are possible as well.

➤ ATM is a good choice for delivering streaming audio and video over a network.

➤ LAN switching services can be used to connect branch offices and campus buildings using standard Ethernet equipment and protocols.

Chapter 8

Building Your Home Network

In This Chapter

➤ Connect hardware together to form a simple home LAN

➤ Set up file sharing and print sharing among the computers on your LAN

➤ Configure the computers on your LAN to use a high-speed (DSL or cable modem) connection to the Internet

So far you've learned a lot of theory about networks. Now it is time to build one. For starters, you'll go through each step of connecting and configuring the computers in your home to form a LAN. The LAN is (as described in an example earlier in the book)

➤ Three personal computers (running Windows operating systems)

➤ Three network interface cards (one for each computer)

➤ Three Ethernet cables (twisted-pair 10BaseT, RJ-45 connectors)

➤ A small hub (with four to eight RJ-45 ports)

After you have the computers connected, you'll learn how to configure them so you can share printers and files among the computers. The next step will be to get connected to the Internet. For that, you'll learn how to

➤ Set up client computers to connect to the Internet via a high-speed service (DSL or cable modem) or dial-up service (56Kbps modem) connected to your LAN.

➤ Configure the computers on your LAN to communicate with the Internet (using TCP/IP addresses and routing).

The result of these procedures will leave you with a setup in which all the computers in your home can share files, share printers, and surf the World Wide Web. If you are ready, let's take the first step.

Connecting Your LAN Hardware

Before you begin running this procedure to connect your home LAN, read through it. Then you should then go out and purchase the equipment you need.

You can either purchase the items separately or in an Ethernet starter kit. Kits typically include a hub, with four or five ports, two NIC cards, and two cables (which could cost you about $150). You can then purchase the additional NICs and cables you need as you get more computers.

This procedure does assume that the computers are near each other and that you don't mind running physical cables between them. If this is a problem for you, you might find wireless, phone-line, or power-line LAN connections more suitable. Those types of equipment can be a bit more expensive and can run at significantly lower rates of speed.

Step 1: Installing the Network Interface Cards

Each computer on your LAN needs to have a NIC. Some computers already have a NIC installed. If that's the case with you, you should see one of several different types of connectors coming out of the back of your computer (see illustrations of these connectors in Chapter 4, as well as other ways to check if a NIC is installed).

The way you traditionally add a NIC involves opening up the computer (a scary thing to some people). Today, however, there are easier ways. There are some slightly more expensive NICs that can connect into special ports on your computer. Unlike home wireless, phone-line, or power-line networks, there is no loss of performance with these NICs.

Before opening up your computer, if your computer has one of these types of ports available you could choose one of these types of Ethernet adapters to use instead:

➤ **PCMCIA**—If your laptop (or desktop computer) has one or more of those little Personal Computer Memory Card International Association (PCMCIA) credit-card size slots, you can get an Ethernet adapter that you just click in. These cards are a bit more expensive than other adapters, but I have never noticed any performance problems. Your Ethernet cable just clicks into the card adapter and the card clicks into the slot on the laptop, as shown in Figure 8.1.

➤ **USB**—If there is a Universal Serial Bus (USB) port on your desktop or laptop computer, they make Ethernet adapters for that type of port as well. One end clicks into the USB port and the other connects to a standard Ethernet cable. Figure 8.2 shows a NetGear EA101 USB Ethernet Adapter.

Techno Tip

To quiet the fears of potential home networkers who don't want to open their computers or run wires around their houses, vendors have come up with several alternatives to the NIC/hub/cable LANs. Here are some examples of these technologies that you can look into (see Chapter 4, "Choosing Your Networking Hardware," for more information):

➤ **Wireless LANs**—These rely on radio frequencies or infrared (less often) methods of transmitting data. Intel AnyPoint offers wireless LAN adapters that plug into an external USB port and transmits at rates of 1.6Mbps (faster than a modem, but much slower than today's standard 10Mbps or 100Mbps wired alternatives).

You can have distances of about 150 feet between units (through walls and doors too). Each AnyPoint adapter, however, will cost you about twice as much as a comparable internal wired NIC (or more when compared to cheaper NICs). For more information, check out http://www.intel.com/anypoint.

➤ **Phone-line LANs**—Tut Systems, Inc. created the HomeRun Ethernet LAN technology that lets computers communicate using the existing phone lines in your home. Although it no longer markets that product, it has licensed the technology to several different vendors, including Intel, 3Com, IBM, and Compaq.

With HomeRun technology, you install a PCI card in each computer that then plugs into the standard POTS (plain old telephone system) lines in your home. Other computers in the home that are connected to the same line can communicate at speeds of 1Mbps without interfering with your regular phone calls. The Home Phoneline Networking Alliance (http://www.homepna.com) is an alliance of vendors who seek to make their phone-line LAN technologies compatible. Check out that Web site for links to products.

➤ **Power-line LANs**—The other wires running through most homes—power lines—can also be used to connect computers on a LAN. It is much the same concept as the phone-line technology: It lets computers communicate without disrupting regular phone or power service. Check out Passport from Intelogis, Inc. (http://www.intelogis.com/products) for more information.

Figure 8.1

PCMCIA Ethernet adapters click into your laptop.

Figure 8.2

Use a USB port to add an Ethernet adapter (without opening the computer).

Check This Out

The steps shown here should be used as guidelines for installing a NIC. Instructions for different NICs can vary to some extent. In particular, with older NICs more manual intervention might be needed to physically set jumpers on a board to properly assign the card's IRQ.

Older computers don't have USB ports and PCMCIA ports are used primarily for laptop computers. If you don't have one of those types of ports available on your computer, you can install your own NIC:

1. *Get the right type of card.* You need an Ethernet card that matches the type of bus slot available in your computer, has the type of connector you need, and runs at the speed you choose. Slots will be related to one of the following bus types:

   ➤ **PCI** If you have a new computer (only a few years old), you probably have PCI (Peripheral Component Interconnect) slots on your computer. This type of bus supports 32-bit and 64-bit cards (the more bits, the faster data can travel between the card and your computer's mother board). PCI bus slots are white or light tan, so you can identify them by sight.

   ➤ **ISA** Before PCI, ISA (Industry Standard Architecture) was the standard bus architecture. So if you have an older computer (more than a few years old), you might need an NIC that plugs into an ISA slot. Some older computers might instead have an Extended Industry Standard Architecture (EISA) bus. These were 32-bit cards that were meant to replace ISA but were rather short-lived. ISA bus slots are black, and EISA bus slots are brown. They are both the same size, although they are longer than PCI slots.

   Check the manual that came with your computer to see what kinds of slots are available. There might be both PCI and ISA slots available, so you might need to figure out which ones are not currently in use. If the manual has disappeared, you might need to look inside the computer to see the type of bus.

As for the connector on the card, you will probably want it to support a RJ-45 connector. For this example, we are using RJ-45 connectors. Although some BNC connectors are still in use, they are used less often these days. (See Chapter 4 for a description of different connector types.)

As for speed, 10Mbps NICs are inexpensive and 10/100Mbps NICs are reasonably priced. If there is one 10Mbps NIC on your hub, all the 10/100Mbps NICs will ramp down to that speed (the 10/100 NICs can detect and adapt their speed). If you want your LAN at 100Mbps, attach only cards that can handle that speed.

2. *Open the computer.* Power down the computer and unplug it. Remove whatever side of the computer you need to remove to expose the card slots. After the computer is open, you need to determine which slots are available and what type they are. Figure 8.3 shows the inside of a computer that has six PCI slots and one ISA slot.

Figure 8.3

This Dell PowerEdge 1300 has six PCI and one ISA slot.

3. *Prepare to open the NIC.* Remember that NICs are delicate pieces of equipment. When you work with NICs, or other cards, you should remove all jewelry from your hands and arms. You should also only use non-magnetic, insulated tools that don't conduct electricity.

4. *Open the NIC.* Carefully remove the NIC from its box, with it still inside the anti-static bag. Look to make sure that it is not damaged.

5. *Remove the slot's back plate.* Using a screwdriver, unscrew the single screw from the slot's back plate, remove the back plate, and set it aside. (You should keep the back plate in case you ever decide to remove the NIC. A computer shouldn't have open slots because it harms the cooling process and allows dust inside.)

6. *Insert the NIC.* Holding the metal part in one hand and placing your other thumb against the card, gently insert the NIC into the slot. Make sure that it is pressed in snuggly (although not so hard that you risk damaging the motherboard). Then screw the NIC into place where you just removed the slot's back plate. Figure 8.4 shows an example of this process.

7. Replace the cover.

8. Reconnect the power and turn on the computer.

Figure 8.4

Gently press the NIC into the PCI or ISA slot until it fits snuggly.

If you are fortunate, your computer should automatically detect your NIC and make it operational. If that is not the case, you might need to do some configuration for the card (as described later in the step for installing NIC drivers). Install a NIC for every computer on your LAN.

Step 2: Installing the Hub

There is not much to installing a hub. Place it somewhere in reach of your computers (within the lengths of cables you have) and plug in the power. For a small home LAN, you will want a hub that has one port available for each computer and probably one for the high-speed DSL or cable modem connection to the Internet.

A five-port hub is a common one for the home. (In Chapter 9, you learn how to expand your LAN by adding more hubs and possibly switches.) Get a hub that handles the speed of your NICs (10/100Mbps hubs are most common).

Step 3: Connecting the Cable

You probably will be using RJ-45 connectors over twisted-pair wiring. Other types of cable and connectors are described in Chapter 4. More detailed descriptions of the relationship between Ethernet speeds, distances, and cables are contained in Chapter 2, "Having Your Own Network (LAN)."

For the simple LAN with just one hub and a few computers, just make sure no two computers are more than 100 meters apart. That means you shouldn't use cables more than 50 meters long to connect two different computers.

On the hardware end, you have done everything you need to do to have a functional LAN. Next you need to make sure that the computer systems have been properly configured on the LAN so that they can communicate together.

Configuring the Computers on Your LAN

At this point, it is quite likely that your hardware is ready to communicate on your LAN. However, a bit more configuration is needed so that the computers can actually talk together.

In the event that the NIC wasn't automatically detected and configured on each computer, you might need to add a driver (that is, the software that makes a piece of computer hardware work) for each NIC that isn't running. You might also need to change some settings for driver. After the NICs are working, you'll probably want to use the local network for file sharing and print sharing (Internet access is described in its own section at the end of this chapter). This requires that you configure the NetBIOS network protocol to identify each computer's name, turn on the services it will use, and enable file and print sharing. After that, your LAN will be ready to share files and printers. (See "Step 2: Configuring Computer Names and Access," later in this chapter for details about NetBIOS.)

Step 1: Installing NIC Drivers

After you boot up your Windows 95/98/NT/2000 computer, the operating system will try to detect your new NIC card and install the proper drivers. If that occurs, your NIC might be already ready to roll.

Windows 2000 offers a nice interface for checking that your connection to the LAN is operational. Click **Start**, **Settings**, **Network and Dial-up Connections**. Then look for an entry such as Local Area Connection and click it. The window that appears should look like the one shown in Figure 8.5.

Figure 8.5

The Windows 2000 LAN Connection window shows packets being sent and received on a working LAN NIC.

This figure shows that the NIC is working, not only because it appears as Connected but because it shows the activity of packets being sent and received. This particular LAN connection has been running for 19 hours, 58 minutes, and 41 seconds. It is operating at 10Mbps and several thousand packets have been sent and received. The driver appears to be functioning just fine.

If the NIC were not working, a new driver might be called for. To install the new driver, run the Add/Remove Hardware Wizard as follows:

1. Select **Start**, **Settings**, **Control Panel**.
2. When the Control Panel appears, double-click the **Add/Remove Hardware** icon. The Add/Remove Hardware Wizard appears.

141

3. Click the **Next** button to continue.

4. Click **Add/Troubleshoot a device** and click **Next** to continue. Windows 2000 tries to detect your new hardware. If it finds the new hardware and has a driver for it, Windows 2000 will install the new driver. If it does not have a new driver, it will ask you to provide a driver.

5. If you have a floppy disk that contains the driver, insert it and indicate the location of that driver. Windows 2000 will install the driver. If all goes well, a window will appear with the newly installed NIC listed, such as the one shown in Figure 8.6.

Figure 8.6

The NIC that was just detected by Windows 2000 was successfully installed.

6. Click the **Next** button to continue. A window appears telling you that you are finished.

7. Click **Finish**.

At this point, you can go back and look for the Local Connection window to see if the LAN is working (**click Start**, **Settings**, **Network and Dial-up Connections**, and then select **Local Area Connection**). Hopefully, everything is running now. You can check properties for the window by clicking the **Properties** button. When the Local Area Properties window appears, click **Configure**.

From the Properties window that appears for your NIC, you can see a lot of information relating to the NIC. Click the **Troubleshoot** button to troubleshoot the device. Click the **Advanced** tab if you have a new driver for the device that you want to install.

Now that everything is working properly, you can start adding the services you need to share files and printers with the network.

Check This Out

Sometimes, the only place a workable driver for your NIC can be found is on the Web site for the vendor of the NIC. Perhaps the "Chicken or the Egg" effect of this scenario has occurred to you. How do you get on the Internet to get the NIC driver you need when your NIC isn't working to get you there? You might need to visit a friend's house or the local library.

In my case, I used another computer to visit the D-Link Web site (http://www.dlink.com), selected Support, selected to download drivers, selected my NIC, and downloaded it. I ran the driver executable that I downloaded and it unzipped all the files into their proper places. I ran the Add/Remove Hardware Wizard and the NIC was installed fine.

Step 2: Configuring Computer Names and Access

Microsoft Windows operating systems share files and printers using a network protocol called NetBIOS. *NetBIOS* is easy to configure on a small, one-hub LAN such as the one in the example. It can be more challenging to configure NetBIOS to share resources over multiple LANs.

Before you can share anything, however, you need to add the computer name and workgroup information to Windows. The procedures are different in Windows 95/98 and Windows 2000:

1. Display the Identification tab as follows
    - ➤ In Windows 95/98, click **Start**, **Settings**, **Control Panel**, and then double-click the **Network** icon. From the Network window that appears, click the **Identification** tab.
    - ➤ In Windows 2000, right-click the **My Computer** icon, and then select **Properties**. From the System Properties window that appears, click the **Identification** tab.

2. For this example, two pieces of information are needed from the Identification tab: the Computer Name and the Workgroup Name:
    - ➤ In Windows 95/98, type in a Computer name to identify the computer, and then type in a Workgroup name. Use the same Workgroup name for all the computers on your LAN. Then click the **OK** button to save the changes.

143

➤ In Windows 2000, click **Properties**. In the window that appears, type in the Computer name and Workgroup name. Then click the **OK** button to save the changes.

3. Next, you want to define how access to your computer's files and printers are controlled:

➤ In Windows 95/98, click the **Share-level access control** button. Then click **OK**. This will later let you assign access to file folders and printers individually.

➤ In Windows 2000, no special access control needs to be set. A more refined level of control is possible when you share file folders and printers later.

Repeat these steps for each computer on the LAN. Next, you need to make sure that all the services needed to share files and printers are added to your computer.

Step 3: Adding Services and Protocols

The protocols and services needed to share files and printers on your LAN need to be added for your NIC. Again, there are different procedures for Windows 95/98 and Windows 2000. In Windows 95/98, you open the Network Properties window and assign all the services and protocols you need. In Windows 2000, you open the Properties for your NIC and assign the services and protocols for the NIC.

1. Open the Properties Window.

➤ In Windows 95/98, double-click the **Network** icon in the Control Panel. You will see a listing of all the protocols and services assigned for your computer.

➤ In Windows 2000, click **Start**, **Settings**, **Network and Dial-up Connections**, and then right-click the **Local Area Connection icon** and select **Properties**. Figure 8.7 shows an example of this listing.

Figure 8.7

In Windows 2000, the Local Area Connection Properties show protocols and services assigned to your NIC.

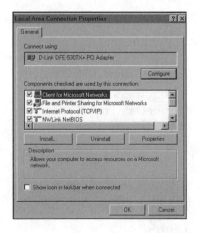

In both cases, you will see networking protocols and services that are installed for your computer. For Windows 2000, you will be viewing protocols and services specific to your NIC.

2. Turn on File and Print Sharing by clicking the **File and Print Sharing for Microsoft Networks** check box. In the box that appears, make sure the check boxes are on for each service.

3. Look to see if Client for Microsoft Networks is listed (and in Windows 2000, make sure the check box is marked). If it isn't listed, add it by clicking **Add**, **Client**, **Add**, **Microsoft**, **Client for Microsoft Networks**. Then click **OK**. (If it's already added, Windows will tell you that you can only have one instance of Client for Microsoft Networks on the system. No harm.)

4. Make sure that NetBEUI (NetBIOS Extended User Interface) protocol is assigned to the NIC. Here's how you do that:

   ➤ In Windows 95/98, click the name of the NIC, and then click **Add**, **Protocol**, **Add**. From the Select Network Protocol window that appears, click **Microsoft**, **NetBEUI,** and then click **OK**.

A new line should appear in the Properties window that shows NetBEUI pointing to your NIC. Figure 8.8 shows the Network Properties window with the NetBEUI protocol added to the NIC.

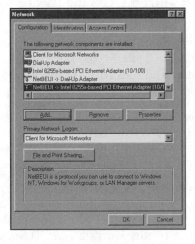

Figure 8.8

To use File and Printer Sharing, NetBEUI protocol must be added to your NIC.

   ➤ In Windows 2000, NetBEUI might already be installed for your NIC. Look in the Properties window for NetBEUI. If a check mark is next to that entry, NetBEUI is already installed. If there is no check mark, click the box to add one. Then click **OK**.

Windows might need you to install the installation disk for your operating system at this point. When this is done, you will have to restart your computer to make the new protocol available.

Repeat these steps for every Windows computer on your LAN.

Techno Tip

So far, you've learned about the minimum number of services and protocols you need to get your LAN working and sharing files with other Windows computers on your LAN. You could also add other protocols for other network services. For example, later you will need to add and configure TCP/IP to use the Internet and related services. If you have a NetWare server on your network, you will need IPX/SPX protocols and related services.

Sharing Files

If you have connected your LAN hardware and configured the computers on your LAN, you should be ready to start sharing files and printers. Any Windows computer on a LAN can share its files and printers with others on the LAN (as long as the computers were set up in the configuration described in the beginning of this chapter).

Although file sharing is the term given to sharing your files with others, you actually select folders or an entire disk (hard disk or CD-ROM) to share on the network. After that folder or disk is shared, all subfolders and files within that shared item are also shared.

Windows 95/98 file sharing doesn't allow much flexibility in what you share. When you make a folder available, anyone who can open that folder can use all files and folders within it with the same level of permissions. With Windows 2000, you have much more control over individual shared files and folders.

File sharing on Windows LANs is considered to be a peer-to-peer activity, because you are basically just sharing a few resources from a computer being used as a workstation with other computers of equal stature. In other words, you won't probably be sharing from massive, dedicated server computers to tiny workstations. Despite that, however, file sharing can still be seen as a client/server activity, because

➤ One computer is making its files or printers available to other computers. Hence it is acting as a server.

➤ One or more, likely several, computers are choosing to use those files and printers. Hence they are acting as clients.

This is an important distinction because it makes it easier for you to know which computer to sit in front of when you do the upcoming procedures. So there are really just two basic steps here: In Step 1 a computer shares a folder and in Step 2 another computer opens the folder.

Step 1: Serving Up a Folder of Files

Sharing folders or disks in Windows is easy, just follow these steps:

1. Click the **My Computer** icon or any folder you choose and explore.

2. When you identify a folder you want to share, right-click it and select **Sharing** as shown in Figure 8.9.

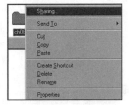

Figure 8.9

*Right-click a folder you want to share with others, and then select **Sharing**.*

The Sharing Properties window for the folder should appear.

3. To share the folder, click the **Shared As** button. Other fields on the window will become accessible.

4. Type a Share Name identifying the shared folder and a comment.

5. Choose the Access Type you want to allow for the file and folders in this folder. Your choices are:

   ➤ **Read-only** To only let others view and copy the files, but not change them.

   ➤ **Full** To let others view, copy, modify, or add files in the folders.

   ➤ **Depends on Password** To require a password to determine whether the person trying to use the folder has Read-only or Full permissions.

6. Type a password for each type of Access Type you just selected (Read-only and/or Full). When a person tries to open the folder from another computer, the password that person enters determines the permissions each has to use the associated files and folders. Figure 8.10 shows an example of the Sharing information for a Folder in Windows 95/98. (The steps are similar for Windows 2000, but not exactly the same.)

Check This Out

Passwords are really the only protection for your resources in Windows file and print sharing. If you fear someone might tamper with your files, choose a secure password. If you want permissions to the folder to be wide open on your LAN, a blank password is allowed. When someone from another computer tries to access the shared folder, it will open without prompting for a password.

Figure 8.10

Share a folder of files with others on your LAN from the folder's Sharing page.

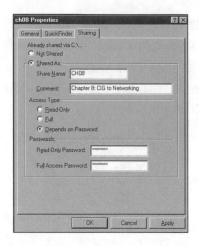

7. Click **Apply** to apply the changes. You are asked to confirm the passwords you entered for the shared folder. Retype the password (or passwords) and click **OK**. The folder is now shared.

For Windows 2000, the Sharing window allows you to enter more varied access permissions. Figure 8.11 shows the Sharing window for a Windows 2000 folder.

Figure 8.11

In Windows 2000, you can limit shared folder access by number of users or to specific users.

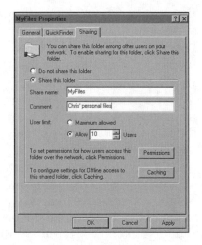

On the Windows 2000 Sharing window for a folder, you can limit simultaneous access to the folder by a set number of users (User limit). This can help prevent your computer from being overburdened by file sharing requests. The Permissions button lets you assign read, change, and full control access rights to the folder to individual computers, users, and groups. The Caching button lets you specify how cached copies of shared files are handled. (Caching is the technique for storing shared files on the client's machine so they can be accessed later without having to go back to the server.)

Step 2: Using a Shared Folder as a Client

There are several ways to use the shared folders (and the files they contain) from another computer on your LAN. One of the easiest ways to scope out the shared folders on your LAN is from the Network Neighborhood window (Windows 95/98) or the My Network Places window (Windows 2000). These windows are accessible from icons on your desktop.

Here is a simple procedure for finding and using shared folders from your LAN:

1. Open the window that shows the computers on your LAN.

   ➤ In Windows 95/98, double-click the **Network Neighborhood** icon.

   ➤ In Windows 2000, double-click the **My Network Places** icon.

   After a few moments, Windows displays icons for the computers it finds on your LAN. Figure 8.12 shows an example of a Network Neighborhood window in Windows 95/98. (For Windows 2000, you would see a similar My Network Places window.)

Figure 8.12

Computers on your LAN that could have shared folders appear in your Network Neighborhood window.

2. If you know that one of the computers listed has a folder containing files you want to share, double-click that computer's icon. A listing of shared folders and printers from that computer appears in the window.

3. To use the contents of the shared folder, just double-click it as you would any folder on your local computer. If the folder is password protected, you will be prompted for a password. Go ahead and enter it. The contents of the folder will be displayed in the window.

4. With the contents of a shared folder displayed, you can do anything with that folder you would do locally. For example:

   ➤ Open a subfolder of the shared folder to view its contents.

   ➤ Open a data file, such as a Word or Excel file, to have that data file opened in its application so you can work on the file.

   ➤ Open an application file to launch the application locally.

149

Addressing Shared Files and Folders

Although the files and folders in a shared folder look like those of any other folder, you might notice that the Address of the folder looks different. Figure 8.13 shows an example of a shared folder from a computer called Maple.

Figure 8.13

Shared folders look just like other folders after you open them.

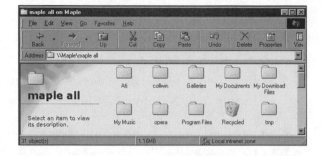

Notice that the address of the folder in this example is \\Maple\maple all. The address for a shared resource in Windows includes the computer name preceded by two backslashes (*Maple* in this case) followed by one backslash and the shared resource name (*maple all* in this case). That can then be followed by other backslashes and names as you go down the folder tree.

Remember this form of naming shared files and folders. You can use it to open shared files in different applications. For example, to open the shared file named mine.doc from this folder in Microsoft Word, you could click **File**, **Open** and type this into the **File name** box:

```
\\Maple\maple all\mine.doc
```

Shortcuts to Shared Files and Folders

If the shared folder is one that you want to use often, you can create a shortcut to the folder. Here's one way to do that:

1. Right-click the remote folder you want, and then click **Create a Shortcut**. Windows will respond that you can't create a shortcut there and ask if you want it on your desktop instead.
2. Click **Yes**. An icon for the folder appears on your desktop.
3. To open that folder from another computer in the future, you double-click the shortcut you created and the contents of the folder will appear in a folder window.

You can also add the folder to your Favorites list. From a folder window, click the folder you want to share, and then select **Favorites**, **Add to Favorites**. From the box that appears, add the name and where you want the folder to appear in your favorites. Then click **OK**. Later, you can open the folder by clicking the **Favorites** button and selecting the folder you just added.

Sharing Printers

After the whole sharing mechanism is set up as described in the "Sharing Files" section of this chapter, it's easy to share printers as well as folders. There are really just two main steps. First, the computer that the printer is attached to needs to make the printer available (share it). Second, another computer (the client) needs to identify the printer as one it wants to use.

Step 1: Serving Up Shared Printers

Follow these steps to share a printer that is connected to your computer with other computers on your LAN:

1. From Windows, click **Start**, **Settings**, **Printers**. The Printers window appears, displaying all the printers configured for your computer.
2. Find the printer you want to share from the icons shown and right-click it. (If you have not added the local printer you want to share yet, do so by opening the **Add Printer** icon and following instructions.)
3. Click **Sharing**. A Properties window for the printer appears that displays the Sharing tab. Figure 8.14 shows an example of this window for Windows 95/98.

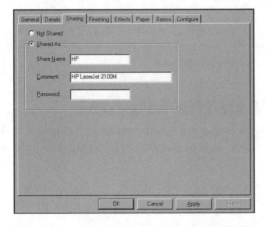

Figure 8.14

Allow a printer to be shared from the printer's Sharing window.

4. Add a Share Name, optional Comment, and optional Password for the printer. (For Windows 2000, there is an Additional Drivers button that lets you assign different print drivers to the shared printer so it can be used properly by earlier Windows systems.)
5. Click **OK**. The printer is now available to the computers on your LAN.

Step 2: Using a Shared Printer as a Client

You add a shared printer so it can be used on your computer in much the same way that you add a local printer. Here are the steps you can use:

1. From Windows, click **Start**, **Settings**, **Printers**. The Printers window appears, displaying all the printers configured for your computer.

2. Double-click **Add Printer Wizard**. The Add Printer Wizard window appears.

3. Click **Next**. The wizard asks how the printer is attached to your computer.

4. Click **Network printer**, and then select **Next**. The wizard asks for the network path or queue name of your printer.

5. Click **Browse** to find the printer or type the address (if you know it). If you are browsing, select the plus sign (+) next to the computer to which the printer is attached. The printer should appear. Select it and click **OK**. The network path to the printer should appear in the box.

6. Click **Next**. The wizard asks you to add a driver for this printer or to keep the existing driver if one is already installed.

7. Select to keep the existing driver (if there is one) and click **Next**. The wizard asks you to name the printer.

8. Select the name for the printer and click **Next**. You are asked if you want to print a test page.

9. Click **Yes** to print a test page. Then click **Finish**. If the test page prints properly, you are done.

With the shared printer set up, you can use it as you would any printer that's connected to your computer. For example, you can set it as the default printer or select it to print from your word processor or Web browser.

Preparing to Connect to the Internet

For file and printer sharing, NetBEUI is the preferred protocol that needs to be set up on your computer. To use the Internet, and just about everything else, you need to configure TCP/IP.

Setting up TCP/IP on the computers on your LAN entails:

➤ Adding the TCP/IP protocol to your LAN NIC or dial-up modem

➤ Configuring address numbers (IP address) and address names (DNS)

➤ Identifying the Gateway (the address of the computer that routes messages from your LAN to the Internet or other TCP/IP network)

Luckily, all this information can be added to the Properties window associated with the device you want to use to get to the Internet. That device is the NIC attached to your LAN or the dial-up modem on your computer.

Typically, you get the information you need to set up TCP/IP from your Internet service provider (ISP). Also, if the ISP has a procedure for setting up TCP/IP (which it should), you should use that instead of what is described here because it might vary somewhat.

The following shows you how to set up your computer for TCP/IP based on whether you are connecting to the Internet using

➤ A dial-up modem

➤ A high-speed connection from a DSL or cable modem attached to your LAN

If you have a DSL or cable connection, you can probably skip the dial-up modem section completely (unless you need to configure dial-up connections as well, for example, on a laptop). However, to allow your computers to communicate using TCP/IP on your LAN, you still need to set up TCP/IP.

After your Internet connection is up and running, you can use all the software described in Chapter 10, "Taking Your Network for a Drive," to surf the Internet, download files, and use email. You can also begin to explore other types of applications to use on the Internet.

The following sections describe how to set up your computer so that it can communicate over the Internet using either a dial-up modem or a high-speed DSL or cable modem attached to your LAN.

Check This Out

There are many compelling price and performance reasons for using a high-speed DSL or cable modem connection. Those reasons are described in detail in Chapter 7, "Making Those Internet Connections." If those services are not available in your area, however, a dial-up Internet connection might be your only choice.

Dial-up Connections to the Internet

Recall that the best way to get the procedure for setting up dial-up to the Internet is from your ISP. However, if your ISP just gives you a bunch of names and numbers and says "have at it" you can try the following procedure. (The example shown is from a Windows 98 computer.)

1. Connect your modem to your computer, probably from a serial port (COM1 or COM2). If your computer has a built-in modem, look for a regular phone jack connector.

2. Start dial-up networking by double-clicking **My Computer**, and then double-clicking **Dial-up Networking**. The Dial-up Networking Wizard pops up. (If it doesn't, double-click the **Make New Connection** icon.)

3. Click **Next**. If it hasn't already, Windows tries to detect your modem. (Click **Next** to let Windows attempt to detect the modem.) If Windows finds your modem, you should see a window similar to the one shown in Figure 8.15.

Figure 8.15

Windows tells you if it can detect your modem.

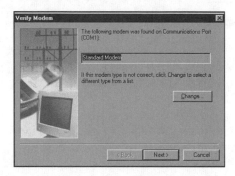

4. If the modem was not detected properly, click the **Change** button to assign a different driver to it. Otherwise, click the **Next** button to continue. A message telling you that the installation was successful appears. Click **Finish** to proceed.

5. Back in the Make New Connection window, type a name to represent the connection you are making (typically, a name identifying the ISP). If the modem needs any special configuration (which it probably shouldn't), click **Configure** and change anything necessary. Click the **Next** button to continue. A window appears, asking you to enter the telephone number to dial.

6. Type the telephone number that will connect you to the modems at the ISP (along with an optional area code and country code, if the number isn't in your local calling area). Click the **Next** button. A window appears telling you that the setup was successful.

7. Click **Finish**.

Next you need to set up properties for the dial-up connection:

1. Open the Dial-up Networking window (double-click **My Computer**, and then double-click **Dial-up Networking**). You should see an icon representing your dial-up connection.

2. Right-click the icon representing your connection, and then click **Properties**. A Properties window appears for the connection.

3. Click the **Server Types** tab. Information appears relating to protocols and such that you need to communicate with the ISP.

4. Make sure that TCP/IP is checked (that is, turned on) and that all other protocols are unchecked (that is, turned off) under Allowed network protocols. Also turn off all Advanced options. You only want TCP/IP here.

5. Click **TCP/IP Settings**. From the TCP/IP Settings window that appears, you add information about your connection to the ISP. Here are your choices (which are specific to your ISP):

> ➤ **IP Address**   If your ISP gave you your own IP address, click **Specify an IP address**, and then type the IP address in the box that appears. More likely, however, you should click **Server assigned IP address**, so the ISP's server can assign a temporary IP address at the time you connect to it.

> ➤ **Server Addresses**   Again, your ISP might automatically assign the information you need to connect to it at the time you connect (so select **Server assigned name server addresses**, in this case). If the ISP wants you to add this information yourself, click **Specify name server addresses** and type in the IP address for the primary DNS server and optionally a secondary DNS server.

6. Click **OK**. You should be ready to go.

To connect to the ISP using the connection you just configured, double-click the icon representing the connection from the Dial-up Networking window. You should hear the modem dial out and establish the connection. The Connecting to window will probably minimize when the connection is established. Go ahead and open Netscape Navigator or Internet Explorer to see if you can access the Internet.

Check This Out

The Domain Name System (DNS) is described in Chapter 3, "Using a World-Wide Network (the Internet)."

Check This Out

This procedure assumes that the DSL or cable modem is already connected and configured on your LAN. Often the phone or cable provider will send a technician to do this. If this is not the case, you'll find a description of setting up a DSL modem in Chapter 9.

LAN Connections to the Internet

If your connection to the Internet comes via a DSL or cable modem connected to your LAN, you need to configure your NIC to use that connection. You need to repeat this procedure for every computer on your LAN. Here's what you do:

1. Open the Properties window for your NIC.

   ➤ In Windows 95/98, click **Start**, **Settings**, **Control Panel**. Then double-click the **Network** icon. The Network window appears with configuration information for all the protocols on your computer.

   ➤ In Windows 2000, click **Start**, **Settings**, **Network and Dial-up Connections**, **Local Area Connection**. The Local Area Connection Status window appears. Click **Properties**. The Local Area Connection Properties window appears for your NIC.

2. Add TCP/IP protocol to the NIC.

   ➤ In Windows 95/98, in the Network window click the entry for your NIC, and then click **Add**. Click **Protocol**, **Add**. Select **Microsoft**, **TCP/IP**, and then click **OK**. Cancel the Select Network Component Type window. A new entry should be added that shows TCP/IP associated with your NIC. On my computer, it looked like this:

   ```
   TCP/IP -> 3Com EtherLink III ISA in PnP mode
   ```

   ➤ In Windows 2000, look for the Internet Protocol (TCP/IP) box in the Properties box. Make sure that the check mark is on for that protocol.

3. Open the Properties window of the TCP/IP protocol for the NIC.

   ➤ In Windows 95/98, in the Network window double-click the **TCP/IP -> NIC** entry (*NIC* is replaced by the name of your NIC).

   ➤ In Windows 2000, in the Local Area Connection Properties window for your NIC, double-click the **Internet Protocol (TCP/IP)** box.

In both cases, the TCP/IP Properties window for the NIC should appear. Figure 8.16 contains an example of the TCP/IP Properties window in Windows 95/98.

Figure 8.16

Configure TCP/IP addresses for your computer and servers.

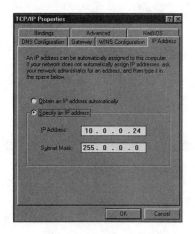

4. Configure IP Address, Gateway, and DNS Configuration. There is one piece of information you need to proceed: Will you get IP addresses automatically or from a server?

If you have configured a DSL unit to do routing, you might be able to set it up to automatically assign the IP address, the location of the default gateway, and DNS servers to all the computers on the LAN. If that was done, you might only need to specify to Obtain an IP address automatically on the IP Address tab of the TCP/IP Properties window.

If you want to specify each IP address statically for a computer on the LAN, here is the information you need. For Windows 95/98, click the appropriate tab to enter the information. For Windows 2000, all the information can be added to the Internet Protocol (TCP/IP) Properties window for the NIC:

Check This Out

Refer to Chapter 3 for information on public and private IP addresses, as well as the Domain Name System (DNS).

➤ **IP Address**   Click **Specify an IP address** and then type the IP address and Subnet Mask into the appropriate fields. If the ISP didn't give you a whole set of IP Addresses for your LAN, you can use private IP addresses. For the sake of this example, I chose to use a network number of 10.0.0 so the computers on the network are numbered 10.0.0.2, 10.0.0.3, 10.0.0.4, and so on. The subnet mask I used is 255.0.0.0.

➤ **DNS Configuration**   Click this tab, and then select **Enable DNS**. Your ISP should have provided you with a host name, domain name, and IP addresses for one or two DNS servers. Add that information to this tab.

➤ **Gateway**   Click the **Gateway** tab. Then type the IP address for your gateway and click the **Add** button. The gateway is the machine that provides the route from your LAN to the Internet. In this example, I assigned the gateway number of the LAN as 10.0.0.1. In my case, this is a DSL unit that provides the route to my ISP.

5. Click **OK** when you are done. You should now have configured your NIC to communicate with the Internet through a DSL unit, cable modem, or other device that provides routing features.

Where To From Here?

You have just read about how to set up a basic home LAN to share files, share printers, and connect to the Internet. In Chapter 9, you can learn how to create a small office network that expands on many of these basic concepts.

The Least You Need to Know

➤ Using a few computers, NICs, cables, and a hub, you should be able to connect a small LAN.

➤ With tools that are built in to Windows 95/98/2000, you can set up your computers to share files and printers.

➤ To get connected to the Internet, you can follow procedures to create a dial-up or LAN connection.

Chapter 9

Hooking Up Your Small Office Network

In This Chapter

➤ Expand your LAN using additional hubs

➤ Segment your LAN to improve performance using a switch

➤ Set up a DSL modem to route messages to the Internet

➤ Use DHCP to assign addresses on the LAN

➤ Use NAT to mask your LAN's IP addresses from the outside world

---

A home and office network can have similar components such as Ethernet, file and printer sharing, and a connection to the Internet; however, an office network has to be somehow more serious. Although a family can add a computer or two, even a smaller business might need to add a dozen new computers or a branch office. Whereas it's important to protect the computers you do your homework on, security takes on a new meaning when you are protecting payroll and inventory records.

This chapter builds on procedures in Chapter 8, "Building Your Home Network," where you built a small network, shared files and printers, and prepared the LAN for the Internet. Here, you'll learn how to expand the LAN with more hubs and switches. Then you'll go through the process of configuring the boundary between your LAN and the Internet, using the setup of a DSL connection as an example of routing and network address translation.

Expanding the LAN with Switches and Hubs

Because Ethernet is a broadcast technology in which all information is broadcast to all computers on the LAN, how you grow the network depends a lot on how big it needs to get and how much data it needs to carry. Should you just add on another hub to expand? Should you incorporate switches?

One of the great things about Ethernet LANs is that you can grow your network without discarding old equipment. But, before you start randomly adding new hardware to your office LAN, you should consider several different techniques for growing without hurting performance. Here are some possibilities you should consider:

➤ **Migrating to higher speeds**   Purchasing 10/100Mbps cards lets your network communicate today at the slower speed, while readying some of the equipment to move to the higher speed.

➤ **Adding hubs**   If your current LAN hasn't reached its capacity yet, but you have run out of ports, adding hubs can be an economical next step to upgrade your LAN.

➤ **Segmenting**   Dividing your LAN into segments can help growth in several ways. First, traffic intended for computers within the segment never gets broadcast outside the segment. Second, some segments of the LAN can start operating at higher speeds, while others can stay at the slower speed. As a result, you can take advantage of the capability of newer, higher-speed technology while still being able to use the older technology.

➤ **Dedicated segments**   A high-volume server or workstation can plug directly into a 10/100Mbps switch, giving that computer its own segment. By adding a 10/100Mbps NIC to that server or workstation, it has a dedicated 100Mbps-bandwidth channel. It can also get better performance by not having to deal with data intended for other computers.

➤ **Faster backbone**—If your LAN continues to grow, you can not only attach hubs to switches, but also you can attach switches to switches. By creating 100Mbps or even gigabit (1000Mbps) backbones between switches, you can alleviate bottlenecks between LAN segments.

The following sections step you through connecting hubs and switches.

Adding a Hub

For connecting a few additional computers to a LAN that isn't already overloaded, adding a hub can be a simple and effective solution. Hubs can be connected using a technique called *daisy chaining*. As the name implies, you effectively chain one hub to the next. As long as the LAN traffic is not too demanding, chaining two or three hubs together is no problem.

The only small trick to daisy-chaining hubs is that each hub expects its ports to communicate with computers, not other hubs. As a result, if you just connected two ports on a hub together with a standard Ethernet cable, both hubs would try to send data on the same wire and receive it on the same wire. This is solved in one of two ways:

➤ **A crossover cable** Using a crossover cable reverses the send and receive wires. In that way, each hub can send and receive data on different wires.

➤ **A crossover switch** Some hubs have a button that internally changes the send and receive wires. The result is that the two hubs can be connected using a standard Ethernet cable. Because the button is associated with a particular port (called an *uplink* port), the cable must connect that port to any other port on the other hub.

Figure 9.1 shows an example of three 3Com OfficeConnect hubs being daisy-chained together.

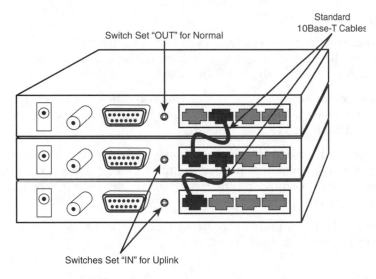

Switch Set "OUT" for Normal

Standard
10Base-T Cables

Switches Set "IN" for Uplink

Figure 9.1

Daisy-chain hubs together by connecting to up-link ports (shown here) or by using crossover cables.

There are a few points to make about these hub connections:

➤ Because these particular hubs have uplink buttons, daisy-chaining can be done using standard Ethernet cables.

➤ If the uplink port is the last port (as it is here), the convention is to connect the cable to the last port on the lower hub and the next-to-last port on the hub

161

above. In that way, the end port on the second hub can be used to daisy-chain to the next hub.

➤ As noted in the figure, the cables between each hub can be up to 100 meters (328 feet) long. In a small office environment, however, these hubs are often just stacked together and connected with short cables, as shown.

➤ Although 10BaseT cables are shown in this example, often thinnet cables with BNC connectors are used to connect hubs. The advantage is that thinnet (10BASE2) cables between the hubs can be much longer (up to 185 meters or 607 feet). These cables, however, cannot be shorter than half a meter (1.6 feet).

In small offices where space is at a premium, you might want to get hubs from the same manufacturer that stack together. If there's no room for a wiring closet, you can purchase hubs that have more attractive designs so you can leave the hubs out where people can see them.

Adding a Switch

Switches are more expensive than plain-old repeater hubs, but they're a lot smarter too. As noted earlier, switches can serve to segment parts of the LAN from each other, only delivering data to segments for which it is intended.

Segmenting also creates *separate collision domains.* A collision domain reduces the amount of traffic in each segment to significantly reduce the chances of frames running into each other and having to recover from that.

A switch looks a lot like a hub, except that it tends to have more ports and use different types of ports. Each port is devoted to its own segment. One of those ports will usually be a high-speed port for connecting the switch to another switch, whereby creating a high-speed backbone.

Figure 9.2 shows how a LAN that is joined together with a single hub can be segmented with a switch to improve performance.

Figure 9.2

A switch can segment hubs, as well as individual servers or workstations.

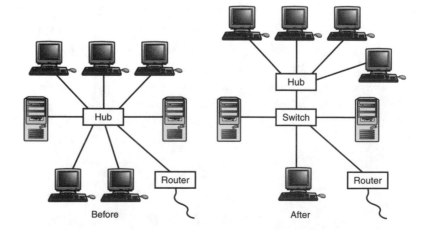

In this example, data being transferred among a set of workstations was negatively impacting the entire performance of the LAN. As a result, a file server and a Web server were unable to handle the amount of traffic they were being asked to deal with from remote sites.

The solution was to add a switch. In this way, the group of workstations that need to exchange data together could do so without harming the capability of the servers to handle requests for data that came in over the router.

Completing the High-Speed Internet Connection with DSL

Although a home user might be satisfied to have a technician come in and configure the home's high-speed Internet connection, a business owner might want more control over the configuration and security of the business LAN. This section provides an example of how you can configure a high-speed Internet connection from your LAN using DSL technology.

Some DSL modems can do a lot more than just pass packets of information along to the Internet. They can also be used to assign addresses to the computers on your LAN (using DHCP), manage translation of private and public IP addresses (using NAT), and most essentially act as a router between your LAN and the ISP's network.

Check This Out

Chapter 4, "Choosing Your Network Hardware," describes DSL technology and notes some of its pros and cons.

Using a Cisco 675 DSL modem as an example, you'll see the steps necessary to configure DSL to provide DHCP, NAT, and routing services. Although your DSL modem might work differently, you should be able to apply many of the same concepts described here to the configuration of your DSL modem.

Check This Out

Although the information in this chapter is explained in detail, it is fairly technical in its nature. Procedures will also vary for different types of DSL modems. At the very least, this section should help you understand how concepts such as DHCP and NAT are actually implemented. If you feel unsure about setting up your own DSL modem, contact your ISP for help.

Connecting Your DSL Modem

To route data from your LAN or workstation to the ISP's Internet connection, the DSL modem needs to have connections to both networks. Here is how it connects to each network:

➤ An Ethernet port on the DSL modem (typically an RJ-45 port) allows you to plug the modem into your LAN or, if you have no LAN, directly into your workstation's NIC using a crossover cable.

➤ A port for a standard phone jack (RJ-11 port) lets you reach the ISP by connecting to the telephone line that is shared with the phones in your house.

➤ In the case of the Cisco 675, the modem also has a port that connects to your workstation's nine-pin (DB9) serial port. This connection allows you to configure the DSL modem from your workstation.

After those connections are made, and the telephone company and your ISP have turned on your DSL connection, you are ready to start configuring your DSL modem.

Configuring Your DSL Modem

Using a terminal program such as HyperTerminal (click **Start**, **Programs**, **Accessories**, **Communication**, **HyperTerminal**), open a communication to the serial port (COM1 or COM2) that is connected to the DSL modem. (A terminal program is a window that lets you type text commands to talk to a modem or other device connected to a serial port.)

You will need to create an entry for the terminal program that identifies the serial port and sets the proper speed (38,400), data bits (8), parity (None), stop bits (1), and flow control (None) for the connection to the port.

Press **Enter**. You should be prompted for a password as follows:

```
User Access Verification
Password:
```

Press **Enter** (there is no password yet). You should see a cbos> prompt. This indicates that you are ready to use the Cisco Broadband Operating System. The series of steps described next will vary for different DSL modems and different ISPs. These steps will do the following for a WAN and LAN:

➤ **WAN** Define the connection between the DSL modem and the ISP as a Point-to-Point Protocol (PPP) connection. This is the wide area network (WAN) connection that is made from the DSL modem to your phone line.

➤ **LAN** Configure the DSL modem's interface to the LAN to do network address translation (NAT) so the LAN can use private IP addresses and still communicate on the Internet. Then the DHCP will be set up to automatically assign all the computers on the LAN the information they need to have their own IP addresses and know the locations of the servers they need to resolve Internet host names (DNS) and get email (SMTP).

Configure Point-to-Point Protocol (PPP) to the WAN

PPP is the same protocol you use when you typically use a dial-up connection to get to the Internet. When you start up your DSL modem, it tries to create the WAN connection to your ISP using a login and password that you provide to PPP. Here is an example of what you might type:

```
set ppp wan0-0 ipcp 0.0.0.0
set ppp wan0-0 login mylogin
set ppp wan0-0 password mypassword
set ppp restart enabled
write
```

The first line (ipcp) indicates to the DSL modem that it should get its IP address (for the connection on the WAN side) from the ISP's server on the WAN. The next two lines define the login name (mylogin) and password (mypassword). The final line enables PPP to restart its connection after the line goes down. After that, the word "write" permanently writes the changes to the modem.

Configure Network Address Translation (NAT) for the LAN

One way that Internet authorities slow down the inevitable fact that the world is running out of IP addresses is to allow private IP addresses. These private IP addresses (described in Chapter 3, "Using a World-Wide Network (the Internet)") can be reused by anyone with a network that wants to use them.

The trick is that before requests from computers using private addresses are routed from the private network to the public Internet, they must be translated in a way that makes the requests look like they come from valid addresses. That's where Network Address Translation (NAT) comes in.

By configuring your DSL modem to do NAT, requests from the LAN are translated into requests from the DSL modem. Because you probably only have one valid IP address (the one assigned to the DSL modem's connection to the ISP), all requests look to the Internet like they are coming from that address.

This is also a nice little security feature. Because only one IP address is exposed, someone snooping around the Internet cannot see how the IP addresses are arranged for the computers on your LAN. The DSL modem and NAT essentially mask that.

So the first thing you want to do from your DSL modem to set up NAT is assign an IP address to your DSL modem's interfaces that faces your LAN to a private IP address. In this case, 10.0.0.1 is used and the following is typed:

```
set nat enabled
set interface eth0 address 10.0.0.1
set interface eth0 netmask 255.255.255.0
write
```

The first line enables NAT. The second line assigns the DSL modem's LAN address as 10.0.0.1. (To the computers on the LAN, address 10.0.0.1 will be seen as the *gateway* to the Internet.) The third line sets the netmask (also called the subnetwork mask) to 255.255.255.0. As a result of the netmask, the network number is 10.0.0 and the other available IP addresses on the LAN are any numbers between 2 and 254 (that is, 10.0.0.2 through 10.0.0.254). The last line writes the changes. See Chapter 3 for a description of netmask.

Configure DHCP for the LAN

Instead of having each computer on the LAN set up its own IP address, plus enter IP addresses for other computers that those on the LAN need to know about, you can configure the DSL modem to be a DHCP server. DHCP stands for Dynamic Host Configuration Protocol.

To configure DHCP, the DSL modem must choose a pool of IP addresses to assign to the computers on the LAN. The DHCP server can also provide other information those computers need. Here is what you might type to set up DHCP on the DSL modem:

```
set dhcp server pool 0 ip 10.0.0.2 enabled
set dhcp server pool 0 dns 111.111.111.111
set dhcp server pool 0 secondary 111.111.111.112
set dhcp server pool 0 smtp 111.111.111.113
set dhcp server pool 0 pop3 111.111.111.114
write
reboot
```

The first line begins the pool of IP addresses that will be assigned to each computer on the LAN with the number 10.0.0.2. Later, when each computer boots up on the LAN, the first to come up will be assigned to the number 10.0.0.2, the next to 10.0.0.3, and so on. The IP addresses shown on the next four lines are made up. Don't use them! Get the real IP addresses for each of the following features from your ISP:

➤ **dns**   The IP address of the primary Domain Name System server.

➤ **secondary**   The IP address of the backup Domain Name System server.

➤ **smtp**   The IP address of the computer that you will send your email through.

➤ **pop3**   The IP address of the computer that you will download your incoming email from.

After all these changes are made, you can type **write** (to write the changes) and **reboot** (to restart the DSL modem with the new settings).

To make all this work, when you set up the client computers on your LAN (as described in Chapter 8), they must be configured to obtain their IP addresses automatically.

Where To From Here?

After you have read this chapter, you can proceed to Chapter 10, "Taking Your Network for a Drive." That chapter describes Web browsers, email readers, and other software programs you can use across the network connections you have just created.

The Least You Need to Know

Right now, the least you need to know about setting up your small office network is this:

➤ Hubs can be used to expand an office by a few extra computers.

➤ If performance is becoming a problem with your LAN, you can segment part of the LAN by using a switch.

➤ If you are using a DSL modem for high-speed access to the Internet, you need to connect it to an Ethernet interface on one side (your LAN or workstation's NIC) and the phone line connection to the ISP on the other.

➤ Using Network Address Translation, you can configure your DSL modem to mask the real IP addresses of the computers on your LAN.

➤ Using Dynamic Host Configuration Protocol, you can automatically assign all necessary IP addresses to the computers on your LAN.

Chapter 10

Taking Your Network for a Drive

In This Chapter

➤ Try out the Internet using a Web browser

➤ Learn about email programs

➤ Participate in online chats

➤ Find and play multi-user games on the Internet

➤ Use shared folders, files, devices, and printers on your LAN

If you just want to use your network, and couldn't care less about building or understanding it, this is the chapter for you. The features described in this chapter are ultimately why you have a network: to browse the Web, have online chats, play multi-user games, and share stuff.

This chapter assumes you are connected to the Internet and ready to try it out. Some of the tools and toys described here might already be on your computer, although you might have to acquire others. Don't worry, you'll find out where to get them (most are either free or have demo or trial versions to test out).

Your #1 Internet Tool: The Web Browser

Nothing was more responsible for the astronomical growth of the Internet than the creation of the World Wide Web. The foundation of the Web consists of the language for creating Web pages (HTML, Hypertext Markup Language) and the program for displaying Web pages: the Web browser. The most basic features of a Web browser include the capability to display

Check This Out

The inside back cover contains short descriptions and Web addresses for many of the applications described in this chapter.

➤ Text (with embedded tags to describe fonts, colors, and position)

➤ Images (mostly in GIF and JPG formats in the first browsers)

➤ Hypertext links (things you can click to take you to other Web pages)

Since their humble beginnings, HTML and the browsers that display HTML have gone through dramatic improvements. Now Web pages can include a variety of data types: document formats, audio, video, forms, virtual reality, and even full-blown application programs.

Although there are dozens of Web browsers around, two have captured the lion's share of the browser market: Netscape Communicator and Microsoft Internet Explorer. One other browser that could benefit from the coming boom in handheld and portable Web devices is called Opera. (Although Opera currently has only a small share of the market, it deserves at least a mention here. Check out the sidebar on Opera later in this chapter.) You'll learn about Netscape Communicator and Internet Explorer browsers in this chapter.

If you have a browser installed on your computer, chances are there is an icon representing that browser on your desktop. Figure 10.1 shows three icons, representing Netscape Communicator, Internet Explorer, and Opera. Double-click any of those icons to start your browser.

Figure 10.1

Look for Netscape Communicator, Internet Explorer, or Opera Web browsers as represented by icons on your desktop.

General Browsing Features

Some browsing features apply no matter what Web browser you are using. For example, most browsers use plug-ins and helper apps to handle different types of data, history lists to keep track of where you have been, and bookmarks (or favorites) to save and organize your favorite sites. Here are descriptions of those features.

Plug-ins and Helper Apps

For a Web browser to handle every type of data that comes along would require it to be so huge that nobody would want to download it. So, to allow users to play or display different kinds of content that the browser couldn't handle natively, Netscape came up with the following two approaches:

➤ **Plug-ins**   A plug-in is a software program that is installed to work with the browser. The plug-in is assigned to handle specific types of data. When a file of that data type is encountered, the plug-in is started up to play the content within the browser window.

➤ **Helper Apps**   A helper app is like a plug-in, except that when data is encountered of a certain type an external window is launched to play that data. For example, if you like to use a certain image viewer to read bitmap files (an image file that has a .bmp extension), you could configure it as a Netscape helper app. When you open a bitmap image in the browser, the image would display in your viewer.

You can look for a variety of plug-ins to add to your browser from the Netscape Plug-ins site (`http://home.netscape.com/plugins`). Although they were originally called "Netscape Plug-ins," you can use them in Internet Explorer and other browsers as well. Here are a few plug-ins you should consider downloading from the Netscape Plug-ins site to use with your browser:

➤ **Adobe Acrobat**   Displays files in its native Portable Document Format (PDF). Many Web sites offer documents in this popular format.

➤ **Macromedia Flash Player**   Plays Flash presentations, containing animation and vector graphics (images that are represented by shapes, rather than just dots). After you install the plug-in, try out some content from `http://www.macromedia.com/software/flash/gallery/collection`.

➤ **Macromedia Shockwave**   Plays Macromedia graphics, multimedia, audio, and video presentations. Shockwave features are now built into the Flash plug-in.

➤ **RealPlayer by RealNetworks**   Plays audio and video content in RealMedia formats.

Using History Lists

Web browsers keep a history of Web sites you have visited. In Netscape, click **Communicator**, **Tools**, **History**. In Internet Explorer, click the **History** button. In both cases, you can see lists of Web sites you have visited in the recent past. You can search the list to find a particular site that you can't quite remember. Or, you can go down the list and select the site to reopen it.

Keeping Bookmarks or Favorite Web Pages

Both Internet Explorer and Netscape have ways of saving and organizing the addresses of your favorite Web sites. Netscape calls this feature Bookmarks, whereas Internet Explorer calls it Favorites.

You can organize your favorite sites into folders, so you can easily find them again later. Both browsers also start you off with a list of their favorites. Click the **Bookmarks** or **Favorites** button, and then click **Add** (**Bookmark** or **Favorite**) to add it to the list of sites you save.

Browsing with Netscape Communicator

Netscape Navigator was the first popular commercial Web browser. In version 4, Netscape evolved into Netscape Communicator to include a full suite of Internet applications along with the browser function. The Netscape Communicator suite includes

➤ **Netscape Navigator** The basic browser that lets you display Web pages and a variety of Web content. Toolbars let you step Forward and Back, return to your home page, search the Web, print the current page, display security information about the current page, and stop loading the current page.

➤ **Netscape Messenger** A tool for reading and composing email. It can also be used to select and participate in newsgroups.

➤ **Netscape Composer** A simple HTML editor for creating and modifying Web pages.

Other components that you can download with Netscape Communicator include the AOL Instant Messenger (discussed later in this chapter), the Real Player (which is great for playing streaming video and audio content), and the Address Book Palm Sync (for synchronizing your address book with a PalmPilot).

If you do not have Netscape Communicator, you can download it by going to http://home.netscape.com and clicking the **Download** link. Follow the instructions for installation. After you've installed it, start **Netscape Communicator** by clicking its icon on your desktop or from the **Start** menu in Windows. Figure 10.2 shows an example of Netscape Communicator.

Figure 10.2
Browse the Web with Netscape Communicator.

Several of the most common things you'll do in Netscape Communicator are described here:

➤ **Visit Web Pages**   To display a Web page, type the address into the Netsite Address box at the top of the page. For example, try **http://home.netscape.com** and press **Enter**. Move the mouse pointer over any Web page. If the pointer turns into a hand, the text or image represents a link. Click it to visit the Web page pointed to by the link.

➤ **Go Back and Forward**   Click the **Back** button to go back to the previously visited Web page. Click the **Forward** button to go forward again. Right-click your mouse on either of those buttons to see a list of sites you could go forward or back to. (The Forward button is grayed out until you click the Back button.)

➤ **Change Preferences**   Click **Edit**, **Preferences**. The Preferences window that appears lets you change many attributes related to the look and feel of Netscape. You could change fonts, colors, languages, mail and newsgroup attributes, composer features, and advanced features related to caching (saving content that you previously visited) and proxy servers (computers that let you indirectly access the Internet).

➤ **Get Help**   Click the **Help** menu to find out more about Netscape Communicator. For example, click **About Plug-ins** on the **Help** menu to see what plug-ins are installed or click **About Communicator** to see what version is installed. There are also complete Help Contents and Reference Library features available.

Browsing with Microsoft Internet Explorer

Like Netscape Communicator, Microsoft Internet Explorer (IE) is not just a Web browser. Instead, it is a bundle of software applications that let Internet clients manage email, have conferences, play audio and video, and publish Web pages. Here's what IE includes:

➤ **Browser**   Not only does this allow you to browse Web pages on the Internet, but lets you play a variety of graphical, audio, video, and other content.

➤ **NetMeeting**   Lets you connect to audio, video, and typed (chat) conferences on the Internet.

➤ **Outlook Express**   Lets you compose, send, receive, and manage email and newsgroup messages.

➤ **Media Player**   Plays live audio and video broadcasts.

➤ **FrontPage Express**   Can be used to create basic Web pages that you can put on the Internet.

➤ **Web Publishing Wizard**   Lets you manage the Web content you create and publish it to the Internet.

Figure 10.3 shows an example of an Internet Explorer window.

Figure 10.3

Internet Explorer provides a popular way to access the Internet.

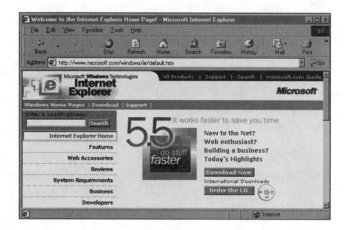

Controls for using Internet Explorer to browse the Web are similar to those for Netscape Communicator. Here are a few more common tasks you can try with Internet Explorer:

➤ **Search the Web**   Click the **Search** button. Choices for searching the Web appear in the left column of the IE window. Type a word or several words into the text box and click the **Search** button. Search results appear in the left column. Click any of the results to have the page appear on the right side of the window.

➤ **Change Options**   Click **Tools**, **Internet Options**. The Internet Options window lets you change many of the features associated with your IE browser. You can change your home page, set security levels (to limit insecure features), add content controls (to block inappropriate Web content), choose an Internet connection, and set many advanced accessibility and browsing features.

➤ **Use Favorites** Click the **Favorites** menu button. Click **Add to Favorites** to add the current Web page to your Favorites list. Click **Organize Favorites** to create folders and arrange your favorites in a useful way. Click any saved Favorite in your list to have that Web page displayed.

Although Internet Explorer and Netscape Communicator are the most popular browsers, with the expected growth of mobile and wireless Internet devices there is one more browser to note here. The Opera Web browser (described in the sidebar) can run efficiently on mobile devices.

Check This Out

Internet Explorer comes built in to Windows 98. If you have Windows 95, but do not have Internet Explorer, you can download Internet Explorer free from Microsoft. Go to `http://www.microsoft.com/ie` and choose **Download IE**.

Check This Out

The Opera Web Browser from Opera Software (`http://www.opera.com`) is more like an entire desktop than just a browser. Although Opera isn't nearly as popular as Netscape or Internet Explorer, it deserves a mention because of Opera's capability to run efficiently on wireless and mobile devices.

Within the Opera window, you can open multiple Web pages, display links to folders or favorites in the left column, and use a variety of navigational features. Figure 10.4 shows an example of the Opera Web Browser window.

One of Opera's unique features is that it is one of the first Web browsers to support Wireless Application Protocol (WAP) and Wireless Markup Language (WML). These features allow Opera to run on wireless devices, such as mobile phones and handheld devices. Click on the download link from the Opera Software home page to download a trial version of the Opera Web Browser or to purchase a copy.

Figure 10.4

The Opera Web Browser can run on desktop PCs or wireless devices.

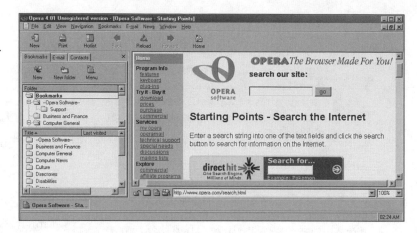

Sending and Receiving Email

Electronic mail (email) is a quick and easy way to send a message to just one person or to hundreds of people simultaneously. In most cases, the message arrives at the person's mail server within minutes, ready to be read. Since the first computer networks were created, email has been—and continues to be—one of the most important uses for computer networks.

Email Basics

In its most basic form, an email message consists of some plain text and an address. The address identifies the recipient in a form that is recognizable by the network that forwards the mail to the recipient.

The first email messages were created with simple text editors (such as the UNIX ed or vi commands) and could be read on dumb character terminals (in other words, no fancy graphics or colors). Although mail messages can still be just as simple, today's programs for composing and reading mail offer a lot more features. Following are some examples:

➤ **HTML format** The latest email programs enable you to create email messages in either plain text or HTML formats. By creating messages in HTML, you can add images, color, font changes, and text formatting. You can even include an entire Web page in a mail message.

➤ **Attachments** Any type of computer file can be attached to an email message. When an attachment arrives with the message, the recipient can choose to save the attachment or open it in a program that is designed to play or display the file. (Attachments are often compressed, using utilities such as WinZip, so messages can transmit faster and avoid hitting message size limitations from mail servers.)

➤ **Address book**   Most email programs come with a way of storing the names and email addresses of the people you send mail to. You can also gather names together into an email group (sometimes called a distribution list) so you can send a message to a group of people at once. Some address books also enable you to store other information about each person, such as address, job title, phone/fax numbers, and Web page location.

➤ **Mail download**   When the computing world was mostly mainframes, mail was usually stored on the same computer where you did your work. However, with more people working on PCs, to receive email the user often sends outgoing messages and downloads incoming messages by connecting to a mail server. Many mail readers use the *Post Office Protocol (POP3)* or *Internet Message Access Protocol (IMAP4)* to get messages from the mail server. (POP and IMAP4 are discussed later in this chapter.)

➤ **Multiple email accounts**   Some people have several email accounts (possibly one work and one personal account). Some mail programs enable you to query several mail servers for your email.

➤ **Managing messages**   Some people get so much email that managing the messages they receive is a big issue. Most mail programs offer a way to save messages to your hard disk or sort them to special mail folders you create. Within folders, there are also ways to sort messages by subject, time/date received, and sender.

➤ **Managing newsgroups**   Because newsgroups just consist of a bunch of email messages grouped together, many mail message programs offer a way of reading and working with newsgroups as well as email. Some special features (such as allowing threads that follow the responses to a particular message) are included for working with newsgroups.

When you choose your mail message program, consider some of these special features to distinguish between the different programs offered. Because most mail readers today are either free or available on a trial basis, you might as well try out a few.

Choosing an Email Program

If you have an Internet browser on your computer, chances are an email program came with it. Netscape Communicator and Microsoft Internet Explorer each have email programs that work quite well (Netscape Messenger and Outlook Express, respectively). A popular email program that you can add on is the Eudora email reader, from Qualcomm.

Netscape Messenger

With Netscape Messenger, you can read, send, and manage your email using the Messenger Mailbox window. If you have Netscape Communicator installed, you can open the Messenger Mailbox by clicking **Mailbox** on the Netscape component bar or by selecting **Communicator**, **Messenger** from the Navigator window.

Figure 10.5 shows an example of the Netscape Messenger Mailbox window.

Figure 10.5

Read, send, and manage mail messages with Netscape Messenger.

Mail messages that have been received appear in the upper part of the Messenger Mailbox window. Select one of the messages and the contents of the message appear in the lower window. You can sort the messages by Subject, Sender, Date, Priority, Status, or Size by clicking the headings above the columns.

Following are some of the things you can do with Netscape Messenger:

➤ To download your messages from the mail server, click the **Get Msg** button.

➤ To create a new mail message, click the **New Msg** button. From the Composition window that appears, add the recipient's address, the subject of the message, and text. You can also add attachments and change the fonts. When the message is complete, click **Send**.

➤ To reply to a message, click the message and then click the **Reply** button. Then select either **Reply to Sender** or **Reply to Sender and All Recipients**. A Composition window appears with the recipient and subject filled in, and the message you're replying to included in the text pane.

➤ To forward a message, click the message and then click the **Forward** button. A Composition window appears with the message you are forwarding added as an attachment.

➤ To open a different folder, click **File** and select the folder you want. The Inbox folder holds messages you receive and the Sent folder has copies of messages you have sent. Other folders are used to hold draft messages or temporary messages (waiting to be sent).

While you are composing a message, there are a lot of features you can use. Click **Address** to choose recipients from the address book. Click **Attach** to attach a file to the message. Click **Spelling** to spell check your message. Click **Security** to find out how to add security features, such as passwords and certificates, to the message.

Microsoft Outlook Express

Outlook Express has some advanced features for collaborating with others and integrating with Microsoft Office and other applications. Although it's a reduced-feature version of Microsoft's Outlook 2000, this program has a lot of the functions you might expect from a full-featured email program.

Starting Outlook Express

You can start Outlook Express from an icon in the taskbar or by clicking **Go**, **Mail** from the Internet Explorer window. Figure 10.6 shows an example of the Outlook Express window.

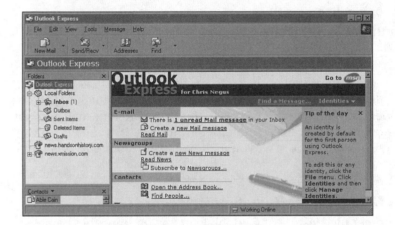

Figure 10.6

Outlook Express adds mail services to the Internet Explorer suite.

The layout and buttons on the Outlook Express window are similar to the Netscape Messenger Mailbox window. Mail messages are listed in the upper pane and the current message contents appear in the lower pane. Mail folders are shown along the left column.

If you are accustomed to managing folders in the Windows Explorer window, you might notice that the layout of mail folders in Outlook Express is the same. You can create folders and subfolders that can be used to sort your mail messages.

Creating Mail Sorting Rules

One of the best features of Outlook Express is the Mail Rules window. With mail rules, you can set what happens to different email messages when they are downloaded. Instead of having all incoming messages sent to your Inbox, messages can be moved, copied, or forwarded to different locations based on what is in the address or subject lines.

To add rules to the mail messages as they come into Outlook Express, select **Tools**, **Message Rules**, **Mail**. The Rule Editor appears.

You can have each email that comes in checked for a particular message size, specific words in the subject line, certain people in any of the address lines, or a specific mail account name. If an incoming message matches your conditions, you can take the following actions:

➤ Move or copy the message to a specific folder.

➤ Delete the message.

➤ Forward the message to specific people.

➤ Reply with a specific email message, such as "I'm on vacation so don't bother me."

➤ Flag the message or highlight it with a color.

➤ Don't download the message from the server.

➤ Delete the message from the server.

If you receive a lot of mail, you can save yourself hours of sorting and reading time using the mail rules feature. For example, if you get messages from a mailing list, you can sort them to a folder that you can check later. If you have different mail accounts for work and home, those messages can go into different folders. If you have something to say to all or a few people who send you mail, you can respond to them automatically with a preset mail message.

Using the Address Book and Multiple Email Accounts

The address book is another nice feature of Outlook Express. You can store names, email addresses, phone numbers, and other information for users with whom you want to communicate. You can also create user groups, so that by sending a message to that group, you can automatically have it go to dozens or hundreds of users.

If you have multiple email accounts, you can have your messages from each account downloaded in turn when you download your mail. These accounts can exist on several different servers, as long as they are accessible from your network.

Adding Backgrounds to Messages

For creating new mail messages, Outlook has a stationery option that enables you to add a background to your messages. There are different motifs for birthdays, formal invitations, and holidays, to name a few. As with Netscape Messenger, you can also use HTML markup to add color, images, and font changes to your messages.

Check This Out

If you get a long message in which you need to find a specific piece of information, you can use the Find Now feature to locate it. Click in the message text and choose **Edit, Find, Find Message.** Then type the word (or words) you are looking for in the Message box, and click **Find Now**. A list of messages containing that text appears.

Using Eudora Email

Eudora is the free email program from Qualcomm (http://www.eudora.com). Because Eudora has been around for a while, it offers many features that make it compatible with older mail features. Eudora doesn't look as fancy as Outlook Express and Netscape Messenger, but it is extremely powerful and flexible.

Because of its support for older mail features, Eudora is a good mail program to use in a diverse corporate environment. For example, besides creating attachments in MIME (the common Internet mail attachment format), you can also use older types of mail attachments including BinHex (used with Macintosh) and Uuencode (used with older UNIX systems) for attaching mail.

There is a version of Eudora that is available for use on the Palm Computing platform as well. The Eudora Internet Suite for Palm Computing lets you manage email, browse the Web, and synchronize Palm and desktop email. The platform runs on Windows, Macintosh, Linux, and other UNIX-based systems.

If you want to make changes throughout the mail message you just typed, the Message Plug-in feature enables you to do some interesting things. After you have typed a mail message, click **Edit, Message Plug-ins**, and then select one of the following:

➤ **Sort** Alphabetically sorts the lines in the message.

➤ **Unwrap Text** Joins the lines of text together into paragraphs.

➤ **Upper Case** Changes all text to uppercase.

➤ **Lower Case** Changes all text to lowercase.

➤ **Toggle Case** Changes upper- to lowercase and lower- to uppercase.

➤ **The Word Case** Changes the case for the selected word.

➤ **Sentence Case** Begins sentences with uppercase.

181

You can also add other plug-ins to Eudora that enable you to manipulate the content of the messages in different ways. If you have trouble with any of the features, Eudora comes with context-sensitive help. Just click the question mark, and then click the button or window with which you need help. A pop-up box shows you a description of the item.

Understanding Email Addressing

By far, most email addresses today use domain-style addressing. This method assumes an address structure based on TCP/IP domains (which are used with the Internet). The form is a username, followed by an "at" sign (@), followed by the domain name. For example:

jjones@twostory.com

Check This Out

To learn more about the domain name system (DNS) and addressing, please see Chapter 3, "Using a World-Wide Network (the Internet)."

This address directs mail to the user named jjones at the domain twostory.com. Mail can also be directed to a particular sub-domain or host within the domain. For example, to send mail to the same user on a computer named jumbo in the same domain, you can use the following address:

jjones@jumbo.twostory.com

If you are sending email to someone within your own domain (or subdomain), you can sometimes get away with only using the username. So, in this case you can just type the name:

jjones

This results in the mail being sent to jjones in the local domain.

Adding Mail Attachments

Using attachments, you can send many different kinds of information along with a mail message. For example, if you have a Word or WordPerfect word processing file, a sound file, a video file, or a graphics file, you can attach it to your mail message without it actually appearing in the text of the message.

While you are composing a mail message, look for a button marked Attach, or one that is represented by a paper clip. Click that button, and then browse for or type the location of the file you want to include with your message.

When you receive a mail message with an attachment, a paper clip usually appears alongside the message title and within the message frame (for Outlook Express, Netscape Messenger, and other mail programs). AOL represents attachments with a floppy disk behind an envelope icon. Click the paper clip or other icon, and then select the attachment (there might be more than one). You are usually then asked either to save the message to a file or open it with a program.

Windows systems keep a list of data types and applications that can run those data types. For example, Windows knows that a Web browser can open an HTML file and that a WAV file plays in an audio player. The system recognizes the type of file by the file's extension (such as .htm or .wav) or by its MIME type.

Check This Out

Some mail programs, such as Netscape Messenger, enable you to attach the contents of a Web page to your email. You do this by clicking on the **Attach** button, selecting **Web page**, and typing the URL of the Web page.

MIME stands for *Multipart Internet Mail Extensions*. It is a protocol designed specifically to handle file attachments used on the Internet. A MIME type consists of a category (such as audio, video, image, and so on) and a specific type within that category (such as bmp for bitmap or mov for a Quicktime movie.) Here are some examples:

Bitmap Graphics File   image/bmp

Adobe Acrobat Document   application/pdf

Protocols for Downloading Email

If your computer is not a mail server—and most PCs are not—rules are needed to define how you can get the email that is being held for you on a mail server. Two protocols that are used to download messages are POP3 and IMAP4.

POP3 and IMAP4 do essentially the same thing: authenticate the identity of a user (in other words, get the username and password) and enable the user to pick up mail messages. Of the two protocols, POP3 is perhaps used more often, although IMAP4 contains more features.

When you add an Internet account to your computer, you might have already set up the information needed to connect to a POP3 or IMAP4 server. For example, if you are using Netscape Messenger you can check information about your mail server by doing the following:

1. From the Netscape Messenger window, click **Edit**, **Preferences**. The Mail and Groups Preferences window appears.

2. Click **Mail Server**. Information about your mail server appears, including the following:

> ➤ **Mail server username**   The username associated with the mailbox.

> ➤ **Outgoing mail (SMTP) server**   The name of the mail server that transfers outgoing mail to the intended recipients. This server must use an SMTP protocol. (SMTP stands for Simple Mail Transfer Protocol and is the standard method of distributing email between mail servers on the Internet.)

> ➤ **Incoming mail server**   The name of the mail server that stores your incoming mail. This server must use POP3 or IMAP4 protocols.

> ➤ **Mail server type**   Choose either POP3 or IMAP4 as the incoming mail server type.

The options available for POP3 and IMAP4 servers illustrate some of the differences between the two types of servers. POP3 doesn't allow much management of the email on the server; basically, all you can do is indicate that you do not want messages to be deleted from the server after they are retrieved.

Check This Out

The option of disabling the capability to delete messages from a server after you download them is a valuable feature for people who read email from different locations. For example, you can use this option from home when you check your work email. That way, the next time you download your mail from work the messages can be permanently stored on your work PC.

The IMAP4 options in Netscape Messenger show how you can manage email messages on the server. You can set new folders for offline download, move deleted messages into a Trash folder, and use an encrypted SSL connection (which prevents messages from being intercepted in transit) to communicate with the server. You can also set the locations of your local mail directory and your IMAP server directory.

When it comes to which protocol to use, as a mail recipient you probably have to use the type of protocol that is supported by your mail server. You can contact the mail server's system administrator to get that information.

Chatting Online

Online chat has become a popular way of keeping in touch with friends and family, or even finding new friends and family. There are literally millions of people using such services as ICQ and AOL Instant Messaging to exchange messages in real time.

ICQ

With ICQ (which stands for "I Seek You") you can chat with your friends, send messages, play games, or send files. The ICQ home page (http://www.icq.com) says that more than 71 million people have signed up for the service. Here is basically what you do to participate:

1. In your Web browser, go to http://www.icq.com.
2. Click the **Free ICQ Software** link.
3. Select the latest ICQ software for your computer.
4. Follow the instructions that appear for downloading and saving the ICQ software.
5. Run the ICQ installation by opening the install program from the folder you saved it in.
6. Follow the registration instructions (be cautious about what personal information you give out).
7. Run the ICQ Tour (http://www.icq.com/icqtour) to learn how to use the service.

After ICQ is installed and running, you can create a list of friends and you will be notified when anyone on your list is online. With one click, you can try to contact them. Methods for communicating include typed chats, message boards, voice, or data conferencing. You can also play Internet games and do file transfers.

AOL Instant Messenger

AOL Instant Messaging was restricted to people with AOL accounts in the past. Now, anyone can sign up for an Instant Messenger account and chat with their friends on AOL. To subscribe to AOL Instant Messenger, go to http://www.aol.com/aim.

If you are using Netscape Communicator, you can start AOL Instant Messenger by clicking **Communicator**, **AOL Instant Messenger Service**. Log in using your screen name and password. The first time you use the service, a wizard will help you get set up. AOL Instant Messenger Service includes:

➤ **Quick Overview**   See the basic features of the service.
➤ **Add/Find a Buddy**   Find your friends and add them to your buddy list.

185

➤ **Create your profile**   Here you can set up the "personality" associated with your account. This is where you enter personal interests and other information about yourself. (Don't enter any information you want to keep private.)

As with other online chat software, when you sign on you can see which of your friends are online and choose to chat with them if they are. You can add people to lists of Buddies, Family, Co-Workers, or other categories you create. Figure 10.7 shows the Buddy List Window:

Figure 10.7

Add Friends and Family to your AOL Instant Messenger Buddy List.

Playing Online Multi-User Games

There are amazing multi-user gaming resources available on the Internet. To participate in many multi-user online games, you don't need any additional software or hardware. You can just open your Web browser and go to one of the many gaming sites on the Internet. For others, you can try out demos (and then later buy the games you fall in love with). Here are a few places you can visit to play some online games:

➤ **Yahoo! Gaming (http://games.yahoo.com)**   To get used to the feeling of playing a game online, try out some of the simple, but fun games at Yahoo! Gaming. Choose from board games, card games, tile games, and other games to compete online. Numbers next to each game show how many people are currently playing in each area. There are also fantasy sports games for major sports that are currently in season.

➤ **Gamecenter.com (http://www.gamecenter.com)**   The Game Center is another good site for the first-time online gamer. Click **Game Hardware** for good reviews of gaming hardware (a must to be competitive with graphic-intense games). Tips, Cheats, and Strategy Guides are just a click away.

To compete online, click the **Play Games Online** link. There's a big list of the best places to play games online on the Play Games page. Find a link to the game you like and click it.

➤ **Heat.net** (`http://www.heat.net`) To play commercial strategy and action games online, sign up for a membership to Heat.net. You can participate in more than 150 games against online competitors, including Age of Empires, Civilization II, Diablo, NASCAR 2, Quake, Railroad Tycoon 2, and Total Annihilation. Demo versions are available for most games (although after you get hooked, you will probably want to purchase full versions).

A couple of examples of multi-user games that have excellent graphics and fun game playing are Quake and Starcraft; they are described in the following sections.

Playing StarCraft

StarCraft from Blizzard Entertainment (`http://www.blizzard.com/starcraft`) is a popular real-time strategy game. Your mission is to gather resources, train and expand your forces, and take them into battle. You can control different species: Terran, Protoss, and Zerg. Each species has different strengths and weaknesses.

Download a demo version of StarCraft from `http://www.download.com` and try it out. The demo contains three missions, leading up to the galactic war. After you become good at it, you can try it against other players on your LAN or on the Internet. Here is how you play StarCraft over the network:

1. Start the StarCraft program (**Start**, **Programs**, **StarCraft**, **StarCraft demo**).
2. Click **Multiplayer**.
3. Select one of the following connection types and click **OK**.
   - ➤ **Battle.net** Connect to a StarCraft server at the battle.net site.
   - ➤ **LAN** Play against others on your local area network.
   - ➤ **Modem** Play over a direct dial-up connection to a StarCraft server.
   - ➤ **Direct cable** Play over a direct cable connection between your computer and another computer.

   After you make your selection, StarCraft will try to connect to a StarCraft server.
4. If you are connecting to a Battle.net server, you will be asked to enter your name and password.

Up to eight players can compete at a time over a LAN or Internet connection. With modem and direct connections, you compete directly against another player.

To support your game play, there are strategies available for each species, battle reports, cheats, and FAQs. You can even get StarCraft wallpaper for your desktop, such as the wallpaper shown in Figure 10.8.

Figure 10.8

StarCraft lets you supply and deploy troops against network opponents.

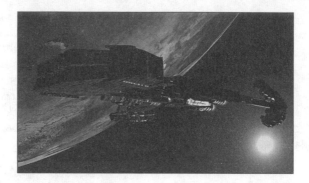

Playing Quake

Quake, from id software (`http://www.idsoftware.com`), combines 3D interactive action with mission-oriented game play. Many people consider Quake to be the premier multiplayer Internet action games available. As you encounter objects along the way, some will help you to your goal and, as you might expect, others will try to blast out of existence. You try to blast them first.

Quake resources on the Internet are plentiful. You can begin from the id software site, where you can find information on Quake, Quake II, Quake III: Arena, Quake World, and Quake Clans. Click the link to the **Quake archives** and select **Get Quake**. You can then download a shareware version of Quake to try it out. Figure 10.9 shows the PlanetQuake Web site (`http://www.quakeworld.com`).

Figure 10.9

PlanetQuake provides a focal point for Quake news, files, and community.

To play multiplayer Quake over the Internet, you will want a high-speed Internet connection. Features in the multiplayer game allow users to acknowledge each other by saluting, waving, or pointing. Some of the services that support multiplayer Quake include Mplayer (click the **Gamers** tab, and select **Quake III**) and Heat.net. To play, you need to have Quake already installed and you need to sign up for an account with the gaming service you are using.

Sharing Folders, Files, Printers, and Devices

So far in this chapter, you've learned about programs you can use to communicate and play over the Internet. However, within your local network, there are resources that you will probably want to share that wouldn't be appropriate to share over the Internet. These include things like your printers, files and folders, and various devices.

Using Shared Files and Folders

Someone on your LAN has made a folder that's on his computer available to you. You want to copy, change, or add to the files from his folder. Here's a simple procedure for accomplishing that task:

Check This Out

Windows file and print sharing is inherently insecure (it's not that difficult for a computer to access another computers printers or files by pretending to be a different computer). Therefore, you should generally only share resources among computers on your LAN and only if those computers are trusted.

Check This Out

Before you can use someone's printer, folder, or device from your LAN, the other person has to make those items available to you. Chapter 8, "Building Your Home Network," contains procedures that allow someone to offer a printer or folder (connected to a PC running Windows) so that others on the LAN (and presumably you) can use it.

1. From your Windows 95 or 98 system, open the **Network Neighborhood** icon from the desktop. (In Windows 2000, it's called the **My Network Places** icon.)

2. Select the computer icon that contains the folder you want to use and open it. (You might need to open the **Entire Network** icon first, if the computer is in a different workgroup or is grouped with different types of computers, such as NetWare servers.) A window containing the shared items appears with the computer name appearing in the title bar, as shown in Figure 10.10.

Figure 10.10

Shared folders and print-ers appear in a computer's Network Neighborhood window.

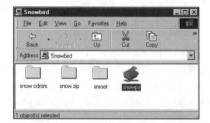

In this example, four items are shared. The first three are shared folders representing different locations on the computer named Snowbird. The first (snow cdrom) is a shared CD-ROM drive, the next (snow zip) is a shared Zip Drive, and the third (snroot) is the top, or root, folder on the hard drive. (The fourth is a printer icon, which we will get to in the next section.)

3. Notice that using folders from CD-ROM or Zip devices is no different than using a folder from a hard disk. To use any of these items you can:

   ➤ Open the folder, and then copy, add, or remove files in that folder as though it existed locally on your hard disk.

   ➤ Drag and drop the folder onto the desktop or any local folder. This action can be used to add a link to the shared folder on your desktop.

Using Shared Printers

To use a shared printer, such as the one that appeared in the Network Neighborhood window in the previous section, you can drag and drop it on to your desktop or any folder. Then you can print files by dropping them on the printer shortcut you just created.

If you want to set up a printer on your LAN so that it can be used by Windows applications such as MS Word or Corel WordPerfect, you should run the Add Printer procedure as follows:

1. Click **Start**, **Settings**, **Printers**. The Printers window appears, showing the printers that are configured for your computer.

2. Open the **Add Printer** icon. The Add Printer Wizard appears.

3. Click **Next**. A window appears asking whether you want to add a Local or Network printer.

4. Click **Network Printer** and select **Next**. A window opens asking you to provide the network path to the printer.

5. Either type the path to the printer, or click the **Browse** button to select the printer from the list of computers in your Network Neighborhood that appears. If the computer name were Snowbird and the printer name were snowps (my own notation for a PostScript printer on Snowbird), the path to the printer would appear as follows:

   \\Snowbird\snowps

   Click **Next** to continue. A window appears asking you to either keep an existing driver for the printer or add a new driver. (A print driver communicates between the computer and specific printer you are using.)

6. Select to either keep or replace the existing printer driver and click **Next**. Usually you will keep the existing driver, unless the printer comes with a CD or floppy disk that contains a more recent driver than is available with Windows. (Add the driver next, if that's what you selected. Otherwise, go to the next step.) You are asked to provide a name for the printer.

7. Type a printer name and click **Next**. You are asked if you want to print a test page.

8. Select **Yes** (to print a test page) or **No** to not print one. I recommend you print a test page to make sure the setup worked.

9. Click **Finish**. The printer you just added appears in the Printers window. More importantly, however, it appears in a list of printers that you can select from when you print a document from most applications that run on Windows.

Where To From Here?

After reading this chapter, you should have your network working the way you want it to and have tried a few networking applications. If you are still hungering for more networking knowledge, you could continue on to the next chapter to learn about procedures for linking your home and work networks. If you are interested in cool networking applications of the future, skip to Chapter 17, "Preparing for an Explosion of Network Content."

The Least You Need to Know

Right now, the least you need to know about running network applications is this:

➤ The Web browser is the most important application for using and taking advantage of the massive amounts of content available from the Internet.

➤ Netscape Communicator and Internet Explorer are the most popular Web browser suites available today. Opera is a Web browser that is gaining popularity, in part because it can run on handheld devices.

➤ Netscape and IE each come with their own email applications. Other email applications, such as Eudora, are also available.

➤ Popular email features include such things as adding attachments, using an address book, creating HTML messages, and managing mail messages.

➤ To chat online, there are applications available such as ICQ and AOL Instant Messenger.

➤ There are many online gaming sites available. Many popular strategy and action games, with sophisticated graphics, can also be played in multi-user mode on the Internet. These include such old favorites as StarCraft and Quake.

➤ Sharing files, folders, printers, and devices on your LAN can be simple. You gain access to these shared items through your Network Neighborhood window.

Chapter 11

Linking Your Home and Office Networks

> ### In This Chapter
>
> ➤ Prepare your home office to connect to work
>
> ➤ Learn the different types of telecommuting sites
>
> ➤ Understand what kinds of networking hardware and software are needed for telecommuting
>
> ➤ Get secure network connections for telecommuting

If you're just going to sit in front of a computer screen all day, why not do it in the comfort of your own home? Or, if you have to put in those extra hours of overtime, why not put on your pajamas and do the work from your own PC? Inexpensive network access and improved security measures are making that link between the home and business offices a much more common practice.

This chapter focuses on practical ways of linking your home computers to your business. For the employee, it can mean more flexibility in where and how work gets done. For an employer, it could mean keeping employees, or getting more work out of them if they don't always need to be onsite to contribute. It can also save a company on overhead costs, by allowing it to maintain less office space.

Preparing a Home Office to Connect to Work

If you just want to use your home office to occasionally read email or download a document from the office, it probably won't be that hard to set up. To use your office for full- or part-time telecommuting requires a bit more thought and planning. The following sections describe how to get at some common work services from home and how to set up your office for full-scale telecommuting.

Check This Out!

Before you start setting up your home computer to grab email or documents from your company computers, do some checking first. Find out what your company's security policy is related to remote access to its computers. If it is a large company, chances are that it has policies in place for remote access to its computing resources.

Setting Up a Proxy Server

Your employer might require you to set up a firewall in your home office. You could then use a proxy server to act as a buffer between the computers on your home LAN and the outside world. Procedures for setting up a proxy server are contained in Chapters 8, "Building Your Home Network," and 9, "Hooking Up Your Small Office Network." Firewalls are described in Chapter 14 "Securing Your Fortress."

Getting Work Email from Home

Some companies maintain mail servers outside of the company firewall. This means that, as long as you know how to locate the mail server, and have a valid account and password, you can access your business email from anywhere on the Internet.

Configuring your home mail reader to access your email from work is basically the same as configuring it to read your personal email. However, you might want to set up your home email program to view your email without deleting it from the mail server. The following procedure describes how to access your email from work using Microsoft Outlook Express.

Before you begin this procedure, contact your system administrator at work and get the Internet address (name or IP address) of your company mail server and its type (POP or IMAP). See Appendix A, "Speak Like a Geek: The Networking Bible," for definitions of POP and IMAP. You will also need your account name (often your email address, up to but not including the @ sign) and associated password.

Now you're ready to start.

1. Open Outlook Express (probably by double-clicking an icon on the desktop).

2. Click **Tools**, **Accounts** from the Outlook Express window. An Internet Accounts window appears.

3. Click the **Mail** tab. The window changes to show the mail accounts you have set up (presumably, just for your personal email account at this point). Figure 11.1 shows an example of an entry for a personal email account.

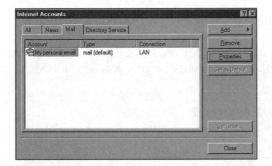

Figure 11.1

Add your business email to your home mail reader.

4. Click **Add**, **Mail**. An Internet Connection Wizard window appears.

5. Type the name that you want to appear on outgoing email from this account and click **Next**. Remember, this is your business account so don't use a name like Snugglebug, unless, of course, that is appropriate for your line of work. You are asked for your email address.

6. Type the email address you use for work and click **Next**. You are asked for information about your email server.

7. Select the correct server type (POP or IMAP as instructed by your administrator from work). Then type the name or IP address of your incoming mail server (that is, where your email is stored) and your outgoing mail server (which is used to forward the mail you send). These might be the same server. When that information is entered, click **Next**. You are asked for your account name and password.

8. Type in your mail account name and password. You can also click a check box to indicate that you want to be prompted for a password each time you collect your email. (By default, Outlook Express just uses your saved password to get your email.) Click **Next**. You are asked to select your Internet connection.

9. Select your method of reaching the email server (phone line, LAN, or manual connection). Then click **Next**. If all went well, you should see a Congratulations message telling you that you are finished.

10. Click **Finish**. At this point you should see the new email account listed in the Internet accounts window. Although the new entry is now ready to begin gathering your business email, you should make one change.

11. Double-click the new email account. A Properties window for the account appears.

12. Click the **Advanced** tab. The window changes to show information about ports and delivery methods.

13. You might want to click the **Leave a copy of messages on server** box, if you want to keep a record of the email you receive at work all in one place. By selecting this box, you can view the mail messages but still have them appear on your work email reader when you return to work. Otherwise, the messages you download will be deleted from the server.

14. Click **Apply** and you are done.

The only other suggestion for managing work email from home is that you be sure to send the email through your business account. After you have composed an email message, instead of just clicking the **Send** button, click **File**, **Send Message Using**, and then click the entry for the business email account you just added.

Getting Work Files from Home

Some companies will let you place documents or software programs on an FTP server so you can access them from wherever you happen to be. If these files are in any way proprietary, you will probably need a login account and password to access them (that is other than the public "anonymous" account).

Although you can access an FTP server (a computer that allows you to download and possibly upload files) from your Web browser, it's fairly awkward to enter an account name and password. For that reason, you should use a real FTP program to access your work files on an FTP server. There is a cute FTP program called, oddly enough, CuteFTP that will do the job nicely. Although there are other FTP programs that will also work, CuteFTP has a firewall option that might be useful to you (described later).

CuteFTP is a program that you can download from many locations on the Web. I found a copy by searching from Download.com (`http://www.download.com`). When you are trying the program, you have 30 days to evaluate it and during that time you have to look at ads. If you like it, send its creator GlobalScape (`http://www.globalscape.com`) $29.95 and the ads go away. Also, CuteFTP monitors your use of the display ads. So if such things make you nervous you might want to buy CuteFTP or skip it altogether. There are also several freeware FTP programs available on the Internet.

Configuring CuteFTP

Another useful feature of CuteFTP, as well as other FTP programs, is that you can set up information needed to connect directly to FTP sites that you often access. That could include the login and password you need for your FTP server at work. In that way, you are just a few clicks away from connecting.

Here is a procedure for setting up CuteFTP to access the FTP server at work:

1. The first time you start CuteFTP, the Connection Wizard appears. Select your ISP from the list or choose **Other**. You are asked to identify the FTP site you want to connect to.

2. Type a name representing the site you want to connect to and click **Other**. You could type something like "My FTP server at work." You are prompted for the location of your FTP site.

3. Type the URL for the ftp site. It will look something like: `ftp://ftp.handsonhistory.com`. Of course, the FTP site will include the domain name of your company. You are asked to choose a default local directory.

4. Type the location of a directory on your local computer. This should identify the directory where you would want to put the files that you download from the FTP site. For example, you could enter: `C:\chris\work` as the directory name. Click **Next** and you are done. If you like, click boxes to connect to this site automatically each time you open CuteFTP or to add CuteFTP to right-click shell integration.

5. Click **Finish**. The CuteFTP window should appear as shown in Figure 11.2.

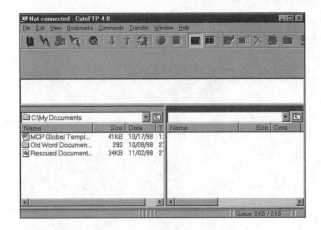

Figure 11.2

Use an FTP program, such as CuteFTP, to get files from an FTP server at work.

Connecting to the FTP Site at Work

To connect to the FTP site you just set up, follow this procedure.

1. Click **File**, **Site Manager**. You will see a list of anonymous FTP sites that you can connect to, along with the one you just added.

2. Double-click the name of your FTP site to connect to that site.

If the connection goes through, you should see your local folder in the left column and the open folder from the FTP site in the right column. In the window pane above the column, status messages appear. The window pane below shows the progress of downloads.

Move up and down the directory structure on either side by double-clicking folders (to go down) or the folder with the up arrow (to go up). When both folders are the ones you want, double-click a file to send it from one folder to the other. The progress of the file transfer appears in a pane below the current window. When you are done, click the **Disconnect** button.

After you are done working with a file, you can reconnect and send the file back to the FTP site. This presumes that you have write permission to the site and that you have probably renamed the file appropriately (if you don't want to overwrite the original).

Getting FTP Through Your Firewall

If you have set up a firewall at home to protect your home network, you might need to access a proxy server to make your FTP connections. CuteFTP includes features that let you connect to an FTP site on the Internet (or otherwise on the other side of the firewall from your LAN). FTP requests from your computer will appear to come from the proxy server.

Follow this procedure to configure CuteFTP to use a proxy server:

1. Open CuteFTP (possibly from an icon on your desktop).
2. Click **Edit**, **Settings**. The Settings window appears.
3. Click the plus sign (+) next to **Connection**, and then select **Firewall**. The Firewall settings appear in the window, as shown in Figure 11.3.

Figure 11.3

Use CuteFTP through a firewall by adding proxy settings.

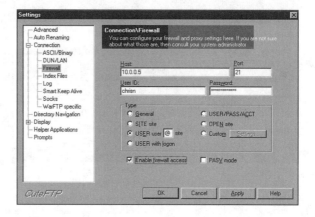

4. Add the following information to identify your proxy server:

   Host   The IP address of the computer on your LAN that is acting as the proxy server.

   Port number   The port number on which the proxy server is listening for FTP services. Port number 21 is the standard FTP port number. Use 21, unless you know the server is using a different port number.

   User ID   The name of a user account on the proxy server that is granted permission to use that server for FTP transfers.

   Password   The password associated with the User ID.

   Type   Select **USER user@site** to have CuteFTP connect to the proxy server using the USER ID and password you just entered.

> **Enable firewall access**   Click this check box to enable CuteFTP to use the proxy service when you try to connect to an FTP site.

5. Click **OK**.

If you are unable to access the proxy server the next time you use CuteFTP, you might need to select the Custom Settings for configuring your connection to the proxy server. You might need to research the proxy server to see what type of user/password or other authentication it is looking for.

Getting Secure Connections

To ensure that the connection to your company network from your home is secure, there are a few different methods you and your company can use. Some of your choices include the following:

➤ **Virtual private network (VPN)**   A VPN is a way for a network administrator to create a private network that passes over public network media (such as the Internet). With a VPN, a telecommuting employee can rely on a secure connection that results in the same level of connectivity he gets in the main office.

➤ **Remote node**   By adding remote node software, an employee can connect to the company's network from home in a way that makes the telecommuter's computer appear to be on the company's local network.

➤ **Remote control**   With remote control software, a telecommuter can connect to her own PC back at the office (usually via a modem that's attached to the office PC). With the remote connection established, the user has access to everything that is available when the user is sitting in front of the computer at work.

Virtual Private Networks

Although virtual private networks can help address the needs of someone connecting to a company from home, VPNs can go far beyond that by creating a cost-effective, flexible way to expand access to a company's network. Every day company networks are providing access to more mobile users, satellite offices, and client locations. VPNs are a way of managing that growth.

VPNs rely on public computer networks, particularly the Internet, to connect remote users to the company's network. Although using the public network (which provides an inexpensive and accessible method of communication), the connection between the user and the company network looks like a dedicated link. The drawback to this arrangement is that the encryption techniques that make the communication secure can slow the performance of your network connection. You are also at the mercy of the traffic on your Internet connection.

A method called *tunneling* is used to achieve connectivity between VPN nodes (such as the user's PC and the entry to the company network). With tunneling, the *tunnel initiator* uses the public network to set up a connection with a *tunnel terminator*. Following is an example of how this might work:

1. An end user with a laptop (tunnel initiator) dials up a local *Internet service provider (ISP)* and establishes a connection to the Internet using a dial-up protocol that is VPN-enabled.

2. Across the Internet, the dial-up software establishes a connection to a tunnel terminator device on the company's enterprise network.

3. Requests for all services are encapsulated and directed to the tunnel terminator, which is often located at the company's firewall. Even requests for Internet resources are directed to the tunnel terminator, and then directed back to the Internet. In other words, nothing that a user of a VPN-enabled computer requests from the Internet or the company's network is interpreted until it reaches the tunnel terminator.

Tunneling enables users located anywhere to act as members of a company's LAN (hence the term *virtual LAN*). To protect the security of the connection between the user and the virtual LAN, a variety of encryption schemes can be used so that someone snooping on the public network can't read the transmissions.

Check This Out

Dial-up VPN was not fully supported in the original release of Windows 95. To check if your computer has VPN support, open the **Networking** icon from the Control Panel. Then click **Add, Adapters**, and **Microsoft** to see if the Microsoft Virtual Private Networking Adapter is listed.

If you do not see VPN support in your Network window, you probably need to install the Dial-Up Networking 1.3 upgrade. Download the file Msdun13.exe from the Microsoft Web site (http://www. microsoft.com) and install it.

The features for connecting to a VPN from a Windows 95/98/2000/NT computer are available for each of those operating systems.

Remote Node (Connect to Remote LAN)

Like VPNs, *remote node* connections enable a remote user to connect to the company's network as though the user's computer were physically connected to that network. Typically, with remote node connections, the user dials a modem that is directly connected to the company LAN.

LANLynk from Lynk (http://www.soholynk.com) is an example of third-party software that makes a remote PC into a workstation on the network. By allowing the PC to transmit standard LAN data, several remote computers can connect to a single LAN-connected host.

Remote Control (Connect Directly to PC)

Instead of remotely connecting to a company network, remote control features enable you to directly dial a modem connected to a PC. After you are connected, you can operate that PC remotely as though you were there locally.

Remote control software can enable you to

➤ Transfer files between the remote and local PCs.

➤ Synchronize files between the remote and local PCs.

➤ Manage remote peripherals (printers, servers, and so on).

➤ Troubleshoot problems on the remote computer.

The Microsoft Remote Access Service (RAS) software is included in Windows 95/98/NT/2000 operating systems. Configuring RAS, however, is somewhat difficult, and there are no special features available for remote control (such as file synchronization).

There are several third-party software products available for providing remote control of a PC, including

➤ LapLink 2000 and LapLink Host from LapLink.com Inc. (http://www.laplink.com)

➤ pcAnywhere from Symantec Corporation (http://www.symantec.com/pcanywhere)

➤ ReachOut Enterprise from Stac Inc. (http://www.stac.com)

➤ Carbon Copy from Compaq (http://www.compaq.com/carboncopy)

Choosing Telecommuting

Some estimate that nearly 80% of all telecommuting is done from the home. Home telecommuting can offer cost and efficiency benefits to employers and time and lifestyle benefits to employees. Telecommuting can be done full-time, part-time, or on an after-hours basis.

Telecommuting equipment for the home can be as simple as a computer with a modem. In such cases, the home office might just be used for situations that require simple communications (such as email and Web browsing) and basic applications (such as word processing and spreadsheets).

For full-time telecommuting from the home, more equipment and sophisticated integration with the company computing resources might be necessary. So, from a PC, modem, and telephone line, either the employee or the company might want to choose some of the following enhancements:

➤ **Higher-speed connections** An old 28.8Kbps modem might perform poorly when using more demanding applications, such as videoconferencing. Upgrading to a 56Kbps modem or an ISDN connection can make a big difference. For secure dial-up connections, ISDN has long been the service of choice.

201

However, with inexpensive DSL and cable modem connections becoming more readily available, those services are being used more often.

➤ **Special communications software**   Software packages are available to simplify communication with the company computing resources. By setting up a virtual private network, the home telecommuter can be assured of a secure connection to the company's computers while taking advantage of low-cost DSL or cable connections.

➤ **More equipment**   Everything an employee takes for granted at the office—FAX machines, copiers, printers, scanners—can be sorely missed by the telecommuter. With a network connection to the main office, some equipment can be shared (and possibly picked up the next day at work).

➤ **Special support software**   When something goes wrong with your computer, you probably won't have a friendly neighborhood technician down the hall to help you. Luckily, you can add software to your computer to allow others to dial in and debug your problems. The computer can also be used to access an online company help desk, if one is available.

➤ **Critical company applications**   If you need to run programs that only reside on company computers or that access company database records, some special setup might be required. You may need to install company software on your home computer. However, there are ways an administrator can allow you to launch an application that runs at the main office but displays on a remote computer.

As a part-time telecommuter, you can often rely on equipment from the home office or, on special occasions, commercial copy centers to get things done. If you plan to use your home office for those tasks that require limited resources but concentrated work (such as writing a report or sending emails), it can be implemented with minimal extra effort.

Telecommuting Organizations

The following are some organizations that have an interest in supporting telecommuting:

➤ **AT&T**   AT&T claims to have 36,000 U.S.-based managers that are telecommuting at least part time. The company supports a telework site that discusses telecommuting issues: `http://www.att.com/ehs/telecom.html`.

➤ **International Telework Association**   A non-profit organization that promotes the benefits of teleworking. Its Web site is located at `http://www.telecommute.org`.

➤ **European Community Telework/Telematics Forum**   Resource for telecommuting projects and studies. You can visit its Web page at `http://www.telework-forum.org`.

Besides these organizations, there are many networking equipment vendors that offer products and information relating to telecommuting. These companies include 3Com, Cisco Systems, MCI/WorldCom, and Lucent Technologies.

Locations for Telecommuting

By far, the most common location for telecommuting is the employee's home. A variety of economic and environmental issues, however, have made telecommuting from different types of locations a viable solution. The following sections describe the different types of telecommuting locations that have arisen in recent years.

Satellite Office

When downtown offices become crowded and adding space is prohibitively expensive, some companies choose to set up satellite offices. A satellite office typically has the following attributes:

➤ Located away from the company's more expensive main site, typically in a suburban location near where employees live.

➤ Fully equipped office that is owned and operated by the company.

➤ Used by employees as a place to work one or more days a week, as an alternative to driving into the main office.

A reduction in wear and tear on the employees is one of the major advantages of the satellite office. From a quality-of-life standpoint, satellite offices also serve to take some commuters off the roads, reducing highway congestion and pollution.

Satellite offices can also save on more expensive office space at the company's main site. Shared office space is more of an option when employees are scheduled to be off-site for several days a week.

From a networking standpoint, a part- or full-time administrator can be placed on-site to set up equipment and keep it running. This arrangement offers the company the greatest level of control over resources in a telecommuting environment.

Hoteling

For companies with many employees who are mobile, *hoteling* is a means of drastically reducing the office space needed. With hoteling, employees have no full-time office location. Instead, when they know they are going to be at their company's office, they call ahead and reserve a work space (just like reserving a room at a hotel).

Companies (such as accounting and sales firms) who frequently send their employees to customer locations are good candidates for hoteling. Typically, an office coordinator makes sure that when employees are going to be in the office they have the office space, telephones, computers, and supplies they need.

To support hoteling, employees are typically set up with a *virtual mobile office*, or *VMO* (described later in this chapter). From a computing standpoint, the VMO enables users to have access to any software and data that they have at the company office.

Telework Center

A *telework center* is similar to a satellite office except the telework center is not maintained by the employee's company. Telework centers tend to be private companies that rent out office space to anyone who needs it.

In addition to space, the telework center allows you to rent whatever office equipment you need. Space and equipment are typically rented per day. Employees who use these centers typically choose one that is close to their homes. Like other telecommuting options, telework centers save commuting time and effort.

Suburban areas outside of Washington, D.C. and parts of California—where commuting is difficult—are popular areas for telework centers. Besides offering such facilities as reception areas, conference rooms, private offices, board rooms, and presentation rooms, telework centers often offer the following computing facilities:

➤ Personal Computers

➤ High-speed modem connections

➤ Popular publishing and presentation application software

➤ Personal email and voicemail

➤ Postal mailroom services

➤ Printing, faxing, and copying equipment

Although telework centers don't enable a company to tailor employees' computing needs exactly to the job, they do offer a low-maintenance way for employees to occasionally save on commuting.

Anywhere (The Virtual Mobile Office)

Very often telecommuting is done not to save on commuting time, but rather to enable an employee to connect to company computer resources from wherever that employee might be. The virtual mobile office is a way of setting up an employee's computer so that by dialing into the company, the employee can have access to all the resources available at the office.

Following are some of the things that a virtual mobile office might enable an employee to do:

➤ Download email or voice mail messages.

➤ Dial in to the company LAN, enabling the employee to access all networking resources that she has access to at the office.

➤ Dial in to her PC, enabling the user to have total control over the PC.

➤ Run important company applications to, for example, access sales reports, billing data, or employee records.

Some features needed by the virtual mobile office, such as MS Windows 2000, are already built into PC operating systems and require only some configuration to work. See the next section, "Communications Software for Telecommuting," for information about Windows features that provide mobile computing services.

Communications Software for Telecommuting

A speedy connection to your company network won't do you much good if you don't have the applications you need to take advantage of it. Many of the features needed to use your home computer or portable PC for telecommuting are already built in. Still others are quite easy to add.

Telecommuting Features in Windows

Using features that are already in Windows 95/98/NT/2000, you can perform many of the most basic telecommuting functions. Following are some of the features built into your PC's operating system that are useful for telecommuters:

➤ **Dial-up networking**   Enables you to specify everything you need to connect to a remote modem using SLIP or PPP protocols over telephone lines. Other protocols, such as Novell's IPX/SPX, are also supported. Windows 2000 has added an extensive array of secure dial-up features.

➤ **Remote access service (RAS)**   Enables you to set up your computer to allow remote computers to dial in. This is a good feature for allowing remote diagnostics of your computer if you are having a problem while away from your company technicians.

➤ **Direct cable connection**   With this feature, you can directly plug your computer into another computer, using a cable between the two computers' parallel or serial ports. No network is needed to exchange files between two computers.

➤ **Deferred printing**   This allows your portable computer to print, even when you are not connected to a printer or network. With this feature, print jobs are saved on the hard disk until a printer connection is available.

➤ **Briefcase**   Using this feature, you can copy files from your computer at work to a laptop, update the files, and later resynchronize the files with those on your computer at work.

➤ **Docking detection**   Windows can tell whether your portable computer is currently connected to a docking station. With this feature, you can use different configurations for when the computer is docked.

Applications for Telecommuting

To communicate with people back at the main office, clients, or anyone else reachable by the network, you probably need a combination of common Internet tools and applications that are specific to your job. You can get many of the Internet tools you need by installing Netscape Communicator or Internet Explorer.

Regardless of which tools you choose, following are the common features you need to communicate with others over the Internet or other TCP/IP-based network:

➤ **Email**   Used to send messages with attached documents or graphics to another person on the network.

➤ **Web browser**   Used to display Web pages and a variety of other types of information on the Internet.

➤ **File transfer**   Used to copy files from one computer (typically an FTP server) to another (typically your computer).

➤ **News reader**   Enables you to participate in online newsgroups by displaying, sending, and managing sets of messages that pertain to a particular topic of discussion.

➤ **Video conferencing**   Enables you to participate in video conferences over the Internet.

➤ **Data conferencing**   Enables the users participating in a conference call to view the same running application from their own computers. If allowed by the person running the program, remote users might be capable of manipulating the program as well as viewing it.

➤ **Whiteboard**   Enables all the users in a conference to draw in a shared window that all participants can see.

Although these are some of the applications that might be useful to telecommuters, each telecommuter needs to speak to the company's system administrator to determine what other applications employees will need to get their jobs done.

Supporting Telecommuting

All the safety and support issues that a network administrator can normally resolve at the company office become more difficult with employees who are telecommuting. A network administrator will probably help put together a guide to help employees protect their computing resources when they work off site.

Some kind of protection checklist can help keep data from being lost and destroyed. The following items should be part of that checklist:

➤ Surge protectors for computing equipment and possible UPS equipment (if it is critical that the computers stay up during power outages)

➤ Virus protection software along with a plan for how often computers should be scanned

➤ Incoming dial-up setup (such as RAS) to allow a company administrator to troubleshoot problems with your computer

➤ Time tracking software for employees who need to punch a time clock

➤ Data backup schemes

➤ Online help (for example, access to the company help desk or connections to vendors that support the tools the employee is using) to free up some of the system administrator's time

Where To From Here?

This chapter has helped you understand how to communicate between your home network and the network at work. It also goes on to cover other types of telecommuting issues, such as equipment and support needs.

With preceding chapters covering how networks work and how you set them up and use them, you are ready to learn how to administer and protect them. Chapter 12, "Your Fearless Leader: The System Administrator," describes system administration duties, while later chapters cover other administrative tasks such as backups (Chapter 13, "Devising a Backup Plan"), Security (Chapter 14, "Securing Your Fortress"), and troubleshooting (Chapter 15, "Troubleshooting from the Trenches").

The Least You Need to Know

Right now, the least you need to know about reaching your business network from home and on the road is this:

➤ You can access your work email from home by identifying company mail servers from you home email programs.

➤ You can transfer files from work to home using FTP programs.

➤ Different network approaches can be taken to create secure connections between home and work, including Virtual Private Networks (VPN), remote node connections, or remote control connections.

➤ You can determine what applications software you need for telecommuting.

➤ You should understand support issues related to having a telecommuting site.

Part 4

Defending Your Network Turf

Even the best-planned networks often go astray. And when they do, the person wearing the big "S" isn't superman—it's the system administrator. Although troubleshooting problems is an important job, even more important are the maintenance and security steps taken to prevent problems.

Chapters in this part describe the system administrator's role (Chapter 12, "Your Fearless Leader: The System Administrator"). They also tell you about administrative duties, such as backing up data (Chapter 13, "Devising a Backup Plan"), preventing break-ins (Chapter 14, "Securing Your Fortress"), and troubleshooting (Chapter 15, "Troubleshooting from the Trenches").

HEAD COMPUTER IN CHARGE

Your Fearless Leader: The System Administrator

In This Chapter

➤ Find out about the duties of a system administrator

➤ Familiarize yourself with basic tasks for administering a Windows 2000 system

➤ Learn basic tasks for administering a Linux system

When you have more than a few computers on your network, it makes sense to centralize file, print, and other services on server computers. For the same reasons, it usually makes sense to focus the management of computers and network services on one person—the *system administrator*.

By having a central system administrator, it becomes much easier to provide consistent levels of security and standard procedures for accessing information and computer hardware.

What's in a Name?

Different network operating systems each have a special name for its system administrator. In Microsoft Windows 2000 and Windows NT, for example, that person is called *administrator*; in UNIX, it's *root*; and in NetWare, it's *supervisor*. The system administrator is represented on the system by a special user account of the same name. Whoever has the password to this account has complete control of the local machine—and perhaps of the entire network.

To perform the tasks described in this chapter, you must have access to this special, privileged account. Therefore:

➤ If you're using Microsoft Windows 2000 or NT, log in as administrator and enter the administrator's password.

➤ If you're using UNIX or Linux, log in as root and enter the root password.

General System Administration Checklist

As a system administrator for a group of networked computers, your main duties are to make sure that

➤ The users on the network have the resources they need to get their jobs done.

➤ The resources are protected from abuse.

Assuming you have already connected your network (as described in Chapters 8, "Hooking Up Your Small Office Network," and 9, "Building Your Home Network"), now you must make sure each user has everything he or she needs from your network. Although all organizations and users are different, most new users require at least the following support from the system administrator:

Check This Out

While logged in as administrator or root, take care not to roam around needlessly. Moreover, carefully consider each step you take and each command you issue. Why? While you're logged in as the supreme being you can accidentally or inadvertently cause irreparable damage to your system.

➤ **Creation of a User Account**   Whether working from a PC, thin client (a computer with reduced hardware), or dumb terminal, the user needs to have a user account. The user account and associated password protect the user's work from unauthorized access by others.

➤ **Installation of Applications**   The user needs access to the application programs necessary to get his job done. As an administrator, you can install applications individually on the user's PC or provide access to an application server.

➤ **Access to the Server**   Depending on the types of servers you have set up, you might need to allow new users access to the file server, print server, proxy server, or other type of server available on your network.

Besides the basic tasks for getting a user up and going on your network, there are ongoing tasks for the system administrator. For reasons of security and efficiency, a system administrator usually does the following tasks:

➤ **Backing up and Restoring Files**   Because the information on a company's computers is a valuable company asset, a system administrator usually does backups for all company computers. With networks connecting your computer systems, network backups can be an easy and efficient way of backing up data from individual users' workstations and storing it on centrally located removable media (that is, removable disks or tape). Techniques for backing up and, if necessary, restoring data are contained in Chapter 13, "Devising a Backup Plan."

➤ **Monitoring System Use**   Make sure computers aren't running out of disk space, processing power, or network bandwidth. Tools are available for monitoring these and other resources. Some of those tools are touched on in this chapter, while others are covered in Chapter 15, "Troubleshooting from the Trenches."

➤ **Looking for Trouble**   Along with the basic task of providing enough computing and networking resources to your users, you also need to make sure that nobody is breaking into your computer network or misusing its resources. Chapter 14, "Securing Your Fortress," discusses ways of securing your network, and Chapter 15 describes some techniques for troubleshooting.

Just to give you a feel for system administration, the rest of this chapter is devoted to teaching you some system administration basics for Microsoft Windows 2000 and Linux operating systems. (Many of the techniques covered here apply to other Windows and UNIX operating systems as well.)

Workstation System Administration for Windows

Although Microsoft Windows operating systems were not originally built for networking, many networking features have been added for new versions of Windows. For example, Windows NT included many network and server features. Some Windows NT features have been added to the latest Windows operating system that is intended for desktop use: Windows 2000 Professional.

Check This Out

If your workstations are running happily on Windows 95 or 98 in a peer-to-peer network, you might not want to upgrade to Windows 2000 Professional unless you need a server that runs Windows. The first versions of Windows 2000 failed to recognize many devices from Windows 95 or 98. Also, Windows 2000 doesn't run well on many older, less powerful computers. Windows 95 and 98 will still let you run diagnostic tools and do other basic network security functions.

If you have already connected your Windows computers to your network, as described in Chapters 8 and 9, there are still many other tasks that you might want to do on an ongoing basis. Several network administration tasks are described in the next few sections. A quick reference to other network administration tasks is contained in Table 12.1.

213

Table 12.1 Networking Administration Tasks in Windows 2000

Tasks	Getting There
Add new networking hardware	Physically connect the network adapter, modem, or other hardware, and then go to **Start**, **Settings**, **Control Panel**, **Add/Remove Hardware**. Have Windows detect and configure the hardware. If requested, you might need to provide a driver from CD or floppy disk.
Add networking applications	Either install directly from the application's CD (or other medium) or go to **Start**, **Settings**, **Control Panel**, **Add/Remove Programs**. Then click **Add New Programs** and select the medium (CD or Floppy).
View/change security policy	To see how security policies are set on your system, click **Start**, **Settings**, **Control Panel**, **Administrative Tools**, **Local Security Policy**. Next, open any of the following: **Account Policies** To view password and account aging policies. **Local Policies** To view auditing, user rights, and security options policies. **Public Key Policies** To view information about security certificates. **IP Security Policies** To view policies for encrypting data as it passes between computers on IP networks.
Configure network connections	Click **Start**, **Settings**, **Control Panel**, **Network and Dial-up Connections**. Double-click **Make New Connection** or select a connection that already exists to change its properties.
Configure network services	Click **Start**, **Settings**, **Control Panel**, **Services**. A list of network and other services appear on the right side of the window. Right-click a service, and then select **Properties** to view or change information on the service.
Monitoring network activity	Click **Start**, **Settings**, **Network and Dial-up Connections**. Then double-click the network interface you want to monitor. The window that appears shows you the status of the connection, the speed, and the number of packets sent back and forth. Click **Properties** to view and change how the connection is configured.

Table 12.1   Continued

Tasks	Getting There
Select Internet connections	Click **Start**, **Settings**, **Control Panel**, **Internet Options**. Then select the **Connections** tab. This tab lets you configure the Internet connection to use for Web browsing.

Many administrative tasks in Windows 2000 have been gathered together within the Computer Management window. To open the Computer Management window, click **Start**, **Settings**, **Control Panel**, **Administrative Tools**, **Computer Management**. The Figure 12.1 is an example of the Computer Management window in Windows 2000.

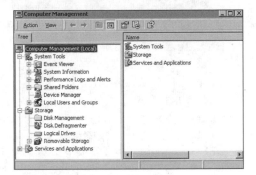

Figure 12.1

Management tasks related to networking, and other features, are available from the Computer Management window.

From the Computer Management window, you can perform useful networking tasks including managing users, managing groups, and setting up a user environment profile (discussed later in this chapter).

Give Me Your Name and Password (User Accounts)

Adding user accounts and passwords is the foundation for any secure network. User accounts provide boundaries between your network's users and provide a barrier against outsiders who are trying to break in.

You can begin adding a user account in Windows 2000 from the Computer Management window. From that window, do the following:

Check This Out

For information on choosing and testing good passwords, refer to Chapter 14.

215

1. Click the **Local Users and Groups** folder.

2. Click the **Users** folder.

3. Click **Action**, **New User**. The New User window appears, as shown in Figure 12.2.

Figure 12.2

Add user and password information to the New User window.

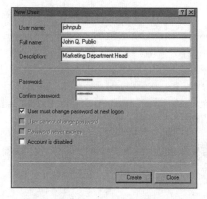

4. Add the information requested to the New User window:

   ➤ **Username**   This field must be filled in. For the sake of convenience, try to choose usernames that reflect either the user's real name or his job function. For example, suppose the user was Bill Wagner, an account executive. You might give him a username of bwagner or accountexec. This way, when you receive email from Mr. Wagner, you can make a split-second educated guess as to who he is.

   ➤ **Full Name**   Filling out this field is optional; it is used for identification purposes. Often, a username is unique but not very descriptive. By providing the user's full name, you ensure that you—or any manager—can identify the specified user. This is especially useful when you are trying to discern between two users with similar usernames.

   ➤ **Description**   Filling out this field is also optional; it is reserved for any comments you might have.

   ➤ **Password**   This field is where you enter the user's password. Typically, you provide only a temporary password and the user sets his or her own later. The user's password can be up to 14 characters long.

   ➤ **Confirm Password**   You must re-enter the password in this field to verify that it was entered correctly. This is to ensure that you didn't mistype the password.

   ➤ **User Must Change Password at Next Logon**   This is a security feature. As administrator, you're responsible for setting each account's initial password. However, it's not necessary—and in fact, it's quite risky—for you to know every user's password. Force users to change their password on their first login; this way, only they know their own password.

➤ **User Cannot Change Password**   This is a seldom-enabled option that prohibits a user from changing his or her own password. Is there ever a reason to use this option? Maybe, and here are two examples: You might someday create an account that's accessible to more than one user, sometimes called a *shared account*. If so, you want to ensure that users cannot change the password. By enabling this option, you prevent renegade users from locking out legitimate folks. Another example is a user account that is used by an application that would cause the application to fail if the password were changed.

➤ **Password Never Expires**   Some accounts sponsor services or other shared resources that are permanently available to all users. On these accounts, you probably don't want the password to expire, so check this option.

➤ **Account Disabled**   This option momentarily freezes the account. You might have several reasons for enabling this option; for example, you might be creating an account for a new employee that hasn't yet transferred over, or perhaps you need to clear his access with other co-workers first.

5. Click **Create** to create the new user account. The new user appears on the list of users.

The user account forms the foundation for security on your network. After that, you can provide the user with access to different features on the computer and network, while keeping out people you don't want to use those features. Features include

➤ **User group accounts**   By adding several users to a group, you have a way of assigning permission to use a feature to that entire group. In one action, everyone can have permission (or be denied permission). This saves you from adding or deleting permissions to each user individually.

➤ **User profile**   Each user can have a user profile that defines the user's desktop environment (that is, how icons, menus, colors, and other items on the user's screen appear) and home directory (that is, the location where a user stores his files). By sharing a profile over a network, the user's profile can be available when logging in to different computers on the network.

➤ **User rights**   Rights to access files and folders in Windows 2000 can be assigned to individual users or groups. Each of these components can even be shared over the network.

Everybody into the Boat (Group Accounts)

Windows 2000 supports *user groups*, entities composed of users with similar permissions and rights. The group system streamlines your job as a system administrator in several ways. For example, Windows 2000 enables you to apply permission changes

217

to a group and have all users within that group inherit the changes. This obviates the need to set these options for individual users.

Perhaps more importantly, however, the group system enables you to build network security and trust relationships that mirror your company's organizational structure. For example, everyone in the accounting department will naturally have access to accounting files, whereas most folks in other departments won't. Therefore, it makes sense to create an accounting group that only accounting personnel can access. This keeps accounting folks grouped together—and keeps everyone else out.

The Groups Membership window provides a very easy-to-use group management interface. You can add users to pre-existing groups or create new groups. Here is how to create a new group and add users to it.

To create a new group, do the following from the Computer Management window:

1. Select **Local Users and Groups**, and then **Groups**.

   You will see your existing groups on the right side of the window, as shown in Figure 12.3.

Figure 12.3

Manage the user's group membership from the Computer Management window.

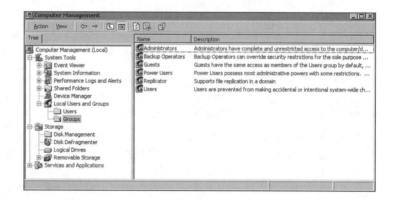

2. Click **Action**, **New Group**. A window appears to let you enter information about the new group.

3. Fill in the group name, description, and members of the group. To add members, click **Add** and select from the list of groups and users that appears.

4. Click **Create** to create the new group.

Let Me See Your Profile (User Environments)

After you assign a username, password, identifying information, and groups, you must edit that user's profile environment. The profile environment describes the user's profile location, home directory, and so on.

Check This Out

There are two built-in groups that you probably don't want to assign users to: Administrators and Backup Operators. Members from these groups have substantial authority and can perform sensitive tasks. When you assign a user to any of these groups, you're granting her a very high security clearance. Think twice before doing it. If a person needs extra authority to run certain applications, consider adding that person to the Power Users group.

With your network in place, you can have a user's profile located on any computer on the network. As a result, a computer can be configured to start up a user profile from another computer. So, you could log in on Jim's machine and have the profile from your computer appear in another office.

From the Computer Management window, click **Users and Groups**, and then **Users**. Double-click the user whose profile you want to set. From the Properties window that appears, click the **Profile** tab. From this tab you can add the following information:

Check This Out

A *profile* consists of customized settings, such as the desktop's appearance or network connections. Profiles can be used to restrict users' access. For example, you can restrict users from changing the appearance of the desktop or their monitor type.

➤ **Profile Path**   This tells Windows 2000 where to find the profile information. You express this path in three parts—the server name, the profile folder, and the user's name: `\\MyServer\profiles\bill`.

➤ **Login Script Name**   Use this field to name the login script file. Note that not every user will have a login script, and that login scripts are not required. However, if you do assign users a login script, you must specify it here.

➤ **Home Directory**   Specify the user's home directory here. If you've ever used UNIX you're probably familiar with this concept. On network operating systems, users can have their own directory where they can store files and run commands; this prevents users from accidentally mixing up their files. When the user saves files, the user can choose to have files saved to this directory.

Typically, you name the directory after the user's username or something similar. Moreover, it makes sense to place all user directories under a shared

219

hierarchy. For example, you can create a directory tree called /myusers and assign all accounts beneath this root, such as /myusers/chris and /myusers/bill.

➤ **Connect To**   If you wanted to indicate the location of the home directory by drive letter instead of server name, you could do that by selecting the letter and location in these two boxes.

It's Nice to Share (User Rights)

You can assign rights to files and folders so they can be shared with others on your computer or over the network. Here is an example of how to share a folder:

1. Right-click a folder that you want to share (for example, your My Documents folder).

2. Click **Properties**. A Properties window appears for the folder.

3. Click the **Sharing** tab. The Sharing tab appears as shown in the following Figure 12.4.

Figure 12.4

Set sharing access to any file or folder from the Sharing tab.

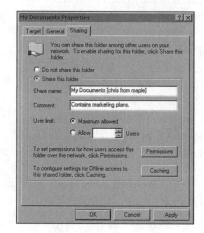

4. To share the folder, click the **Share this Folder** radio button.

5. Type in a name for the shared folder and a comment (optional).

6. Click **Maximum Allowed** or **Allow XXX Users** (replacing *XXX* with the number of users allowed to simultaneously access the folder).

7. Click the **Permissions** button. A Permissions window appears, allowing you to add users and/or groups to have permission to use your folder. You can also select whether users have full control, change access, or only read access to the contents of the folder. (Click **OK** when you are done setting permissions.)

8. Click the **Caching** button. The window that appears allows you to specify files and folders that can be accessed while working offline (that is, when you are not connected to the network).

9. Click **OK**.

When users on other computers open the My Network Places or Network Neighborhood window, and then open an icon associated with your computer, they will see the shared folder as available. They will be able to view and change the contents of that folder based on the permissions you just set.

Server System Administration

If you are looking for a career in managing networks, or you want to put together your own powerful network, I strongly recommend learning about the mystical UNIX operating system. UNIX always has been, and continues to be, the dominant operating system for network servers.

Perhaps the easiest way to get started with UNIX is to obtain a copy of the free UNIX operating system clone: Linux. This chapter gives you a quick tour of some of the tools and procedures you can use for Linux system administration.

Check This Out

A final note if you are administering a Windows NT or Windows 2000 system. Be sure to rename the administrator account. You can copy it as well and give it a name other than administrator. If you leave the account name as administrator, it is too easy for hackers to break into your system.

Check This Out

Linux is a free operating system. However, there are companies that put together distributions of Linux and resell them (along with technical support). To try out the procedures in this section, I recommend either Red Hat Linux or Caldera OpenLinux. The software comes in boxed sets from those companies, as well as in books on the subject. You can also download those distributions from `ftp.redhat.com` and `ftp.calderasystems.com`.

Tools of the Trade

Many of the tools that you need to administer any UNIX or Linux system are basically the same. Before you get started administering your Linux system, I recommend that you arm yourself in the following ways:

➤ **root user** You need to log in as the root user to do most Linux system administration. Of course, this requires that you know the root password. Be very careful what you do while you are logged in as root. Removing or even just misconfiguring system files can wreck your Linux system. (By the way, the root user is sometimes referred to as the super-user.)

➤ **Try out graphical administration** Tools for graphically setting up networks, users, and other features are available with most Linux distributions. For Red Hat Linux, try out linuxconf. For Caldera OpenLinux, try Webmin or COAS.

➤ **Learn a shell** The shell is a command-line environment for typing commands and moving around the file system. Although there are graphical interfaces for administering Linux, the command line can sometimes be the quicker, or possibly the only, way to make a necessary change. Most Linux distributions use the bash shell because it was developed by the free software community.

If you log in to Linux and you see a dollar sign ($) or a pound sign (#) and not much else, you are in the shell. You can just start typing commands (after you know what commands to type). If you begin with a graphical user interface (GUI) that contains windows, icons, menus, and so on, look for a Terminal icon and select it to open a shell window.

➤ **Learn a text editor** By far, most Linux administration is done by adding entries to plain-text configuration files located in the /etc directory. Even with improved graphical tools, there will be times that you have to edit a plain text file by hand. Popular text editors include vi and emacs commands.

➤ **Learn how to get more information** There is no shortage of documentation for Linux these days. While you are logged into Linux, to find out more about any shell command or file, use the man or info commands. In the /doc directory, you can find documents related to individual software packages as well as popular HOW-TO documents.

Following are a few standard procedures you can go through to administer your Linux system.

Adding and Deleting Users

Adding a user is one of the most basic administrative operations in Linux. When you first install Linux, you always add a root account and usually one regular user account (along with their passwords). Nearly every Linux distribution offers different graphical tools for adding users. However, to add a user from the command line, nearly all UNIX and Linux systems support the adduser command. To delete users, most offer the userdel command.

Adding a User

To add a new user account from the command line, first login as the root user. Here is an example of a command line to add a user named sheree:

```
adduser -m -g users -c "Sheree Glass" sheree
```

In this example, a user named sheree is added to the Linux computer. The -m option causes a new home directory to be created and assigned to the user. By default, that new directory is the username in the /home directory (/home/sheree in this case). The primary group name assigned to the user is "users" (-g users). After the comment option is the user's full name (-c "Sheree Glass").

When the new home directory is created, that directory typically starts with some files already in it. Any files that are in the /etc/skel directory are copied to the new user's home directory. After the new account is added, the new user record is stored in /etc/passwd, the name is added to a group in /etc/group, and the password is usually stored (encrypted) in the /etc/shadow file.

Adding a Password

After the user is added, you need to assign a password to that user. The user can't login to the account until she has a password. To add a password for the user sheree from the command line, type the following command:

```
# passwd sheree
New password:
Retype new password:
```

When prompted, type the new password. Then type it again. If the two passwords don't match, the operation fails and you have to enter the password again.

The /etc/passwd file

As noted earlier, entries for all user accounts are stored in the /etc/passwd file. The following is an example of several entries from an /etc/passwd file:

```
root:uXonr7RoTwQWs8:0:0:root:/root:/bin/bash
bin:*:1:1:bin:/bin:
daemon:*:2:2:daemon:/sbin:
adm:*:3:4:adm:/var/adm:
lp:*:4:7:lp:/var/spool/lpd:
sync:*:5:0:sync:/sbin:/bin/sync
shutdown:*:6:0:shutdown:/sbin:/sbin/shutdown
halt:*:7:0:halt:/sbin:/sbin/halt
bwagner:yPf3M5qMgglUc:101:10:Bill Wagner:/home/bwagner:/bin/bash
```

That probably looks very confusing. In reality, however, the file's structure is really simple. Each line consists of seven fields, separated by colons:

223

➤ The user's login ID

➤ The user's password in encrypted form

➤ The user's user ID (uid), a numeric value to identify the user

➤ The user's group ID (gid), a numeric value to identify the group that user belongs to

➤ The user's real name

➤ The user's home directory

➤ The user's shell

Consider this entry:

```
bwagner:x:101:10:Bill Wagner:/home/bwagner:/bin/bash
```

From this, you can ascertain the following:

➤ The username is bwagner.

➤ The password is not stored in the password file (it's in /etc/shadow) so the password is only represented by an "x" character. If the encrypted password were stored in this file, you would see a series of characters between the two colons.

➤ The user ID is 101.

➤ The group ID is 10.

➤ The real name is Bill Wagner.

➤ The home directory is /home/bwagner.

➤ The preferred shell is bash.

Deleting a User

To remove a user, you need only remove his entry from the passwd file and delete his home directory. The preferred way, however, is to use the userdel command. For example, to remove bwagner, you could type the following at the command line:

```
userdel bwagner
```

Or, to delete the user and also remove that user's home directory, type

```
userdel -r bwagner.
```

Enforcing File System Permissions

What makes the root user a superuser? Here it is in a nutshell: Whereas regular users can generally make changes only to their own files, root users can make changes to any file. In the larger picture, however, the root is much, much more. To understand the root and the power it wields you need a crash course in computer security.

In shared networked environments, users can check out files, directories, and other resources at will. To prevent that from getting out of hand, UNIX employs a technique called *Discretionary Access Control*, or *DAC*. DAC is present in any system that enables a centralized, human authority to incisively permit or deny users access based on file, directory, or machine. As the root user, you enforce these rules through *permissions*. There are different types of permissions:

➤ **Execute**   Execute permissions enable users to execute the specified file.

➤ **Read**   Read permissions enable users to read the specified file.

➤ **Write**   Write permissions enable users to alter the specified file.

These permissions are attached to files, directories, and devices. Each permission is represented by a letter called a *token*. Permission tokens are

➤ r   Read access.

➤ w   Write access.

➤ x   Execute access.

To ascertain permissions on a file or directory, list the file in long format by typing the following at the command line:

```
ls -l
```

Here's some sample output:

```
drwxrwxrwx    2 bwagner   other            512 Jun 25 22:35 Consent
drwxrwxrwx    2 bwagner   other            512 Jun 25 22:35 Instructions
drwx------    2 bwagner   other            512 Aug  8 18:41 mail
-rw-rw-rw-    1 bwagner   other            324 Aug 11 16:34 ppp-off
-rw-rw-rw-    1 bwagner   other            121 Aug 11 16:34 ppp-on
-rw-rw-rw-    1 bwagner   other          46188 Aug 11 16:33 pppd-man.txt
-rw-rw-rw-    1 bwagner   other             58 Aug 11 20:43 pppkill
drwxrwxrwx    8 bwagner   other            512 Aug  1 01:32 public_html
```

For purposes of clarity, extract the fourth line. (The other lines show other file and directory listings, although for this purpose one example should suffice):

```
-rw-rw-rw-    1 bwagner   other            324 Aug 11 16:34 ppp-off
```

Notice that the line is broken into fields. File system permissions are indicated in the first field, which consists of 10 characters:

```
-rw-rw-rw-
```

Let's break down what those 10 characters mean. The first character, which in the example is represented by a dash (-), tells you the type of file you're dealing with. There are two tokens that could appear in this first character:

➤ **-**   Represents a file.

➤ **d**   Represents a directory.

In the example, the first character is -; therefore, it is clear that this is a file.

The remaining nine characters are actually three sets of three. Let's break them down, three at a time. The first set (reading from left to right) represents the permissions of the current user:

    rw-

In this case, the current user (that's me) has read and write but not execute permissions.

The second set (again, reading from left to right) represents the permissions of the current group:

    rw-

Again, group users have read and write access.

Finally, the last set represents what permissions the rest of the world has:

    rw-

As you can see, the rest of the world also has read and write access. So everybody has the same permissions on this file.

Suppose, however, that the first column of the permission table looked like this:

    drwxr-xr-x

This is a different situation altogether. First, it is known that this resource is a directory because the first character is a d. Also, it is clear that the root user (the file's owner) has read, write, and execute privileges because the next three characters are rwx. However, the fact that the final six characters are r-xr-x indicates that both the current group and the world can only read and execute; they cannot write.

So, to reiterate:

➤ The first character reports the file type (typically, a regular file or directory.)

➤ The next three characters reflect the file owner's privileges.

➤ The second set of three reflects the group's privileges.

➤ The last set of three reflects the world's privileges.

Setting Permissions: the chmod Command

To set permissions on an individual file or directory, use the chmod command. chmod accepts three operators:

➤ - The minus operator removes permissions.

➤ + The plus operator adds permissions.

➤ = Th equal sign operator assigns permissions.

Table 12.2 summarizes what permissions these operators can remove, add, or assign.

Table 12.2 chmod **Permissions**

chmod **Permission**	**Explanation**
r	Adds or subtracts read permission. Example: chmod +r *filename* adds the read permission to *filename*.
w	Adds or subtracts write permission. Example: chmod -w *filename* takes away write permission from *filename*.
x	Adds or subtracts execute permission. Example: chmod +x *filename* adds the execute permission to *filename*.

chmod *and the Octal System*

Using letters (r, w, x) to assign permissions on individual files and directories is fine. Sometimes, however, you'll want to set permissions *en masse*. For example, you might want to set permissions for the file's owner, the owner's group, and finally, the rest of the world. For this, it's easier to use the octal system.

In the octal system, numbers represent permissions. Table 12.3 summarizes the octal number scheme and what each number represents.

Table 12.3 chmod **Octal Permissions**

chmod **Octal Permission**	**Explanation**
0	The octal value 0 is equivalent to - - - or no permissions at all.
1	The octal value 1 is equivalent to - -x, or only execute permissions.
2	The octal value 2 is equivalent to -w-, or only write permissions.
3	The octal value 3 is equivalent to r - -, or only read permissions.
4	The octal value 4 is equivalent to -wx, or only write and execute permissions.
5	The octal value 5 is equivalent to r - x, or only read and execute permissions.

Table 12.3 CONTINUED

chmod **Octal Permission**	**Explanation**
6	The octal value 6 is equivalent to rw-, or only read and write permissions.
7	The octal value 7 is the whole shebang: It's equivalent to rwx, or read, write, and execute permissions.

You can use the octal scheme to perform widespread permission changes. For example, consider this command:

```
chmod 751 filename
```

In this case, *filename* has the following permissions:

➤ The owner can read, write, and execute it.

➤ The group can read and execute it.

➤ Outsiders can only execute it.

Be careful when applying permissions. You can accidentally place over-restrictive permissions, and then no one will be capable of accessing anything. Conversely, if your permissions are too liberal, folks can overwrite or access files they shouldn't.

A Few Words About Linux and UNIX Security

This book is really too short to give you a decent primer on security (although this issue is covered in Chapter 14). However, here are some basic rules to live by when maintaining a UNIX network:

➤ **Never give anyone the root password** The root password gives you access to everything. If someone gets your root password, he can seize control of your machine. Protect that password with your life. Don't write it down, and make sure that it isn't easy to guess. For example, don't make the root password your birthday, your social security number, or even any word found in the average dictionary.

➤ **Back up the entire system on a regular basis** Backups often comprise the only evidence you'll ever have that a security breach has occurred. If you have more than a few users, back up weekly (at a minimum).

➤ **Buy a good book on security** UNIX security is a very complex field that's evolved over some 25 years. If you really intend to secure your server, you need expert advice. For this, check out *Practical UNIX and Internet Security* by Simson Garfinkel and Gene Spafford (published by O'Reilly & Associates). This takes you step-by-step through the paces of UNIX security. Alternatively, try *Maximum Security*, published by Sams Publishing.

Where To From Here?

Network administration is a complex subject and this chapter only scratched the surface. Over time and through experience, you'll discover ways of improving centralization and simplifying management on your particular platform.

Next in Chapter 13, you'll learn about backing up: why it's necessary and how it is done.

The Least You Need to Know

➤ The system administrator has total control over your computer systems so use administrative tools carefully (and protect administrative passwords).

➤ Whether Windows or Linux systems, make sure that everyone who uses the computers on your network have individual, password-protected user accounts.

➤ Always enforce strong password policies. If you don't do it, nobody will. Users are lazy when it comes to these things.

➤ Exploit the convenience of group-based management whenever possible. This will save you many hours of work.

Chapter 13

Disaster Prevention: Back Up! Back Up! Back Up!

In This Chapter

➤ Understand why you need to back up your computer files

➤ Learn how to perform simple backups

➤ Find out what kinds of media are used to back up data

➤ Learn what goes into creating a backup strategy

Your computer might be struck by lightning. Your child might mistakenly erase the novel you've been working on for the past three years. Your laptop can fall into the lake…. If you've backed up your computer's data, these will be irritations rather than disasters.

As an individual, your data is important to you. To a business, data can be the company's lifeblood. Every individual has the option to back up his or her personal computer files; to most businesses, however, backing up computer data is a necessity.

If your home or business computers are on a network, that network is probably the best way to make sure that everyone's files are backed up. Network backups can be more thorough, cost effective, and efficient than backups done individually.

This chapter describes the advantages of backups in general, and on networks in particular. It then describes how to go about planning and performing backups.

Why Back Up?

The reason for backing up your computer files is simple: Your files can be deleted or destroyed when you still need them. There are many ways in which your files can be lost:

➤ **Hard disk crash**   A computer's hard disk has elements that are electrical, magnetic, and mechanical. Any of those types of technology can fail, causing the disk to crash in such a way that data is not recoverable.

➤ **Deletions**   People delete files all the time, both intentionally and by mistake. If the deleted files existed at a time when the computer's files were backed up, the files can be retrieved later if it becomes necessary.

➤ **Viruses**   A virus can infect the programs and files in a computer. This can result in files being destroyed or infected in such a way that they are no longer useful. A system backup from before the time the virus was introduced can return the computer system (and the data files) to a workable state.

➤ **Computers destroyed**   Fires, floods, or other natural—or unnatural—disasters can destroy computers as much as any other kind of property. The backup medium you created can be used to re-create the computing environment with the new or fixed equipment.

For some companies, the information contained on their computers is far more valuable than the cost of the hardware it's maintained on. That information can include inventory records, accounts receivable, sales data, product specifications, and a variety of other things. Seeing that timely backups are done and managed is part of company policy.

Performing Simple Backups

Generally, a backup consists of copying one or more data files from their permanent location (typically a computer's hard disk) to another location (usually a removable medium, such as a cartridge tape or removable disk). The removable medium can then be stored in a safe place in case it is ever needed.

There are a few simple types of backups that you can do with existing software on your Windows 95/98/2000 computer. Although these procedures do not enable you to perform complex or automated backups, they will help you realize that backups are not so scary.

A Simple Copy-to-Floppy

Perhaps the easiest backup—and the one done by most first-time PC users—is to copy a few important files to a floppy disk. Let's say, for example, that you want to back up a folder containing your latest novel (C:\mybook) to a floppy disk from Windows 95. The steps for doing so are as follows:

1. Insert a floppy disk into the floppy disk drive (usually A:).

2. Double-click the **My Computer** icon.

3. Double-click the **C:** icon; arrange the My Computer and C: windows on your desktop so you can see them both.

4. Drag and drop the **mybook** icon onto the 3.5 Floppy icon.

As long as the floppy disk can hold the amount of data contained in the folder, the files are copied to the floppy disk. At that point, you can pop out the floppy disk and store it in a safe place. That's it!

Using Windows 98 Backup

Although a simple copy-to-floppy technique is okay for a few files, more sophisticated tools need to be when a lot of files must be backed up on a consistent basis. The Microsoft Backup utility that comes with Windows 98 is a good tool for setting up a backup procedure that you can run more than once.

The Backup utility comes with a Backup Wizard that starts automatically the first time you open Backup. Here's an example of how to use the Backup utility:

1. Click **Start**, **Programs**, **Accessories**, **System Tools**, **Backup**. The Backup window appears, as shown in Figure 13.1. (If the wizard doesn't open, click **Tools**, **Backup Wizard** from the main Backup utility window.)

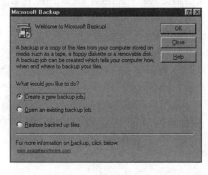

Figure 13.1

Run simple backups with the Windows 98 Backup utility.

2. The Backup Wizard window asks you what to back up. Select either **Backup My Computer** (to backup all files) or **Back up selected files, folders and drives** (to select which files to back up), and then click **Next**. (If you chose to select back up items, select those files and continue to the next step.) You will be asked what to back up.

3. From the next screen of the Backup Wizard, select **All selected files** (to do a full backup of all selected files) or **New and changed files** (to only back up files that are new or have changed since the previous backup), and then click **Next**. You will be asked where to back up.

233

4. Select **File** (to create a single backup archive of all the selected files), select the location (drive letter, folder, and filename) where you want the backup archive to be placed, and then click **Next**.

I recommend that you click the folder icon to select the location for the archive. When the Where to Back Up window appears, click the down arrow to see the drives you can select, as shown in the following Figure 13.2.

Figure 13.2

Choose the drive and folder to store the backup archive.

Check This Out

An archive is a single file that contains all the files you backed up. Although this file can become quite large, having it as one file makes it convenient for moving from one medium to another.

5. When the How to Back Up window appears, select both the **Compare original and backup files** (verifies that the backup medium was successful) and the **Compress the backup** (lets you save space by compressing the data) options. Then click **Next**.

6. On the next screen of the Backup Wizard, type the name of the backup job you are creating. At this point, you also have a choice of adding a password to the backup set. Then click **Start**.

The Backup Progress window appears, showing you the progress of the backup.

7. When the backup is done, click **Report** (to see if there were errors during the process), and then click **OK** to close the window.

At this point, you should see the main Backup window, as shown in Figure 13.3.

From the main Backup window, you can do the following:

➤ **Backup** On the Backup tab, select what, where, and how to back up as you did with the Backup Wizard. You can also click the **Options** button to select additional features (such as password protection for the backup archive).

➤ **Restore** Click the **Restore** tab. Then you can select a backup you have already made and restore all or some files to your computer from the backup medium.

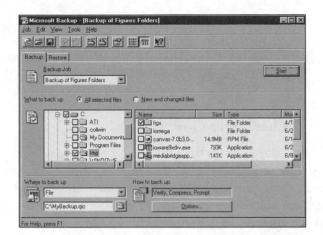

Figure 13.3

Configure backups from the main Backup window.

Check This Out

Here's your opportunity to back up the files over the network. File servers on your network appear in the Network Neighborhood folder. On the Where to Back Up window, choose **Network Neighborhood** and select the file server to which you want to back up your files. Then you can select any shared file folder, tape drive, or CD-RW drive to write your backup to. It's a simple way to share your backup devices over a network!

After you are done creating a backup to a removable medium, you can remove the backup medium and mark it with an appropriate name and date. You need to store this medium in a secure place. If the data is critical, you should consider storing your media in another building in a locked room or a safe.

Using Iomega Zip and Jaz 1-Step Backup

Simple backup tools are often delivered with the backup medium itself. For example, Iomega Zip and Jaz drives come with a 1-Step Backup utility. This utility provides a simple way to identify files to back up, run the backup, and save the backup settings for later use.

Check This Out

The Windows 98 Backup utility allows you to back up files to multiple removable media (such as tape, floppy disk, or Zip cartridges). However, with the Backup utility in Windows 95, backup can't span more than one medium. In other words, if you fill a 100MB Zip cartridge before the backup is done, you can't just pop in another cartridge and have it continue. To get around this problem, you can use the DOS utility Xcopy to do the backup. From a DOS window, first change the attributes to indicate that files are ready to be archived (the following line changes all files on your C: drive):

```
ATTRIB +A C:\*.* /S
```

Then, with the medium loaded into the drive (let's say the Zip drive in drive D:), type the following command:

```
XCOPY C:\*.* D:\ /S /M
```

The C:*.* asks XCOPY to copy all files from the C: drive. The D:\ asks to place the copied files to the top (\) of the D: drive. The /S says to copy all directories and subdirectories (except empty ones). The /M tells XCOPY to copy files with the archive attribute set, and then turn off that attribute.

After the medium is full, a message tells you so. Put in another blank Zip cartridge and run the command again. Repeat the command until the command exits without showing you a disk–full message.

To start the Iomega 1-Step Backup, select **Start**, **Programs**, **Iomega Tools**, **1-Step Backup for Zip and Jaz**. The utility assumes you are backing up to your Zip or Jaz drive, but enables you to select the files to back up. You can add password protection to the backup and compress the data (so more fits on the removable disk).

See "Removable Disks," later in this chapter, for more information on Iomega removable storage devices.

Why Network Backups?

The focus of this chapter is network backups, which entail a lot of issues you might want to consider. Network backups imply that you are dealing with multiple computers and users, so you need to think about the following:

➤ **How much data needs to be backed up?** If you have a network of three PCs, you might get by with a 100MB Zip drive for all your backups. If the network has 100 PCs, you probably want at least one mass storage device.

➤ **How critical is the information?** If there is little new data being added to the computers, you might do a backup just once a week. If important data—such as financial or medical records—are being added constantly, you might need to do backups every day or even every few hours.

The more computers and users that are on your network, the more beneficial network backups can be. Many of the advantages you get from sharing other network resources also apply to centralizing your backup administration. Some of these advantages are

➤ **Shared hardware** Instead of spending money on a removable drive for each PC, you can have one large backup device, such as a CD tower or tape device, that is shared on the network.

➤ **Central administration** Because a company's information is so important, most companies have a policy about how and when computer files are backed up. Having one person responsible for running the backups and securely handling the backup medium helps ensure that backups are done properly for all computers and users. Using the network, the administrator can back up all the computers without actually visiting each one.

➤ **Convenient scheduling** Using some of today's advanced backup tools, backups can be scheduled to run over the network at times when the computers aren't being used much. This can help prevent the performance hits that occur during backups.

Choosing a Backup Type

Different users change different amounts of data, add and delete different numbers of files, and place different levels of importance on their files. Each of these issues has an impact on the types of backup you need and how often those backups are run.

Most locations use a combination of backup types. The reason for doing different backups at different points in the backup schedule is to make your backups efficient. For example, if a computer has 1GB of data on it, but only 2MB of data changes between Monday and Tuesday, there is no reason to do a full backup of the computer each day. Therefore, on some days you do a full backup, whereas on other days you do either an incremental or differential backup.

Full Backup

With a full backup, you copy the entire contents of a computer (that is, its whole hard disk) to the backup medium. After a full backup is done, you have the capability to restore that entire hard disk to where it was when the backup was done.

Incremental or Differential Backups

A typical backup schedule backs up the entire contents of a hard disk once a week and then backs up the changes that occur on every other day of the week. The backups that are done on those other days are either incremental backups or differential backups.

For an *incremental backup*, the backup program determines which files have been added or changed since the previous (most recent) backup. Only the added or changed files are put on the incremental backup tape. The next backup will again store only those changes made since the previous incremental backup. This continues until the next full backup, at which time the next incremental backup uses the new full backup as the baseline.

For a *differential backup*, all backups that are done after the initial full backup track all changes since the full backup. So, for example, if a full backup is done on Sunday night, a differential backup on Monday contains all files that are new or changed since Sunday. The next differential backup done on Tuesday also contains all files that have changed since Sunday (including files changed on Monday and Tuesday).

Check This Out

A full backup backs up all files on the system and clears all archive bits. An incremental backup backs up all files that have been changed since the previous backup and clears their archive bits. A differential backup doesn't clear the archive bit, so the next backup will result in all files being copied since the previous full backup. If that made sense to you, don't read this paragraph again!

The differences between incremental and differential backups include the number of backup media you use and the difficulty in restoring the files if necessary:

➤ **Backup amounts differ**   Incremental backups result in less information being stored each day than with differential backups. Therefore, with incremental you can use fewer media (fewer tapes or disks) and get each backup done faster. Think of continuing the backup schedule each day through Saturday in the preceding example. With incremental, Saturday's backup includes changes between Friday and Saturday. With differential, Saturday's backup contains all changes since last Sunday. Figure 13.4 illustrates this concept.

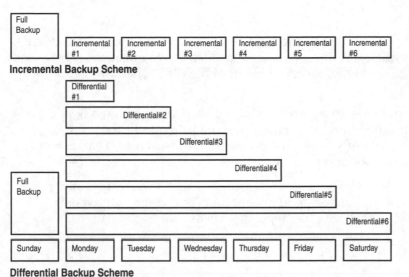

Figure 13.4

Restore incremental backups (use full and all incrementals) or restore differential backups (use full and last differential).

> ➤ **Restore convenience differs**   With a differential backup you only need two sets of media to restore files from any day: the full backup and the day you want to restore to. Restoring with incremental media requires you to have the full backup (from the week being restored) and the backup media for each day up to the restore day.

Because most backups are done automatically overnight, the differential backup is usually the most convenient. By reducing the restore to two media, one full and one differential, the administrator's restore job is much easier.

Choosing Backup Media

Remember that a backup means creating a copy of a file or files in some place other than the original medium. Although this typically means a removable medium, a backup can also be done to a hard disk on another computer or to a second hard disk on the same computer. Various types of backup media are available:

➤ Hard disk

➤ Tape

➤ Recordable CD (CD-RW)

➤ High-density floppy disks

➤ Removable disks

Check This Out

Although it is possible to back up files onto the same hard disk, that generally defeats the purpose; if the hard disk crashes, you lose both copies.

239

Hard Disk

It can be much faster to copy files to another hard disk—possibly even if that disk is on a network server—than it is to copy them to tape. This type of backup can be used for backing up data in real time, where waiting until the night's backup isn't soon enough.

Although hard disks are more expensive than tape devices (discussed next), prices have decreased significantly in recent years. If the data being protected is critical, ongoing backups can efficiently copy data to a file server's hard disk. That data can then be offloaded to tape when it is convenient.

This type of backup is sometimes referred to as *real-time replication*. Essentially, you are creating a replica of the data on another hard disk. That disk might be on a NetWare file server or a variety of other types of systems.

Tape

Before inexpensive removable disks and recordable and rewriteable CD-ROMs (discussed next) were around, magnetic tape was the backup medium of choice. In fact, one of the first UNIX system backup utilities was called tar—short for tape archiver. Although there are still the old 60MB and 120MB cartridge tapes around, much higher capacity tape drives are available today for reasonable prices. These include

➤ **Digital Linear Tapes (DLT)** DLTs are considered to be the leading format for high-end tape backup. Although originally created by Digital Equipment Corp. (which is now part of Compaq Computer Corp.), DLT is an open standard for magnetic tapes. DLT is a half-inch tape. Its cartridge is 4.1 square inches and 1 inch high. A DLT 4000 can hold 20GB (or up to 80GB compressed), whereas a DLT 7000 can hold 35GB (or up to 70GB compressed).

➤ **QIC** QIC tapes use a 5.25-inch cartridge. The latest versions can hold up to 13GB of data.

➤ **DAT** DAT holds up to 8GB compressed data (DDS-2 format), 24GB compressed data (DDS-3 format), or 40GB compressed data (DDS-4 format). These small cartridges are popular in part because they are compact and are produced by several different vendors.

➤ **8mm** This type of cartridge tape was created by Exabyte Corporation. Using 2:1 compression, 8mm tapes can hold up to 20GB of data.

DLT is becoming the most popular tape format for high-end operations. DAT is popular for inclusion on desktop units.

Check This Out

Compression software is used to cause the data you save to take up less space. By compressing backups and software applications, it becomes easier to move them around and faster to write and transport them.

Recordable CD

There are two different types of recordable CDs available:

> ➤ **CD-R** (compact disc-recordable) enables you to write once to a CD, and then read it as many times as you like. This type of media is referred to as *WORM* (write once—read many).

> ➤ **CD-RW** (compact disc-rewriteable) enables you to write and erase the CD multiple times.

Although both the media and the drives are more expensive with CD-RW, the ability to rewrite data can make CD-RW more cost-effective. However, one drawback to CD-RW is that discs cannot be read by all disc players, whereas CD-R can.

For more information about recordable CDs, refer to the CD-Recordable FAQ (`http://www.fadden.com/cdrfaq`). This FAQ contains a lot of information about the different formats and how you can use them.

High–Density Floppy Disks

The SuperDisk 120MB floppy disk drives can be used to replace standard 1.44MB floppy drives. With the new drives, you can use either the new 120MB floppy disks or the standard 1.44MB floppy disks—so you can continue to use your old floppy disks. For low-volume backups, the 120MB floppy disks can be a good alternative to purchasing another backup medium.

Removable Disks

Like high-density floppy disks, removable disk cartridges came along to fill the huge hole between floppy disks (holding 1.44MB) and mass storage devices. These drives are fairly inexpensive, can plug into an existing parallel port, and use inexpensive media (under $12 for a cartridge).

Iomega is the leader in removable storage devices. An Iomega Zip drive uses 100MB and 250MB cartridges. The more expensive Jaz drives can handle 1GB and 2GB cartridges. You can find Zip drives today for under $100 and Jaz drives for under $350. A major competitor to Iomega has been Syquest. (However, Syquest recently filed for Chapter 11 bankruptcy, putting its future as a leader in removable drives in question.) You can find Syquest SparQ 1GB removable drives for under $200. Its cartridges are also less expensive than those of Jaz drives. However, you should consider that a lack of reliable support makes the safety of your backed up data unreliable.

Choosing a Backup Strategy

No single backup strategy fits all cases. Computers that contain constantly changing, critical data need a much more diligent backup schedule than low-use computers containing nonessential data. Large and small amounts of data benefit from different kinds of backup media. This section helps describe the issues that go into choosing a backup strategy.

What Needs to be Backed Up?

Determining what data you need to back up is probably the best place to begin. The kind of information you want to back up from computers falls into two basic categories:

➤ **Data files**   These contain the information that users or applications generate and can include word processing files, database records, and spreadsheets.

➤ **System files**   These contain data that is needed to reconstruct your computer system. System files can include information defining user preferences (such as screen layout and colors) and configuration information (such as network addresses).

If a computer is managed in an organized way, data files are fairly easy to back up. In a UNIX system, users tend to keep personal files in their own home directories. For example, a user named johnj might store his files in the /home/johnj directory. Windows 95 users tend to store files in folders that are specific to an application, although this still represents a limited number of locations.

System files, however, can be more spread out than data files. Although in a UNIX system there are separate configuration files for almost every feature, most of these files are in the /etc directory. For example, the following are UNIX configuration files that you need to back up to re-create your system:

➤ **/etc/password**   Contains usernames and encrypted passwords for each user on the computer

➤ **/etc/inittab**   Contains the programs that are run (mostly system programs) when the computer starts up or enters a different run state

➤ **/etc/printcap**   Contains information about the printers that are configured to work on your computer

On Windows 95/98/2000 systems, system information includes Registry entries, user profiles, and INI files. An inexperienced user probably doesn't even know where most of this information resides. Luckily, there are backup utilities specifically designed to find and back up Windows system information.

Techno Tip

There are a variety of backup utilities available to back up your Windows 95/98/2000 or Windows NT system files so your computer can be re-created in the case of a disk crash. Safety Net Pro (`http://members.aol.com/_ht_a/ron2222/snpro.htm`) backs up your Registry, INI files, and startup files to disk. Emergency Recovery System for Windows 98, NT, or 2000 (`http://www.mslm.com`) can also be used to back up Windows system files.

How Often Is Backup Needed?

Both the kind and the amount of data being created on your computers have an impact on how often you need to back up. Following are a few examples of situations that require data to be backed up at different intervals:

➤ **Personal backups** Say you have a few computers on a small LAN—perhaps in a home or a school—that are not used for anything critical. In this case, you might choose to back up the computers once a week on a regular basis, with an occasional special backup if someone has just created some important files.

➤ **Daily backups** Some small businesses put their sales, inventory, scheduling, billing, and all other critical information on a few computers that are connected by a LAN. Although consistent backups are necessary in this case, once each workday is usually enough. Usually the backup is run after hours so as not to disrupt ongoing work.

➤ **Ongoing backups** Sometimes the data on a company's computers is so critical that it must be constantly backed up. For example, a bank can't afford to go back to yesterday's backup medium to restore its data, as it would lose track of money that has come and gone from people's accounts. In this case, companies might use *mirroring*, in which all the data on a hard disk is mirrored exactly on another disk. Both disks are updated simultaneously. (See the description of Redundant Array of Independent Drives (RAID) later in this chapter.)

The amount of data you need to back up can help you determine the type of backup device you need. By backing up over a network, you multiply the backup volume you do for a single computer. For that reason, instead of using a single tape or CD device, you might want to purchase a unit that can handle multiple backup devices at the same time. This type of device is referred to as a *library*.

One advantage of using a library is that you don't need an operator to change tapes or disks during the backup operation. This is useful because backups are often run during the middle of the night, when it might not be convenient to keep an administrator near the machine. The tapes or disks can be removed, labeled, and stored the next morning.

When Should Backups Be Run?

Running a backup slows the performance of the computer being backed up. For that reason, backups are often run late at night. However, for critical data (such as financial data), live backups (that is, backups that occur while the systems are actively being used) might need to be run constantly—or at least several times a day.

To run backups late at night, UNIX systems use utilities called at or cron. With at or cron, an administrator registers the backup utility (such as cpio or tar) to be started at a particular time with a certain set of options. With Windows 95/98/2000 and NT systems, you can use the backup agent to run automatic backups. From the Network Properties window, you can add backup services, such as Backup Exec (from Arcada Software) or ARCserv (from Cheyenne). Then, to enable the automatic backup, display the properties for the network service and select **Enable Network Backup** (in addition to any options you choose to set).

Backup Tips

The following are some tips to help you perform backups and manage backup media:

➤ **Cycle backup media**   You don't need to use a new tape or disk each time you run a backup. Besides being expensive and difficult to manage, it is also unnecessary. Rewriteable media are designed to be rewritten. So, cycling media is the normal practice.

Have at least two sets of media that you cycle. By alternating them, you always have a good set of media in case the hard disk crashes in the middle of a backup.

Check the manufacturer's specifications for information on how often the medium can be rewritten. Some tapes can handle 100 backup and restore passes and might need to be replaced only once a year.

➤ **Label backup media**   If the day ever comes when you need to restore some or all a computer's files, you will understand just how important a good label is. The label indicates when the backup was done, where the data came from, the type of backup (full, incremental, or differential), the backup tool used (cpio, tar, or other), and the number of the medium in the set (such as tape 4 of 7).

➤ **Store the media safely**   It doesn't help to have the backup medium on the desk next to the computer if the office burns down. Media need to be kept in waterproof and fireproof containers. For very important data, media need to be kept at another site.

➤ **Verify the backup media**   Try restoring a few files from your backup medium after the backup is complete. You don't want to find out that the medium was bad when you go to restore the files from a crashed hard disk.

➤ **Clean the drive**   Check the manual that comes with the tape drive for instructions on how and how often the drive needs to be cleaned.

Protecting Your Data

Although it's nice to be able to recover from disasters that can happen to your computer network, it's even better to prevent disasters in the first place. RAID and UPS technology can help you do just that.

RAID

When it is imperative that your data be protected and always available, *Redundant Array of Independent Drives (RAID)* might be your answer. A RAID unit is made up of two or more disks that appear as a single disk to the outside world. Data on the disks is redundant, so if one disk crashes, another can take over without missing a beat.

Having duplicate data available on several physical disks has other advantages. Performance can improve by allowing access to different records simultaneously, instead of one after another on a single disk. Also, if one disk needs to be repaired or replaced, it can be done without shutting down the system.

UPS

To prevent power problems from bringing down or damaging the computers on your network, you can use an *uninterruptible power supply (UPS)*. A UPS unit can protect your computers by

➤ Protecting against power surges and spikes

➤ Providing an uninterrupted flow of power during power outages

There are several different types of UPS systems available. A UPS system used with computers has a battery backup that immediately kicks in when the power goes out. This allows the computers to continue to work for a short period of time without interruption.

If the power outage lasts for a long time, the UPS can keep the computers up long enough that they can be shut down in an orderly way. If it's critical that the computers stay up, even in long power outages, the UPS can keep the systems up until a backup generator can be started to keep the power flowing beyond the battery capacity.

Where To From Here?

Keeping your data safe from disk crashes, fires, and floods can be done using the backup methods described in this chapter. Keeping your data safe from more insidious attacks, such as viruses and hackers, falls under the heading of security. Matters of security, and techniques for improving your security using passwords, firewalls, and other methods are described in Chapter 14, "Securing Your Fortress."

The Least You Need to Know

Right now, the least you need to know about backing up data is this:

➤ Computer backups, where data is copied from its permanent source to another medium, can prevent the loss of your vital computer information.

➤ For simple backups, no network is needed. You can copy to another medium using drag and drop or the Windows Backup utility.

➤ Network backups can make backing up more efficient by allowing many computers to share backup devices and centralize administration.

➤ Backups are typically done with a combination of full backups (perhaps once a week) and incremental or differential backups (perhaps every day).

➤ Backups can be done from one hard disk to another. More often, however, the eventual destination of a backup is a removable medium (such as tape, rewriteable recordable CD, high-density floppy disks, or removable disks).

➤ When you create your own backup schedule, you need to determine what to back up, how often the data needs to be backed up, and when the backups are to be run.

Chapter 14

Securing Your Fortress

In This Chapter

➤ Discover how to secure a network

➤ Learn about antivirus protection

➤ Learn about firewalls

➤ Find additional security resources

Let the good guys do as much as they need to with your computer network, while keeping the bad guys out. That's the basic rule for computer network security.

Although no computer network is completely safe from malicious intruders, you can take many steps to prevent or correct security breaches of your network. This chapter describes some of the most common practices for protecting your computer networks.

Why Should I Care About Network Security?

Whether your network is just an office LAN or a high-speed connection to the Internet, if you rely on that network for your livelihood, you need to protect it. Network intrusions have become more common than ever, and that trend will only continue.

You might think that nobody would care enough to break into your network. But the truth is that there are both human and automated crackers that randomly scan IP addresses on the Internet to find insecure networks. Likewise, email worms and viruses can spread like wild fires, without knowing or caring who gets infected.

A 1999 Information Week survey reported that 64% of respondents experienced at least one virus in the previous year. (That figure was up from 53% the previous year.) In the United States, the number of companies reporting at least one virus was 69%.

Other types of security breaches that were noted included the following:

➤ Information loss (11%)

➤ Data and system integrity losses (11%)

➤ Denial of service attacks (11%)

➤ Trojan horses (a malicious software program that replaces a program that is supposed to be on your computer) (8%)

You Just Sank My Battleship!

In *denial of service* attacks, attackers render your system inoperable; they effectively blow a machine off the network by crippling its capability to respond to its peers.

For respondents to the survey that had experienced security breaches, 48% said that the breaches were caused by hackers or terrorists. A year earlier, only 14% believed that their security breaches were caused by hackers or terrorists. Some of the increase in reported hacking from outside sources comes from improvements in the tools available to detect network security problems. In other words, it might just be easier to tell that someone has broken into your computers from the network.

The bottom line is that the wires connected to your most precious computing resources can act as portals to anyone from mischief-makers to those bent on destruction. So, what can you do about it? Your means of protection can come in several major forms:

➤ **Physical security** Control who has access to the wires, hubs, switches, computers, and other equipment that make up your network.

➤ **Computer system security** After someone gets on your network, how your computer systems are configured can have a dramatic effect on how much damage the person can do. Computer system security typically starts with separate user accounts and good passwords. An administrator can protect computer systems by limiting system services and by having good tools for monitoring security.

➤ **Human security** You can configure your network with lots of fancy tools for keeping out intruders. However, if employees tell their passwords or other personal information to a stranger, security goes right out the window.

➤ **Network security** It's good to be able to catch someone who has gotten on to your network. However, it is even better to keep them off your network in the first place. Firewalls (discussed toward the end of this chapter) are among the best tools for protecting the boundary between your local network and a wide area network (such as the Internet).

Physical Security

Protecting the physical access to your computer network should be your first consideration when you set it up. No computer is secure if it's left in a place where someone can walk off with it. No LAN is secure if its wires are exposed for anyone to connect to.

The following sections give suggestions for physically protecting your network.

Protecting Physical Data Storage

The information that is the lifeblood of any company is typically stored on computer hard disks. Physical access to those computers can let a person walk off with your data or change the computer operating system in a way that allows him access. Also, copies of the data on these computers are stored on tape, removable disks, or other media when you do backups of your hard drives.

To physically protect against data loss, you should take at least the following four steps:

➤ **Place your servers out of reach**   To protect your servers against hardware attacks, house them in a secure location, such as a room that offers restricted access. (Ideally, only employees with a key should have access.) When you finally develop a written on-site security policy, be sure to clearly specify which employees can physically access your servers and when such access is authorized. (Also, establish penalties for non-compliance. This protects you if you later decide to terminate an employee who violates policy.)

➤ **Secure your backup media**   Many offices use backup devices (discussed in Chapter 13, "Devising a Backup Plan") to hedge against disaster. This is an excellent idea. However, remember that backups—especially total backups—pose a special security risk. (Often, such backups contain vital and sensitive information.) Unless your backups are completely encrypted, store them in a secure location.

➤ **Secure your installation media**   If employees have access to your installation disks, they can bypass traditional access control. (Remember that installation routines place the user in a privileged mode. This enables her to alter file systems and access resources she can't otherwise reach.)

➤ **Use removable storage media whenever possible**   Additionally, if your data is sensitive, I recommend using removable hard disk drives. These drives are typically encased in a carriage that slides along a track. This track leads to an extended data cable, inside the machine. Using these devices, you can remove your hard drives each night and place them in a safe or locked closet.

Secure Your Network Wiring

Your network wire is yet another point of vulnerability. Certain network wiring schemes are susceptible to splice-in attacks. In this type of attack, someone splices a workstation or laptop into your network by attaching it to your network wire. This attack is more common in bus-based networks. However, it is possible to splice into other topologies.

To protect against splice-in attacks, carefully insulate your wire route from outsiders. For example, if your offices are located in a large building (and therefore co-exist with other offices adjacent, above, or below you), beware. Make certain that folks in other offices can't gain physical access to your wire.

Who Can That Be Knockin' at My Door?

On the off chance that you're extremely paranoid, I thought I would mention *Transient Electromagnetic Pulse Emanation Standard (TEMPEST)*. TEMPEST technology is the study of capturing electromagnetic emissions from computers. There are now TEMPEST tools that can capture signals from your monitor and reassemble them on a remote computer (up to two blocks away).

If you're engaged in very sensitive work, you might want to outfit your network with TEMPEST-shielded computers. These are quite expensive but guarantee complete security from prying eyes (or antennae). There are also other ways of hardening your computers to prevent actual physical attacks, such as electromagnetic denial of service attacks. For more information, refer to an article on "Hardening Your Computer Assets" at this Web address:

`http://www.infowar.com/CLASS_3/harden.html-ssi`.

Using Console and BIOS Passwords

Console and basic input/output system (BIOS) passwords represent yet another risk. If you fail to set these passwords, anyone in your offices can gain access to the BIOS or command mode. From there, they can cause serious damage. Many BIOS systems now provide disk-formatting utilities or surface-analysis tools that can destroy drive data. Moreover, most modern BIOS systems provide access to serial and printer ports or other hardware that can be used to export or import information.

This problem is not confined to Intel-based architecture, either. Many UNIX workstations provide access to single-user or command mode through the Programmable Read Only Memory (PROM).

Depending on the workstation's design, users can perform a wide range of tasks from command mode including disk formatting, boot device assignment, serial communication, and so on. For this reason, you need to ensure that both PROM and BIOS passwords are set on all workstations.

Computer System Security

Most of the on-going work for protecting networked resources should focus on configuring and monitoring your computer systems. Here are several of the security measures that you should consider for every computer that you have connected to your LAN or, even more importantly, to the Internet:

Going to the PROM!

PROM stands for *Programmable Read-Only Memory*. The PROM is to a UNIX machine what the BIOS is to a PC: It's a chip with firmware that manages the most basic tasks, including identifying disks, tabulating your machine's memory capacity, and so on.

➤ **Choosing an operating system** Although Microsoft Windows operating systems are the most popular, they were not designed originally for network computing. Especially if you need a file server, print server, or a Web server, other operating systems such as Linux, OpenBSD, or NetWare can provide more powerful and secure network services.

➤ **Adding user accounts/passwords** User accounts and passwords are the first line of defense for computers on a network. On most computer systems, only most public services (such as public files and Web pages) are accessible without logins and passwords.

➤ **Limiting system services** You can make your computers more secure by only offering network services that you need to offer and by securing many of those services with passwords. These include basic services such as file sharing and print sharing.

➤ **Preventing and patching holes** As security flaws are uncovered, computer system vendors produce software patches and bulletins to help close security holes.

➤ **Teach good practices** On the human level, there are many things you can do to keep your network-computing resources secure. Setting policies for handling email, downloading files, and protecting passwords can be as important as locking up your computers.

251

The following sections describe ways of securing your computer resources.

Choosing Operating Systems

The operating system you choose has a weighty impact on your security. When making that decision, take the following into account:

➤ **Access Control** Does your operating system enable you to deny access to files, directories, and network resources?

➤ **Logging** What if there's a security breach? Will your operating system record that event (and the intruder's subsequent activities)?

➤ **Encryption** Does your operating system encrypt passwords and other important data? If so, how strong is its encryption scheme?

Evaluating Security Features

Different operating systems offer different levels of security services. Table 14.1 compares several popular network operating systems and their out-of-the-box security tools.

Table 14.1   Comparison of Network Operating System Security Controls

Issue	Encryption	Logging	Access Control
Linux	Good	Very Good	Excellent
NetWare 2.x	Poor to none	Fair	Fair
NetWare 3.x	Good	Good	Good
NetWare 4.x	Excellent	Good	Excellent
Plan 9	Very Good	Very Good	Excellent
UNIX (General)	Very Good	Very Good	Excellent
VMS	Good	Very Good	Excellent
Windows 3	None	None	None
Windows 3.11	Perfunctory	None	None
Windows 95	Weak at best	None	Minimal/ineffective
Windows 98	Weak at best	None	Minimal/ineffective
Windows NT 3.x	Some but weak	Decent	Good but vulnerable
Windows NT 4.x	Good	Very Good	Excellent
Windows 2000	Good	Very Good	Excellent

Unless you have a reason not to, always choose the operating system with the most security (and naturally, one that you're familiar with). For example, if you're a Windows user, choose Windows 2000.

Using Multiple Operating Systems

In the old days, computers on the same network typically ran the same operating system. In today's business world, however, networks are often composed of workstations running multiple operating systems. (Some offices house systems running NetWare, Microsoft Windows, Windows NT Server and Workstation , MacOS, and UNIX—all under one roof). This naturally makes security more complex.

A typical network configuration in a business will have MacOS and Windows operating systems on peoples' desktops. Then, the computers that contain secure databases, file servers, and other critical services will run on UNIX, Windows NT, OpenBSD, or Linux operating systems.

Note

To learn more about network operating systems, see Chapter 5, "Network Servers and Clients at Your Service."

Adding User Accounts/Passwords

If you are accustomed to using your own PC at home, you might assign a username and password to your computer to protect it from being used by others. In a networked environment, there are even more reasons to establish user accounts.

Reasons for Separate User Accounts

The main reason for having separate accounts is to allow all users on the network to establish their own identities. After an identity is established, resources can be assigned to that identity. Here are some advantages of having separate user accounts for everyone on your network:

➤ Users can have their own environments set up when they login. Each environment can include the assignment of desktop colors, icons, mouse actions, shortcut keys, and startup applications to suit each user. It also typically includes a home directory where the user can store personal data files.

➤ Some operating systems, such as UNIX or Linux, allow you to extend a user environment across multiple computers. For example, a common practice is to use the Network File System (NFS) feature to allow a user from one computer to have access to all the same files on another computer—regardless of which computer the user logged in from.

➤ With individual user accounts, administrators can assign individual permissions to use (or not use) data files, folders, applications, printers, floppy disk drives, scanners, or any other hardware or software on the network.

On more advanced operating systems, there are assigned administrative user accounts to install software, add users, and generally maintain the computer. In UNIX and Linux, the main administrative user is the root login (also called the super user). When someone tries to break into a UNIX or Linux system and take control, he typically tries to obtain root permission.

If users are allowed to log in to the computers on your network from other computers, the only real defense protecting each account from intruders is each user's password. If the intruder obtains the root password, that intruder basically has the keys to the castle. That is why password protection is perhaps the most important security issue for securing your computers.

Protecting Your Passwords

Weak passwords account for a high percentage of network security breaches. Make every effort to educate your users on good password choices. At a minimum, user passwords should never contain

➤ Proper names, birth dates, or social security numbers

➤ Any word that appears in a dictionary

➤ Strings of fewer than five characters

➤ All numbers

➤ All the same letter

➤ Any combination of the preceding

Additionally, institute a password aging system. This is where user passwords expire after so many weeks or months. The purpose of this is to periodically force your users to change their passwords, which reduces the chances of a password compromise.

Some network operating systems have password aging built into their security structure and others don't. If yours doesn't, consider obtaining third-party tools for this purpose.

There are several tools for testing password strength. These tools attempt to crack your network passwords, and their approach is quite effective: Whole dictionaries are encrypted using the same algorithm that your operating system uses. Each encrypted word is then compared to your network password. If the program finds a match, the password has been cracked.

Such tools are available for UNIX, Windows NT, and Novell NetWare. For these platforms, I recommend Crack, NTCrack, or NWPCrack. Let's briefly look at these utilities and what they do.

Crack

Crack is used to check UNIX networks for characteristically weak passwords. The author, Alec D. E. Muffet, explains the program's purpose:

> Crack is a freely available program designed to find standard UNIX eight-character DES encrypted passwords by standard guessing techniques...It is written to be flexible, configurable, and fast, and to be able to make use of several networked hosts via the Berkeley rsh program (or similar), where possible.

Crack runs on UNIX only. It comes as a tarred (single file archive containing many files), g'zipped file (compressed file in gzip format), and is available at `http://www.users.dircon.co.uk/~crypto/`.

NTCrack

NTCrack performs high speed brute force attacks. As reported by the folks at Somarsoft:

> The program...does about 1000 logins per minute, when run on a client 486DX-33 with 16MB of RAM, a server 486DX2-66 with 32MB of RAM, and a 10Mbps Ethernet. This is equivalent to testing 1,152,000 passwords per day. By comparison, there are perhaps 100,000 common words in the English language.

To prevent such attacks, Somarsoft suggests that you enable account lockout, rename the Administrator account, disable network logins for Administrator, and disable SMB over TCP/IP. (SMB permits file and printer sharing among Microsoft Windows computers.)

To try out NTCrack, get the software at `http://www.tux.org/pub/security/secnet/tools/ntcrack`.

NWPCRACK

NWPCRACK is a brute-force NetWare password cracker. It works in much the same manner as Crack, but is slower. You can find NWPCRACK at `http://bigfat.net/novell.html/nwpcrack.zip`.

As a rule, test user passwords once every 90 days. Whenever you find a weak password, notify the user and request that they create a stronger one. This process effectively weeds out crackable passwords and thus increases your system's overall security.

Limiting System Services

How can intruders get into your computer system over a network? They might try guessing passwords through your login service. They might try to enter through your email service, running a destructive program when you open an attachment. Or they might try accessing insecure shared file systems.

Remote login, email, file transfer, and remote program execution are all useful services that your computer might offer. These services, however, can also act as windows that a cracker can use to break into your computer.

The OpenBSD operating system, which many consider to be the most secure operating system, uses the following motto for its network services: "Secure by Default".

The OpenBSD project (http://www.openbsd.org) delivers its operating system with all non-essential network services disabled. In this way, as a novice user you don't have to be a security expert to begin using OpenBSD. As you add each new service, you can study the security implications. Regardless of the operating system you are using, I strongly recommend learning which network services are running, and then learning about how securely those features are configured.

You might wonder how network services are implemented. In UNIX-based servers, *daemons* are used to implement networking services. A daemon is a program that runs in the background on your computer and waits for something to happen. That "something" is typically a request from a user on your computer or from a user from the network.

Note

To learn more about configuring network servers, see Chapter 5.

An example of a daemon in UNIX is the lpd daemon. The lpd program, which stands for line printer daemon, listens for requests to print documents, cancel print jobs, pause printing, or do other related activities. The request is allowed or disallowed based on how the printer has been configured in the lpd configuration files. As requests come in to access the printing service, those requests are logged to predefined log files. So, if you are going to be offering network services from your server computer, you should be aware of:

➤ The daemon process that listens for requests for the service

➤ The configuration files that set permissions to use the service

➤ The log files that keep track of activities that take place with the service

The "Secure by Default" motto is a good rule to follow if you are bringing up your first server. As you add a network service, make sure that you carefully configure the service (erring on the side of being too restrictive), and then keep track of activities of that service on an on-going basis.

Preventing and Patching Holes

No computer system is completely bulletproof. Security holes are being found and corrected on every mass-market operating system that can connect to a network. Likewise, there can be holes in the computer applications that you install and run.

Getting Upgrades and Patches

Organizations that maintain these operating systems also maintain upgrades and patches that you can use to patch known security holes. I recommend that you check on occasion for security patches (every few weeks or more often for critical networks). Important security fixes, such as those for the "I Love You" virus that infected Microsoft Outlook email programs, will often have useful support information along with the patch (visit `http://www.officeupdate.com`). Here are some other Web sites to visit for security patches:

➤ Red Hat Linux   `http://redhat.com/apps/support/updates.html`

➤ Microsoft Windows   `http://support/microsoft.com/directory`

➤ OpenBSD   `http://www.openbsd.org/errata.html`

➤ Sun Trusted Solaris   `http://www.sun.com/software/solaris/ trustedsolaris/ts tech faq`

➤ Novell NetWare   `http://www.novell.com/servlet/Knowledgebase`

There are also other kinds of holes in your security that a malicious intruder can exploit. Here are some suggestions that will help minimize your risks:

➤ Install only software that you need.

➤ Get rid of buggy code. Programs that have memory leaks or loop continuously can be used to bring down your computer.

➤ Don't use insecure protocols (that is, those that don't verify the identity of users and host computers). Examples of insecure protocols include UNIX "r" commands (rlogin, rcp, and so on) which allow data sharing without securely verifying the identity of users and computers.

➤ Don't use configuration options that allow users to bypass security. Again, options that let you bypass passwords and other verifications are inherently insecure.

Dealing with Flawed Applications

Many *commercial-off-the-shelf (COTS)* applications have poor security. There are two reasons for this:

➤ Security is an obscure concern, and one that's sometimes overlooked.

➤ Today's network applications often exceed 500,000 lines of code. Managing such a large project is difficult, and there's much room for error.

Another factor is the time-to-market schedule in software development. The software industry is highly competitive and has only become more so with the increased demand for networked applications. In the rush to market, many software manufacturers fail to adequately test their products for security controls. As a result, the industry is now flooded with insecure applications.

Worse still, because source code is rarely available, you have no way of finding out whether your commercial-off-the-shelf (COTS) software is safe. Typically, insecure programs are exposed too late, only after hackers or crackers have already exploited the weakness.

Unfortunately, there's no easy solution to this problem. The best you can do is watch security mailing lists for vulnerability reports. The location of several such lists is provided at the end of this chapter.

Preventing Viruses

A computer *virus* is a program that attaches itself to files on the target machine. During attachment, the virus's original code is appended to victim files. This procedure is called *infection*. When a file is infected, it is converted from an ordinary file to a *carrier*. From that point on, the infected file can infect other files. This process is called *replication*. Through replication, viruses can spread themselves across a hard disk drive, achieving systemic infection. Often, there is little warning before such a systemic infection takes hold, and by then it's too late.

Different viruses perform different tasks. Some do nothing more than replicate and thus cause a little disruption of service. However, a limited number destroy data, format hard disk drives, or otherwise incapacitate their host system. A recent—and irritating—development is the emergence of data viruses. These are commonly called *macro viruses*. Macro viruses infect documents and document templates, particularly in Microsoft Word and Excel. Such infection invariably leads to the host application's poor (or sometimes bizarre) performance.

Check This Out

One excellent place to learn about viruses is the Department of Energy's Computer Incident Advisory Capability Virus Database. The CIAC Virus Database lists thousands of viruses, their signatures, their file sizes, and what damage they can cause. To check out the Virus Database, go to `http://ciac.llnl.gov/ciac/CIACVirusDatabase.html`.

Where Do Viruses Come From?

Viruses come from programmers who are either malicious or bored. Virus programmers usually release their code to the Internet (or another communal network), where the chances of proliferation and transport are high. From there, the virus might take any number of twists and turns before it gets to you. You might unwittingly download it directly from the Internet, or you might receive an infected disk. In most cases, you'll never know.

There are currently more than 10,000 viruses, the majority of which target consumer-oriented, PC-based operating systems. In particular, all Microsoft products and several Apple products are especially vulnerable. UNIX, on the other hand, is low-risk for virus infection—in fact, there are only two known viruses for UNIX. Does UNIX have some magical, inherent protection against viruses? No; rather, UNIX is a poor target for virus attacks because its access control is exceptionally stringent. Therefore, it's less likely for a virus to spread in a UNIX environment.

Check This Out

An important, and often missed, point about virus scanners is that their effectiveness hinges greatly on time. New viruses are released every month; therefore, to protect your network, you must constantly keep up with virus-scanner updates.

Addressing Risks Associated with Viruses

Protecting against viruses is relatively simple. To do so, install a quality virus-detection utility on each workstation. Most of these utilities can be programmed to scan a workstation's drive each time it boots.

Table 13.2 lists several well-known virus-detection utilities. I have experience using each of the entries in this list, and can recommend them all. Most employ similar techniques of detection.

Table 13.2   Popular Antivirus Utilities

Product	URL
FindVirus	http://www.drsolomon.com/
F-SECURE Professional	http://www.DataFellows.com/
Integrity Master	http://www.stiller.com/stiller.htm
Iris Antivirus Plus	http://www.irisav.com/
McAfee VirusScan	http://www.mcafee.com
Norman Virus Control	http://www.norman.com/
Norton Anti-Virus	http://www.symantec.com/avcenter/index.html
PC-Cillin II	http://www.antivirus.com/pc-cillin/
Sophos Antivirus	http://www.sophos.com/
Thunderbyte Anti-Virus	http://www.norman.com/tbav.shtml

259

Human Security

It's not much use to lock a building if one of your co-workers gives away the keys. The same can be true of passwords and other private company information that can undermine your security.

Check This Out

How often do you need to run virus scans? That depends. If you have network users with Internet connectivity, you should full virus scans every day. Most antivirus software has options to automatically scan for viruses.

Security experts have consistently proven that human beings are the weakest devices in any security structure. Because of this, hackers can often "socially engineer" their way into your system.

Your only defense against social engineering is to educate your users. At the very least, they need to adhere to the following simple rules:

➤ Never offer network information via telephone or email.

➤ Never transmit a password via email in clear text.

➤ Never discuss the network with non-company personnel.

➤ Never write down (or otherwise record) passwords (no sticky notes or crib sheets).

Anti-Social Engineers

Social Engineering is a fancy term that describes the act of obtaining information through fraud. A typical example is a hacker calling your personnel department claiming to be a security administrator. During this initial conversation, the hacker obtains a list of valid users. From there, he calls each user, claiming that he needs to "verify" their password. Incredibly, most employees surrender their password without questioning the caller's authority. The victim of such a ruse has been *socially engineered*.

To understand how silly users are in this regard, consider this: Recently a security expert tried this social engineering approach on a series of banks. In most cases, bank personnel unwittingly provided their passwords without a struggle.

> ➤ Protect your passwords; don't even tell an administrator.

> ➤ Shred information about your network, telephone lists, memos, and so on.

> ➤ Don't give information to anyone you don't know and trust.

Lecturing users on these points is one thing; getting them to adhere to them is another. One way to encourage compliance is to periodically run unannounced tests. In other words, have an outsider call up each department posing as a security administrator. See if your outsider can obtain any real passwords.

Network Security

Keeping a burglar out of your house is a good thing...but keeping him out of the city is even better! If your network is connected to a wide area network (such as connecting your home LAN to the Internet), the first and best place to stop an intruder from the outside world is to keep him off the network completely. Internal security is very important and, traditionally, this is the focus of most LAN security schemes. However, the rules drastically change after you establish Internet connectivity. Internet servers often run the full gamut of TCP/IP services, which means that if you don't use a firewall (a subject to be discussed momentarily), anyone can connect to your system.

This is very different from a traditional private LAN, in which known users can connect, but only at certain times of day. Hence, you can easily identify the source of an intrusion. Moreover, you can quickly identify unauthorized after-hours activity. Conversely, with an Internet server, both known and unknown users can connect 24 hours a day, seven days a week.

To protect the boundary between your local network and the world, you can use such techniques as *sacrificial hosts* or, more often, *firewalls*.

Sacrificial Hosts

If you establish a Web server purely for distributing generic information (promotional materials about your company, for example), securing your site is simple enough. This arrangement is sometimes called a *sacrificial* or *bastion host*. Sacrificial hosts don't house sensitive or even dynamic data, which means that disaster recovery is quick and painless: Restore the hard disk drive and you're good to go.

Additionally, folks rarely spend much money to secure sacrificial hosts. Security on such servers is typically limited to absolute requisites. Sacrificial hosts—at worst—can be brought down by denial of service attacks. If this happens, you implement a disaster-recovery plan.

If, however, you intend to establish Internet connectivity for your entire network, you'll need a firewall.

Firewalls

A *firewall* is any device designed to prevent outsiders from accessing your network. This device is typically a standalone computer, a router, or a firewall-in-a-box (proprietary hardware device). This unit serves as a single entry point to your site. As connection requests are received, the firewall evaluates each one. Only connection requests from authorized hosts are processed; the remaining connection requests are discarded.

Firewalls can also analyze incoming packets of various protocols. Based on that analysis, a firewall can undertake various actions. Firewalls are therefore capable of performing conditional evaluations: "If this type of packet is encountered, I will do this." These conditional constructs are called *rules*. Generally, when you erect a firewall, you furnish it with rules that mirror access policies in your own organization. For example, suppose you have both accounting and sales departments. Company policy demands that only the sales department can have access to your Web site. To enforce this policy, you provide your firewall with a rule; in this case, the rule is that connection requests from accounting are denied.

In this respect, firewalls are to networks what user-privilege schemes are to operating systems. For example, Windows NT enables you to specify which users can access a given file or directory. This is discretionary access control at the operating system level. Similarly, firewalls enable you to apply such access control to your networked workstations and your Web site.

Techno Tip

Attack signatures are command patterns common to a particular attack. For example, when a user tries to log in to your computer over a network (for example, by using Telnet to connect to port 80) and begins issuing command-line requests, this "looks" a particular way to your machine. By training your firewall to recognize that series of commands, you can teach it to block such an attack. This can also be done at a packet level. For example, some remote exploits generate specialized packets that are easily distinguished from other, non-malicious packets. These can be captured, recognized, and acted on.

However, that is only a part of what modern firewalls can do. For instance, most commercial firewalls enable you to screen content. You can exploit this capability to block Java, JavaScript, VBScript, ActiveX, and cookies at the firewall. In fact, you can even create rules to block particular attack signatures.

There are two types of firewalls:

➤ Network-level firewalls

➤ Application gateway firewalls

Network-Level Firewalls

Network-level firewalls are typically routers with powerful packet-filtering capabilities. Using a network-level firewall, you can grant or deny access to your site based on several variables, including

➤ Source address

➤ Protocol

➤ Port number

➤ Content

Network-level firewalls that are built into a router are popular because they're easily implemented. (You plug one in, provide some rules, and you're done.) Moreover, most new routers do a superb job of handling dual interfaces, in which IP from the outside must be translated to some other protocol on the inside.

Additionally, a router-based firewall is a perimeter solution. That is, routers are external devices, so they obviate the need to disrupt normal network operation. If you use a router-based firewall, you don't have to configure a dozen machines (or a dozen services) to interface with it.

Application Gateway Firewalls

Another type of firewall is the *application-proxy firewall* (sometimes called an *application gateway*). When a remote user contacts a network running an application gateway, the gateway acts as a proxy for the connection. In this instance, IP packets (discussed in Chapter 3, "Using a World-Wide Network (the Internet)") are not forwarded to the internal network. Instead, a type of translation occurs, with the gateway acting as the conduit and interpreter.

The advantage of application gateways is that they prevent IP packets from tunneling into your network. The disadvantage is that they demand high overhead and substantial involvement on your part. Here's why: A proxy application must be configured for each networked service including FTP, Telnet, HTTP, mail, news, and so forth. Additionally, inside users must use proxy-aware clients. (If they don't, they'll have to adopt new policies and procedures.)

Do You Really Need a Firewall?

Firewalls are expensive (typically costing $2,000 to $100,000). Before you consider buying a firewall, therefore, ascertain whether you really need one. In fact, there are many instances in which firewalls are impractical.

263

For example, if your network is an otherwise open environment that must accept connections from varied sources, a firewall is probably not the best solution. Universities and Internet service providers are good examples. Often, these networks house mail servers that perform relay services. This enables remote users to check their mail from anywhere in the world (an Internet café, another school, or a friend's home). Because these connections can come from virtually anywhere, there is no feasible way to establish an approved IP address list. Therefore, instituting firewall policies isn't possible.

Also, perhaps your company is using the Internet merely as a conduit, a sort of private leased line. In such an environment, you probably won't accept any traffic from the outside world. If this is the case, you might not need all the functionality offered by a full-fledged firewall. Instead, you might choose a *virtual private network (VPN)* solution. VPNs are systems that allow encrypted traffic between two or more points (regional offices, for instance) and are typically less expensive than firewalls. The best VPN solution is NetFortress. You can learn more about NetFortress at http://www.fortresstech.com.

Resources Roadmap

The security procedures you undertake depend on many factors, including your operating system, hardware, and application set. To provide you with a roadmap of where to start, here is a list of resources:

➤ Security checklists

➤ Security mailing lists

➤ Security newsgroups

These resources will get you pointed in the right direction. Furthermore, as you use the Internet more, you'll find a treasure chest of security information. In fact, the Internet houses most of the computer security information now available.

Check This Out

I recommend using a combination of the checklists described previously. By combining this information, you can tailor your own checklist to meet your needs.

Security Checklists

Here you'll find a wide variety of security checklists:

➤ **LAN Security Self-Assessment by Computer Security Administration—University of Toronto** http://www.utoronto.ca/security/lansass.htm

➤ **Generic Password Security Checklist by Lindsay Winsor** http://delphi.colorado.edu/~security/users/access/goodprac.htm

➤ **Cisco IP Security Checklist by Cisco Systems, Inc.**
   `http://www.cisco.com/univercd/cc/td/doc/cisintwk/ics/cs003.htm`

➤ **Security Policy Checklist by Barbara Guttman and Robert Bagwill**
   `http://csrc.nist.gov/isptg/html/ISPTG-Contents.html`

Security Mailing Lists

Table 13.3 identifies key security mailing lists. The majority of these issue up-to-the-minute advisories.

Table 13.3   Mailing Lists for Holes and Vulnerabilities

List	List Name and Subjects Discussed
`81gm-list-request@81gm.org`	The Eight Little Green Men Security List. Detailed discussion of UNIX security holes, exploits, and fixes. To subscribe, send a message that has the command `subscribe 81gm-list` in the body.
`alert@iss.net`	The Alert List at Internet Security Systems. Alerts, product announcements, and company information from Internet Security Systems. To subscribe to this and other ISS lists, go to `http://iss.net/vd/maillist.html`.
`bugtraq@netspace.org`	The BUGTRAQ Mailing List. Members discuss vulnerabilities in the UNIX operating system. To subscribe, send a message with the command `SUBSCRIBE BUGTRAQ` in the body.
`cert-advisory-request@cert.org`	The CERT Advisories mailing list. These advisories address Internet security problems. They include methods for checking for and fixing known problems. To subscribe, type `SUBSCRIBE email` (where *email* is replaced by your email address) into the subject line.
`firewall-wizards@nfr.net`	The Firewall Wizards Mailing List. Maintained by Marcus Ranum, this list is a moderated forum for advanced firewall administrators. To subscribe, go to `http://www.nfr.net/forum/firewall-wizards.html`.
`linux-alert-request@RedHat.com`	The Linux Alert List. This list carries announcements and warnings from Linux vendors and developers. To join, send a message with the command `subscribe` in the subject line.

Table 13.3 CONTINUED

List	List Name and Subjects Discussed
linux-security-request@redhat.com	The Linux Security List. Now maintained by Red Hat, this list focuses on Linux security issues. To subscribe, send a message with the command subscribe in the subject line.
majordomo@lists.gnac.net	The Firewalls Mailing List. This list focuses on firewall security. (This was previously firewalls@greatcircle.com.) To subscribe, send an email message with the command subscribe firewalls in the body.
majordomo@toad.com	The Cyberpunks Mailing List. Members discuss issues of personal privacy and cryptography. (If a major cryptographic system is broken, you'll probably hear it here first.) To subscribe, send a message with the command SUBSCRIBE in the body.
majordomo@uow.edu.au	The Intrusion Detection Systems List. Members of this list discuss real-time intrusion-detection techniques. To subscribe, send a message with the command subscribe ids in the body.
listserv@listserv.ntbugtraq.co	The NTBUGTRAQ List. Maintained by Russ Cooper, the NTBUGTRAQ list tracks vulnerabilities in Microsoft Windows NT. To subscribe, send a message with the command subscribe ntbugtraq *firstname lastname* in the body.
risks-request@csl.sri.com	The Risks Forum. Members of this list discuss a wide variety of risks that are inherent to an information-based society. (Examples include invasion of personal privacy, credit-card theft, cracking attacks, and so on.) To subscribe, send a message with the command SUBSCRIBE in the body.

Security Newsgroups

You can also collect important security information from Usenet security groups. Table 14.4 lists a few good haunts in that regard.

Table 14.4   Usenet Newsgroups Related to Security

Newsgroup	Topics Discussed
alt.2600	Hacking and cracking
alt.computer.security	General computer security
alt.security	General security issues
alt.security.espionage	For the truly paranoid
comp.lang.java.security	Java programming language security
comp.os.netware.security	NetWare security
comp.security	General computer security
comp.security.firewalls	Firewall technology
comp.security.unix	UNIX security
microsoft.public.cryptoapi	Microsoft cryptography

Where To From Here?

In this chapter, you learned about securing your network from outsiders. In Chapter 15, "Troubleshooting from the Trenches," you'll learn what steps to take when your network gives you trouble.

The Least You Need to Know

Securing a network is no easy task; as mentioned, much depends on your specific configuration. However, there are some basic steps you can take to improve your network security:

➤ Place your servers in a secure location.

➤ Educate users on good password practice.

➤ Regularly check the strength of user passwords.

➤ Secure your backups and installation media.

➤ Protect your wire and hardware.

➤ Run virus scans frequently.

➤ If you establish an Internet server, consider a firewall.

➤ If you use the Internet as a leased line, consider a VPN.

Chapter 15

Troubleshooting from the Trenches

In This Chapter

➤ Track down common networking problems

➤ Learn approaches to troubleshooting

➤ Understand common troubleshooting tools

You open your Web browser, select your favorite Web site, and suddenly you get the dreaded message:

```
No connection to the Internet is currently available
```

In other words, somewhere between you and the information you want far, far away, something is broken. How do you set out to fix the problem? Well, although there are a lot of things that can go wrong between you and the sites you surf, there are simple ways to check and solve common network hardware and configuration problems.

To illustrate some troubleshooting techniques, I'll use a small office or home network example similar to the ones described in Chapters 9, "Hooking Up Your Small Office Network," and 8, "Building Your Home Network." Start with a LAN consisting of a few workstations that are connected to a hub. A DSL modem is also connected to the hub, providing an Internet connection to the ISP from the LAN. We'll break down the procedures into LAN and Internet troubleshooting (on both workstations and servers).

Let's go look for some trouble!

Troubleshooting Your LAN

If you reach the Internet from a workstation connected to a LAN, and you can't communicate with your LAN, you aren't going to get to the Internet. Because you control your LAN hardware and the modem that gets you to the Internet, you can check and fix those hardware problems yourself. There are also software tools for checking your LAN.

Check This Out

Many of the techniques for troubleshooting your network that are described in this chapter are included in the Network Troubleshooter's Cheat Sheet in the front of this book.

Trying to Reach Others on Your LAN

If your network is already set up and configured, the first thing you want to do is see if you can talk to other computers on the LAN. From Windows, you can check your My Network Places or Network Neighborhood folders on your desktop. If that doesn't work, you can try the ping command (from Windows or any other kind of computer system).

Checking Network Places and Neighborhoods

To see if you can reach other Windows computers from a Windows system, do the following:

➤ Open either the Network Neighborhood (Windows 95/98) or My Network Places (Windows 2000) windows from an icon on the desktop.

➤ Open either the Computers Near Me or Entire Network folder. If you are used to seeing the other workstations from your LAN and see only your own lonely computer, as shown in Figure 15.1, your LAN connection might be broken. (I name my computers after ski resorts: Canyons, Snowbird, Alta, and so on)

Figure 15.1

If yours is the only computer in your neighborhood, your LAN connection might be down.

If you can see other computers in your Network Neighborhood or My Network Places, it means that your network interface card is working and that your cable to the hub is connected properly. If you don't see other computers, continue on.

Pinging Other Computers

It is possible that your LAN is working, but that other computers on the network are just not configured to share resources yet. So, to find out if another computer is up and connected to the network, the network administrator's tool of choice is the ping command.

The ping command sends a packet containing an ECHO REQUEST (that is, a request to send back a sort of "I'm here" response) to another computer or gateway on the network. If the computer gets the packet, it's supposed to send back an ECHO RESPONSE packet. If you get the ECHO RESPONSE, you know that the other computer is reachable and is working. Usually, ping sends a few requests and lets you know how many of them were received and returned.

Most operating systems have the ping command. From Windows, open an MS-DOS prompt (or in UNIX, open a shell) and type the ping command followed by an IP address. Figure 15.2 shows the ping command being used to check if a computer at IP address 10.0.0.1 is running.

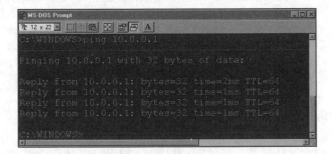

Figure 15.2

A reply from ping indicates that a computer is running on the network.

This figure indicates that the computer at address 10.0.0.1 received all four packets sent to it and replied to each quickly (in either 1 or 2 milliseconds each). A ping command on UNIX systems will keep sending and receiving packets until you stop them by pressing Ctrl+C. Before ping exits, it prints a summary report of how it did. For example, the following output shows that all nine packets sent were received and that each packet took between 0.821 and 1.000 seconds to go out and come back (with 0.851 being the average).

```
--- 10.0.0.1 ping statistics ---
9 packets transmitted, 9 packets
received, 0% packet loss
round-trip min/avg/max/mdev =
0.821/0.851/1.000/0.058 ms
```

Check This Out

Ping is such a common term among network administrators that you can use the word as a verb. You can ask a network guru to "ping my computer to see if it's up." You can even use it in common speech, as in "ping Ralph in marketing to see if he's in his office."

If you can ping another computer on your LAN, it means that your networking hardware is working. If you get no response, continue on.

Check This Out

Ping's name was derived from submarine lingo. During WWII, submarines found one another by sending sonar waves across the ocean. Whenever those waves struck a submarine, a sonar wave was echoed back to the sender (this noise was the *ping*). This notified the sender that another sub was nearby.

Network Interface Cards

If you get no response from your LAN, there might be something wrong with your networking hardware. Your network interface card (NIC) could be the problem. Normally, Windows automatically detects your NIC, installs the right driver (or lets you do it from a disk that comes with the NIC), and sets it to start automatically.

Is the NIC Plugged in Right?

If you suspect that your NIC isn't working, first look to see if the light on the NIC is lit. If it isn't, make sure that the NIC is seated properly. You can open your computer (carefully) and check that the NIC is securely placed in the slot on your computer. If it isn't properly seated, your computer might not know it is there at all. Reboot and see if things are working.

Is the NIC Driver Working?

Like other hardware devices, software drivers on your operating system control the operation of NICs. You can check that the NIC has the correct driver installed and that the driver is working. In Windows 95/98/2000, do the following:

1. Right-click the **My Computer** icon on the desktop.
2. Select **Properties**. The System Properties window should appear.
3. Click either the **Hardware tab, and then the Device Manager** button (Windows 2000) or the **Device Manager** tab (Windows 95/98).
4. Click the plus sign (**+**) next to Network Adapters. You should see the name of your NIC in the list that appears.
5. Double-click the name of your NIC. A Properties window for the NIC appears.

From the Properties window for your NIC, you can find out some things about the NIC. The General tab tells you whether the device appears to be working properly. The Resources tab tells you whether your settings (IRQs and hardware addresses) conflict with other cards in your computer. If there is a conflict, you should check the manual that comes with the NIC to see how to change its IRQ settings (in case it allows you to do such things manually).

If the driver (that is, the software that controls the NIC) is defective, there might be an updated driver that you can install. I suggest you check the Web site of the manufacturer of the NIC to see if they have updated drivers available. Click the **Driver** tab (Windows 2000) and click the **Update driver** button to install the new driver.

If the NIC seems to be working properly, you might check the cables next.

Are There Diagnostics to Run?

Some NICs come with diagnostic programs that you can run to test your NIC. (If the NIC doesn't come with a diagnostic program, you're on your own.) For example, the 3COM 3C509 NIC comes with diagnostic software. Using that software, you can

➤ Check the NIC's physical components, connectors, and circuitry.

➤ For some combination models, check their capability to transmit and receive data on the coaxial transceiver.

➤ Test the capability of the NIC to transmit and receive data while on the network.

If all these tests pass, chances are the NIC is okay. From here, you might want to move on to your cables.

Cables

Cabling problems tend to fall into one of these categories:

➤ You didn't plug the cable into the right place.

➤ The cables are broken within the shielding (which would be invisible to you).

➤ You got your wires crossed.

These issues are described in the following sections.

Improper Cable Connections

First, make sure you have the right kind of Ethernet cable and that it's plugged into the right places. On your computer, the cable should plug into your NIC on one side and either your hub (twister pair with RJ-45 connectors) or the next computer in your bus network (coaxial cable with T-connectors). These are described in Chapter 4, "Choosing Your Networking Hardware."

RJ-45 connectors look a lot like the connectors you use to hook up your phone. If your RJ-45 connector doesn't click into the back of your computer, don't try to force it. You might be trying to jam it into your modem.

On the hub side, the connector should just click into a port on the back of the hub. One thing to be careful of is that you are not plugging the cable into a crossover port. A crossover port is used to connect two hubs together. Usually, there is a button that lets you switch one port between being a regular hub port to a crossover port. The documentation that comes with the hub should tell you how to set that button.

Check This Out

There are crossover cables made specifically for connecting hubs together (in case the hub doesn't have a special crossover button). To connect a workstation to a hub, use a straight-through cable (a crossover cable will *not* work). A straight-through cable will have the same color wiring going to the same number pin on connectors on each end of the cable. When a hub talks to another hub, the crossover cable switches the send and receive wires, so both sides don't talk and listen on the same wires.

Crossed Wires

If you made your own cable and didn't do it right, or if you just got a defective cable, that can be a show-stopper. The easiest way to see if a cable is faulty is to switch out the cable in question with one that you know works.

If you already pulled the wire through the walls, however, and it isn't working, you might want to think about getting a cable tester. With a cable tester, you can determine whether you forgot to crimp a wire. You can test for such things as continuity (can a signal get from one end to the other), crossed pairs (did wires get mixed up), short circuits, or connections that were just wired wrong.

If you are going to be stringing a lot of cable, and you like cool gadgets, you might consider getting a time domain reflector. *Time domain reflectors (TDRs)* are devices that diagnose various cable types (including power and network cables). TDRs rely on a technology called *pulse echo reflection (PER)*. When you test a cable, your TDR sends an electronic pulse down the cable wire. This pulse is then measured and results are displayed graphically on a screen.

As you watch the screen, you can easily see the status of the electronic pulses, much like watching an EKG of a heart patient. When you see a dramatic change in the pulse strength—which means a change in the pulse's velocity—you know that a fault or defect exists in the wire. The TDR can pinpoint the defect's actual physical location within two feet or so. This distance is gauged by the time it takes for signals to echo back to the TDR.

You'll probably never need a TDR because they're employed chiefly in large networks. To learn more about these tools, however, contact a TDR vendor. I recommend Riser-Bond Instruments of Lincoln, Nebraska. You can contact Riser-Bond's staff at

Riser-Bond Instruments, Inc.
5101 N. 57th Street
Lincoln, NE 68507 (USA)
(800) 688-8377

```
http://www.riserbond.com/
```

Hubs

You have two computers connected to a hub and they can't communicate. On way to check if the hub is not working is to connect the NICs on the two computers directly to each other. To do this, you need a crossover cable. (See Chapter 4 for a description of crossover cables.) If the two can communicate, there is probably something wrong with the hub.

The lights on the hub can give you an idea whether the NICs and cables are working properly. There is generally one light for each port on the hub. Here is what each light means:

➤ If the connection is good, the light is on.

➤ If the connection is bad, the light is off. You might have a bad or incorrectly wired cable or a bad NIC.

➤ If the polarity is off in the cable (usually because the wires were connected wrong inside the cable), the light might turn yellow (or on some models, it blinks).

The problem might be that your hubs and NICs are incompatible. Although Ethernet cards should be made to specific standards, some NICs might fail to communicate with NICs from other vendors.

Troubleshooting Internet Connections (from a Workstation)

If you can communicate with the computers on your LAN, but still can't communicate with the Internet (assuming your LAN is connected to the Internet), there are a few things you can check. These include checking your workstation's TCP/IP configuration, your ability to communicate with your router, and your DNS configuration.

Check Your IP Address and DNS Addresses

For your workstation to communicate over the Internet, you usually need to configure your computer to have an IP address. Procedures for configuring IP addresses for your Windows workstations are described in Chapter 8, "Building Your Home Network." Here is a quick review to make sure that TCP/IP is set up right:

Check This Out

Before you go to all the trouble of troubleshooting your Internet connection, just humor me for a second. It might be possible that you can't reach a Web site because it's down. Try a few other Web sites in case that's the problem.

1. From Windows, click **Start**, **Settings**, **Control Panel**.

2. Open either the **Network** icon (Windows 95/98) or **Network and Dial-up Connections** (Windows 2000).

3. Do one of the following:

   For Windows 2000: Right-click the **Local Area Connections** icon and select **Properties**.

   For Windows 95/98: Select **TCP/IP** and select **Properties**.

4. Look for an entry in the Properties window that begins with Internet Protocol or TCP/IP (for Windows 95/98, TCP/IP should be followed by the name of your NIC). Then double-click it. In Windows 2000, here is what the Internet Protocol (TCP/IP) Properties window should look like (see Figure 15.4).

It is possible to have your workstation's IP address and DNS server information picked up automatically. For that to happen, you need a DHCP server (to provide IP addresses) or a DNS server configured to broadcast information about itself (to provide domain name to IP address translation when you surf the Internet).

If you needed to put IP addresses and DNS information in manually, here are some things to look out for:

➤ **IP Address** Make sure this address is unique within your LAN (if you are using private IP addresses) or unique throughout the whole Internet (for public IP addresses). See Chapter 3, "Using a World-Wide Network (Internet)," for a description of IP addresses.

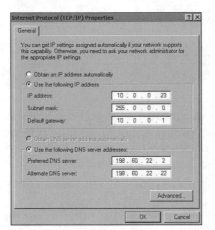

Figure 15.4

Make sure IP addresses are set properly.

Check This Out

DHCP stands for Dynamic Host Configuration Protocol. A DHCP server is assigned a pool of IP addresses. When a client computer starts up on the network, it contacts the DHCP server. The DHCP server provides the client with an IP address, from its pool of addresses, and the client uses it as its own address until it shuts down its network connection. Then the address can be assigned to another client.

➤ **Subnet Mask**   This number identifies the part of the IP address that represents the network. If this number is wrong, your computer might misinterpret which IP addresses are on your local network and which are accessible on the Internet.

➤ **Default Gateway**   This is the IP address of the routing device (computer with two network interfaces, DSL modem, and so on) connected to your LAN. If you get this wrong, your requests for information from the Internet will never be routed to the Internet.

➤ **Preferred DNS Server**   You enter the IP address of the computer that will translate the requests you make for Internet addresses (whatever.com) into IP addresses. If you get this wrong, you will see those "server not found" messages when you try to surf the Web.

➤ **Alternate DNS Server**   This is the same as the Preferred DNS Server, except that it is the IP address of the backup DNS server.

Ping the Router and Internet

You already learned how to use the ping command to determine whether you could reach other computers on your LAN. Well, that same command can also be used to test your connection to the Internet. Use the ping command to ping the following places:

➤ **Router**   By pinging the IP address of the router, you can make sure that your computer can find the device that provides its route to the Internet. Remember that routers have at least two IP addresses: one on your LAN and one on the network connecting to the ISP. You can ping both of them.

➤ **Other Internet Addresses**   To make sure you can get beyond your router, try pinging an IP address that is on the Internet. In other words, try pinging an IP address that the packet would need to cross the router to get to. If DNS is working, you could ping a Web address instead (such as www.yahoo.com).

If you can reach the router but not any IP addresses on the other side of the router, the router might be improperly configured. Check the manual for configuring the router or contact your ISP to see whether there is a problem with the connection at the ISP.

Check Dial-Up Connections

Although this book has focused on connecting a LAN to the Internet with some kind of DSL or cable modem, most individuals still use a regular dial-up modem to reach the Internet. Here are a few problems you might encounter that could keep you from connecting to the Internet:

➤ **Dial tone**   If you see a "no dial tone" message or you just don't hear a dial tone when your computer tries to dial out, your modem might not be connected to a working phone line. Check that a working telephone line is connected to your modem and try again.

➤ **ISP phone number**   You should have a telephone number for your ISP that allows you to dial-in to create a network connection to the Internet. Make sure the connection supports the speed of your modem.

➤ **Account name and password**   Without this information, you will not be able to login and get a connection to your ISP.

Sometimes special dialer scripts are needed to dial in to your ISP. Connections from your Windows workstations to Windows servers at the ISP tend to connect easily over telephone lines. Windows workstations sometimes need special scripts to connect to UNIX servers. The two types of dial-up servers typically do different types of authentication. By far, the best way to handle the problem is to call your ISP for instructions.

Troubleshooting Internet Connections (from a Server)

Servers that were specially set up to manage network resources have more advanced tools for monitoring and troubleshooting your network. The following sections contain some commands that are commonly found on Linux and other UNIX systems for checking out the Internet and other TCP/IP networks. In many cases, there are versions of these commands that run on other operating systems. When possible, I tell you where to get the different versions of those commands.

Traceroute: Checking for Trouble on the Line

Traceroute is a tool for checking the route between two machines to locate where the problem is. Traceroute performs this task by dropping special packets at each stop that echo back to the sender. In this way, Traceroute builds a network map of the precise route taken between two machines. Following is an example (bold is what you type):

```
C:\WINDOWS>traceroute 207.171.0.1

Tracing route to cisco-t3.pacificnet.net [207.171.0.1]
➥over a maximum of 30 hops:
1 149 ms   137 ms   137 ms   tnt1.isdn.jetlink.net [206.72.64.13]
2 141 ms   136 ms   125 ms   jl-bb1-ven-fe0.jetlink.net [206.72.64.1]
3 147 ms   143 ms   139 ms   166.48.176.17
4 138 ms   135 ms   137 ms   core1.Bloomington.cw.net [204.70.4.161]
5 141 ms   139 ms   145 ms   lang1sr2-4-0.ca.us.ibm.net [165.87.156.174]
6 140 ms   138 ms   137 ms   165.87.157.129
7 149 ms   143 ms   135 ms   ded1-fe0-0-0.lsan03.pbi.net [206.13.29.196]
8 161 ms   157 ms   152 ms   cisco-t3.pacificnet.net [207.171.0.1]

Trace complete.
```

Pretty interesting stuff. In the preceding trace, the two machines (206.72.64.13 and 207.171.0.1) are only several miles apart—but it still took eight hops (that is, connections through eight different routers) to complete the trace. But even that's considered a healthy trace. What about a trace where problems are revealed? Let's try it. I'll trace the route between the Central Intelligence Agency and the computer from which I run traceroute. Here's the output:

```
C:\WINDOWS>traceroute www.cia.gov

Tracing route to www.odci.gov [198.81.129.99]
➥over a maximum of 30 hops:1 140 ms 124 ms 127 ms
➥tnt1.isdn.jetlink.net [206.72.64.13]
```

```
2 214 ms 239 ms 169 ms jl-bb1-ven-fe0.jetlink.net [206.72.64.1]
3 145 ms 134 ms 134 ms ana-3-0-2xT1.sprintlink.net [144.228.79.9]
4 136 ms 141 ms 154 ms 144.232.1.37
5 138 ms 135 ms 136 ms  sl-bb4-ana-4-0-0.sprintlink.net
➥[144.232.1.30]
6 151 ms 140 ms 39 ms t16-0.Los-Angeles.t3.ans.net [207.25.133.1]
7 199 ms 211 ms 205 ms f2-1.t60-81.Reston.t3.ans.net [140.223.60.142]
8 213 ms 207 ms 205 ms  f0-0.c60-13.Reston.t3.ans.net
➥[140.223.60.215]
9 222 ms 215 ms 205 ms  enss3624.t3.ans.net [207.25.139.38]
10 225 ms 219 ms 220 ms  207.27.2.46
11 *          *          *        Request timed out.
12 *          *          *        Request timed out.
13     *          *          *        Request timed out.
```

The Request timed out, beginning at hop 11, indicates that a connection is not being made past hop 10. To find out what's wrong, you would have to begin with the last viable address; in this case, that is `207.27.2.46`:

```
1 140 ms 124 ms 127 ms tnt1.isdn.jetlink.net [206.72.64.13]
2 214 ms 239 ms 169 ms jl-bb1-ven-fe0.jetlink.net [206.72.64.1]
3 145 ms 134 ms 134 ms ana-3-0-2xT1.sprintlink.net [144.228.79.9]
4 136 ms 141 ms 154 ms 144.232.1.37
5 138 ms 135 ms 136 ms  sl-bb4-ana-4-0-0.sprintlink.net
➥[144.232.1.30]
6 151 ms 140 ms 39 ms t16-0.Los-Angeles.t3.ans.net [207.25.133.1]
7 199 ms 211 ms 205 ms f2-1.t60-81.Reston.t3.ans.net [140.223.60.142]
8 213 ms 207 ms 205 ms  f0-0.c60-13.Reston.t3.ans.net
➥[140.223.60.215]
9 222 ms 215 ms 205 ms  enss3624.t3.ans.net [207.25.139.38]
10 225 ms 219 ms 220 ms  207.27.2.46
```

Similarly, on your network, if you run a `traceroute` query and receive timeouts, start with the last viable address. Somehow, between that host and your intended target, there's a problem. Trace the physical and logical connections for a possible breach. (For example, a wire might have come undone.) If you can't find any immediate cause, you might need to search even deeper, to the packet level. If so, you'll need a protocol analyzer. (See "Protocol Analyzers: Getting Down to the Nitty-Gritty," later in this chapter for details.)

In particular, Traceroute is useful for diagnosing network bottlenecks and gateway errors in just a few seconds. For example, take a look at these four lines:

```
1 40 ms 44 ms 47 ms tnt1.isdn.jetlink.net [206.72.64.13]
2 34 ms 64 ms 69 ms jl-bb1-ven-fe0.jetlink.net [206.72.64.1]
3 45 ms 89 ms 77 ms ana-3-0-2xT1.sprintlink.net [144.228.79.9]
4 36 ms 41 ms 54 ms 144.232.1.37
```

Notice that the turnaround times are pretty short. The packets went smoothly through the entire route—the longest response time was 89 milliseconds. But what if the Traceroute table looked like this:

```
1 40 ms 44 ms 47 ms tnt1.isdn.jetlink.net [206.72.64.13]
2 34 ms 64 ms 69 ms jl-bb1-ven-fe0.jetlink.net [206.72.64.1]
3 245 ms 289 ms 277 ms ana-3-0-2xT1.sprintlink.net [144.228.79.9]
4 236 ms 241 ms 254 ms 144.232.1.37
```

Notice that the turnaround times increase dramatically after the packets reach 144.228.79.9. That is precisely where the problem starts: 144.228.79.9. So, by examining response times, you can often identify where to begin your serious investigation.

Techno Tip

Traceroute is a command native to UNIX. To use it, you can issue the `traceroute` command followed by the desired address, like this: `traceroute 207.171.0.111`. On Windows, however, the command is `tracert` instead (therefore, the command would be `tracert 207.171.0.111`). Finally, note that to use `tracert` on Windows, you need to run it through a DOS or command prompt window.

If You Don't Have Traceroute or Ping

If you're not using UNIX or a Windows variant, you might not have Traceroute or Ping. Table 15.1 provides locations of these tools for other operating systems.

Table 15.1 Traceroute and Ping Tools for Other Operating Systems

Application	Description/Location
AtcpTraceroute (Amiga)	Traceroute tool for Amiga enthusiasts, located at `ftp://wuarchive.wustl.edu/pub/aminet/comm/tcp/AtcpTraceroute.lha`.
MacTCPWatcher (Macintosh)	Ping/Traceroute utility (with extended TCP/IP debugging) located at `http://www.macintoshos.com/shareware.library/internet/mactcp.utilities.shtml`.

281

Table 15.1 CONTINUED

Application	Description/Location
Trumpet TCP (DOS)	A Traceroute tool for DOS, located at `ftp://ftp.trumpet.com.au/tcp-abi/tcp201.zip`.

The *netstat* Command: Checking the Routing Table and Connections

The netstat command is useful for troubleshooting protocol problems along the routes your transmissions take. For example, netstat allows you to examine protocol statistics (the -s asks for a summary). Following is a sample report:

```
C:\WINDOWS>netstat -s

IP Statistics
  Packets Received                    = 55
  Received Header Errors              = 0
  Received Address Errors             = 0
  Datagrams Forwarded                 = 0
  Unknown Protocols Received          = 0
  Received Packets Discarded          = 0
  Received Packets Delivered          = 55
  Output Requests                     = 58
  Routing Discards                    = 0
  Discarded Output Packets            = 0
  Output Packet No Route              = 0
  Reassembly Required                 = 0
  Reassembly Successful               = 0
  Reassembly Failures                 = 0
  Datagrams Successfully Fragmented   = 0
  Datagrams Failing Fragmentation     = 0
  Fragments Created                   = 0

  ICMP Statistics
  Received     Sent
  Messages                  0            0
  Errors                    0            0
  Destination Unreachable   0            0
  Time Exceeded             0            0
  Parameter Problems        0            0
  Source Quenchs            0            0
  Redirects                 0            0
  Echos                     0            0
  Echo Replies              0            0
```

```
Timestamps                    0            0
Timestamp Replies             0            0
Address Masks                 0            0
Address Mask Replies          0            0


TCP Statistics
    Active Opens                      = 5
    Passive Opens                     = 0
    Failed Connection Attempts        = 0
    Reset Connections                 = 0
    Current Connections               = 0
    Segments Received                 = 51
    Segments Sent                     = 54
    Segments Retransmitted            = 0

UDP Statistics
    Datagrams Received    = 4
    No Ports              = 0
    Receive Errors        = 0
    Datagrams Sent        = 4
```

If you pull such a report and find many receive or transmit errors, the local worksta-tion's NIC might be malfunctioning (see the section on network interface cards, ear-lier in this chapter). Another possibility is a faulty network driver. You may need to contact the manufacturer of the NIC to download an updated driver.

netstat also allows you to view the routing table. To do so, issue the netstat com-mand plus the -r (route) switch, like this:

```
# netstat -r

Kernel IP routing table
Destination    Gateway        Genmask        Flags   MSS Window   irtt Iface
10.0.0.0       *              255.0.0.0      U       0 0          0 eth0
127.0.0.0      *              255.0.0.0      U       0 0          0 lo
default        10.0.0.1       0.0.0.0        UG      0 0          0 eth0
```

The output from this command shows a computer with a simple network configura-tion. The first line shows an interface to an Ethernet LAN (eth0) that is connected to the network 10.0.0.0. The only other interface is a loopback driver (lo) at the stan-dard address 127.0.0.0. To reach any address outside of the local LAN, information is sent to the default gateway machine (UG) at address 10.0.0.1 on the Ethernet net-work (eth0).

If the reported gateway address is incorrect—different from your gateway's actual address—you'll need to change it.

Protocol Analyzers: Getting Down to the Nitty-Gritty

Protocol analyzers are devices that capture network packets. Their legitimate purpose is to analyze network traffic and identify potential areas of concern. For example, suppose one segment of your network is performing poorly—packet transport seems incredibly slow or machines inexplicably lock up on a network boot. To determine the precise cause, use a protocol analyzer. Protocol analyzers vary in functionality and design. Some analyze only one protocol, whereas others can analyze hundreds. As a general rule, however, most modern protocol analyzers can analyze at least the following protocols:

➤ Standard Ethernet

➤ TCP/IP

➤ IPX

➤ DECNet

Protocol analyzers are always a combination of hardware and software. Proprietary protocol analyzers are typically expensive but offer superb technical support. Freeware protocol analyzers, in contrast, are cheap but offer little or no support.

Protocol analyzers are most useful in diagnosing large networks at the hardware or network level. (For example, they can be used to analyze whether NICs, routers, switches, hubs, and gateways are working correctly.) It's unlikely that you'll need a protocol analyzer for a small network. However, the following sections provide a small list of commercial and non-commercial protocol analyzers just in case that need arises.

Commercial Protocol Analyzers

The following protocol analyzers are commercial, but many companies offer demo versions. Prices range from $200 to $3,000.

ATM Network Analyzer from Network Associates

Internetwork Analyzer decodes more than 250 LAN/WAN protocols, including but not limited to AppleTalk, Banyan VINES, DECnet, IBM LAN Server, IBM SNA, NetBIOS, Novell NetWare, OSI, Sun NFS, TCP/IP, 3Com 3+Open, X Window, and XNS/MS-net. Network Associates can be reached at `http://www.networkassociates.com`.

PacketView by Klos Technologies

PacketView is a DOS-based protocol analyzer that is ideal for Ethernet, Token Ring, ARCNET, and FDDI environments. The demo version is located at `ftp://ftp.klos.com/demo/pvdemo.zip`. Reach Klos Technologies, Inc. at `http://www.klos.com/`

EtherPeek

EtherPeek is widely recognized as the premier Macintosh protocol analyzer (although a Windows version is also available). For information, contact the AG Group, Inc. at `http://www.aggroup.com`.

NetMinder Ethernet

NetMinder Ethernet is a Macintosh-based protocol analyzer that offers automated, real-time HTML output reports. A demo version is available at `http://www.neon.com/demos_goodies.html`. Contact Neon Software at `http://www.neon.com`.

NetAnt Protocol Analyzer

NetAnt Protocol Analyzer decodes all popular protocols including TCP/IP, IPX/SPX, NetBIOS, AppleTalk, SNMP, SNA, ISO, BPDU, XNS, IBMNM, RPL, HTTP, FTP, TELNET, DEC, SunRPC, and Vines IP. NetAnt Protocol Analyzer also runs on Windows 95 and exports to popular spreadsheet formats, making human analysis very convenient. Contact People Network, Inc. at `http://www.people-network.com`.

Freely Available Protocol Analyzers

There are also many freeware/shareware protocol analyzers available. These are perfect if you want to learn about network traffic without spending any money.

Gobbler

Gobbler runs on MS-DOS and Windows 9x (through a shell window). You can run Gobbler on a single workstation, analyzing only local packets, or you can use it to monitor an entire network. The program offers complex packet filtering functions, and you can specify alerts based on the type of packet encountered. You can even start and stop Gobbler by configuring it to wait for a specified packet type before it begins logging.

Gobbler provides real-time monitoring of network traffic and is an excellent tool for diagnosing network traffic jams. Altogether, Gobbler is a great tool to learn about protocol analysis; you can get Gobbler at `http://www.computercraft.com/noprogs/gobbler.zip`.

285

ETHLOAD

ETHLOAD is a freeware packet sniffer written in C for Ethernet and Token Ring networks. ETHLOAD is an excellent protocol analyzer for DOS and Novell platforms. Get it at http://www.computercraft.com/noprogs/ethld104.zip.

Some Extra Troubleshooting Tips

When maintaining your network, you might encounter any of a thousand network problems and errors. Unfortunately, there isn't room to address them all here. However, Table 15.2 lists some common network problems and errors and possible solutions. (Network error messages are italicized.)

Table 15.2   Common Network Problems and Possible Causes

Problem	Likely Cause and Possible Solution
Cannot Find Specified Name	You misspelled the server name. Try again.
Cross-device link	This indicates that you're trying to access or create a link across two hosts, one of which either doesn't support linking or doesn't have the specified file or directory. If you've previously accessed linked files or directories on the remote host, check your spelling and try again. Otherwise, contact the remote host's administrator. Perhaps they disabled shared links, or maybe the directory or file has been moved.
Excessive packet collisions	If you run a protocol analyzer and discover an inordinate number of packet collisions, your cable might be damaged, or one or more segments might be incorrectly terminated (using bus topology somewhere, perhaps). Check your cable and your terminators. If neither of these pan out, check for duplicate hardware addresses. Some Ethernet cards/software allow the user to manipulate MAC addresses. Although it is unlikely, two NICs could have the same hardware address. This can cause serious trouble, collisions, and packet delivery failure. Solution: Replace the current MAC address with one that is unique.
File Creation Error	This is a security violation message; it means that you attempted to create a file on a network drive to which you had no privileges. Solution: Get higher privileges.
FTP Error 57	This indicates that the FTP server is currently overloaded. Try again later.

Table 15.2   Continued

Problem	Likely Cause and Possible Solution
Host name lookup failure	This error indicates that you're either not connected to the network (or Internet) or that you failed to specify a domain name server. (Without a name server, your system cannot resolve hostnames.) Solution: Verify that you're connected. If so, check your DNS setup or, if you use UNIX, check /etc/resolv.conf for a valid name server address. (In Windows, you might check your lmhosts or hosts files. It's possible that one or more hostnames or addresses are misspelled. Therefore, when your system tries to reach those hosts, it fails.)
Host or Gateway not Responding	Check your spelling of the hostname. Otherwise, check your assigned gateway's address. It might be incomplete or incorrect.
Illegal buffer length	This is a NetBIOS error. It means that the system tried to send a unit larger than 512 bytes. This rarely happens, and is usually a benign error (you simply resend). However, if you continue to get this error from a particular application, it could be the programmer's fault. If so, discontinue use of the product and notify the vendor.
IPX not installed	This is a NetWare (or NetWare client) error. As it suggests, IPX is not installed. Choose **My Computer**, **Control Panel**, **Network**, **Add**, **Protocol** and install either Novell's or Microsoft's IPX. (IPX is the protocol used on Novell NetWare networks. You won't encounter this if you are not trying to use NetWare.)
Memory Errors	Memory errors are rare and usually occur only in DOS or DOS/Windows 3.11 environments.
Network unreachable	This TCP/IP error typically signifies that your gateway is down, or that there's a routing problem. Check to see that the route to the gateway is correctly assigned. To do so (on both UNIX and Windows), issue the command netstat -r, which displays the routing table. Check the real gateway address against the one in your netstat query. If they differ, change the Gateway settings. (In Windows, choose **Control Panel**, **Network**, **TCP/IP**, **Properties**, **Gateway**.)

Table 15.2   Continued

Problem	Likely Cause and Possible Solution
No route to host	This TCP/IP error indicates that your network connection is down. Check your network connection and whether your interface (Ethernet, PPP, and so on) is working correctly. On UNIX, you can do this with the `ifconfig` command. In Windows, issue the command `winipcfg` and check that your interface is up. (If you discover your interface is down, activate it or investigate further.)
Session terminated	This indicates that the remote host died, reset, or killed the connection. Check the remote host. (There's nothing wrong at your end.)
Transmission of garbage	If a single workstation starts spontaneously transmitting high volumes of garbage or malformed packets, the workstation's cable or NIC has most likely malfunctioned. Solution: Troubleshoot both and replace the offending hardware.
Unable to create directory	This is a security violation message; it means that you attempted to create a directory on a network drive to which you had no privileges. Solution: Get higher privileges.
Workstation(s) often freeze up	First, determine whether the problem is isolated, local, or global. If the problem is isolated, it's almost certainly due to a faulty cable, connection, NIC, or driver on the troubled workstation. Check these first. If the problem is local or global, however, check your hubs, switches, routers, or other networking hardware.
You can't access a network drive	The network drive might not be made available to other computers on the network. See "Setting up Your Shared Resources" in Chapter 10 and double-check that all shares are properly assigned. If this doesn't work, verify that the target workstation is currently connected and accessible.

Where To From Here?

In this chapter, you've learned that network troubleshooting is all about the process of elimination. Often the problem is exactly what you expect it to be: simple and easily fixed. In Part 5, "Charting Your Network Future," you'll find chapters on upcoming networking technologies.

The Least You Need to Know

Right now, the least you need to know about troubleshooting your network is

➤ Try the easy things first. Check that cables and NIC cards are installed and connected properly when you can't access the network.

➤ Ping is your friend. Use the ping command to check if another computer is reachable and alive on the network.

➤ If you can't reach the Internet, make sure the IP addresses of your workstation are set up correctly.

➤ More advanced troubleshooting tools let you trace the route of packets on your network and analyze how network protocols behave.

289

Part 5

Charting Your Networking Future

Every day networking technology gets faster and more networking devices become available. Though it's impossible to know exactly what lies ahead with the networks of the future, there are a few places to look for hints.

Chapters in this part look at future directions of networking by focusing on technologies just now being developed or deployed. Chapter 16, "To the Internet and Beyond," describes the next generation of the Internet. Chapter 17, "Preparing for an Explosion of Network Content," describes new types of networking content. Chapter 18, "Networking Your Kitchen Appliances," focuses on new types of networking appliances and devices.

Chapter 16

To the Internet and Beyond

In This Chapter

➤ Learn how fiber-optic networks will grow and improve in the future

➤ Understand how coming fixed wireless and satellites will compete with cable and DSL for customers

➤ See how your network devices can go from wired to wireless

➤ Understand how the next generation Internet (IPv6) will allow it to expand and become more secure

➤ Learn why IPv6 hasn't been implemented yet and why it might be soon

---

As the Internet advances out of adolescence and moves toward adulthood, it is experiencing some growing pains. Demands for bandwidth are increasing. IP addresses are running out. Yet, for every challenge, there are companies out there rushing to provide the solutions.

Like most teenagers, however, the Internet has great potential that has some hurdles to overcome before it can be realized. Although predicting how it might all turn out is a risky business, there are ways of making some educated guesses. This chapter suggests where the Internet might be going based on plans that are being developed and new initiatives that are recently underway.

In general, this chapter is divided into two major topics:

➤ **Building out the Internet** Some observations on how the Internet's physical infrastructure is changing.

➤ **Preparing for the Next Generation Internet** Descriptions of Internet Protocol version 6 (IPv6), how it will improve the Internet, and when it might be implemented.

Building Out the Internet

The Internet is connecting more people, providing faster transmission rates, and reaching more places every day. Networks are like chains, however. The weakest link along the way determines how quickly that Web page, song, or video is going to land on your computer.

Today, the weakest link in most people's Internet chain relates to the couple of miles between your home or office and the service provider. Phone companies, cable television companies, and others are working to make improvements there.

The long-haul network medium of choice today is fiber-optic cable (discussed in the next section). Miles and miles of cables are being strung to carry voice and Internet data across the country and around the world. Also, better technologies are being created to send data over those wires.

Finally, your own little network will soon be the beneficiary of many new technologies for hooking you (or your local network) into your Internet connection. New LAN technologies, as well as wired and wireless devices, will make it easy to plug into your high-speed Internet connection.

A safe prediction to make related to the initiatives in each area of the global network is this: There's going to be a lot of bandwidth around and it's going to get cheaper! The following sections on the future building out of the Internet focuses on: long-haul networks (networks that carry data hundreds or thousands of miles), the last mile, and hooking in your local network.

Increased Long-Haul Networks: More Fiber!

In 1990, there were about 140,000 miles of fiber-optic cable containing about 2.8 million miles of fiber-optic fibers laid in the United States. Now there are more than 300,000 miles of cable containing 17.4 million miles of raw fiber-optic fibers. As you might guess, all that fiber-optic equipment isn't being used just to make phone calls. Fiber-optic has become the medium of choice for providing long-haul Internet and other data services. In the amount of data it carries, fiber-optic dwarfs other long-haul network media, such as satellite, microwave, and copper cabling. Although a few years ago, there were only a handful of companies investing in long-haul fiber-optic networks (mostly the long-distance and regional phone carriers), today there are dozens.

Check This Out

According to KMI Corporation (http://www.kmicorp.com), from 1997–1999, there were 13 new fiber-optic network carriers. Although AT&T, MCI WorldCom, and Sprint accounted for 72% of the fiber-optic deployment in 1996, by 1999 they only accounted for 30% of fiber deployment. New long-haul carriers, as well as regional carriers, are challenging the dominance of the big long-distance carriers in fiber optics.

The build-out of these high-volume, high-speed fiber-optic networks is expected to continue, although at a slower rate. Projected slower growth has more to do with transmission equipment needing to catch up with the new fiber-optic cable that has been put in place than it does with a lack of demand. The following are some other trends that will impact the growth and performance of fiber-optic networks:

➤ **Dense Wave Division Multiplexing (DWDM)** This relatively new technology from Lucent Technologies (http://www.lucent.com) will greatly improve the amount of data that can be sent across a fiber-optic fiber. With DWDM, up to 80 separate wavelengths can be transmitted simultaneously on a single fiber. The result is that a single fiber can transmit up to 400Gbps of data. To give you an idea of how much data that is, Lucent says with that transmission rate, you could transmit more than 90,000 volumes of an encyclopedia in one second.

   According to Lucent, its researchers have demonstrated that it is feasible for more than 1,000 different light waves to be transmitted at the same time on a single fiber. Products based on DWDM are expected to be available from Lucent by the end of 2000. The product family is called WaveStar.

➤ **Keeping Data at Photon Level** With massive amounts of data being able to pass over long-haul fiber-optic networks, there is more potential for bottlenecks at other points in the network. Some suggest that the long-term solution to that problem is to keep data at the photon level (microscopic bits of light) through as much of the network as possible. This could include equipment at network junctions, such as routers, that can manage data at the photon level. Every time data has to be translated from one form to another, it can slow down transmission.

➤ **Lighting up the Fibers** Many miles of fiber-optic cable that have been put in place have not yet been lit with lasers. Likewise, carriers that have cable capable of providing point-of-presence to a location might not yet have the

equipment in place to terminate the connections. So, the full potential bandwidth of the fiber-optic cables that are already in place have not yet been fully realized.

➤ **Competition continuing** With fiber-optic growth continuing to be spread across more companies, greater competition is being seen in more markets. According to KMI Corporation, the average number of points-of-presence for each long-haul carrier was 67 in 1991, as opposed to 100 in 1998. So more networks are serving more cities.

➤ **Global fiber-optic connections** Undersea cables connected 97 countries by 1998. In 1999, 11 more countries and territories were first connected to these networks. It is expected that undersea fiber-optic cables will reach 134 territories and independent states by 2003, according to KMI Corporation.

Spanning the Last Miles

For most people, the bottleneck that prevents blazing fast Internet performance occurs on the last few miles between your home or business and the provider of your Internet connection. Although cable modems and DSL service on phone lines are high-speed technologies that continue to improve, high-speed Internet service for those media are not available everywhere. If a company wants to offer Internet service, and doesn't happen to already run wires to its potential customers, it basically has two choices: land-based wireless stations and satellites. For out-of-the-way places or people on the go, coming wireless and satellite technologies can offer that last leg of communication.

Fixed Wireless to Your Building

Fixed wireless networks can make the Internet connection to your home or business without the wires. This type of network provides high-speed Internet access from wireless providers directly to homes and businesses. Fixed wireless networks work by transmitting voice and data between a network base station and a customer's home and business.

There are both technological and business reasons why fixed wireless technology is geared up for rapid expansion in the near future. On the technology side, fixed wireless can provide high-speed Internet access to locations that don't have cable television or DSL service available. On the business side, it can give long-haul network players, such as AT&T and MCI WorldCom, control of their customers by providing the last few miles of service to homes and businesses.

If high-speed Internet service hasn't made it to your area yet from the phone company or cable television provider, fixed wireless in your area might let you make that connection. Although it might not be offered yet in your area, it might be on its way.

Fixed Wireless from AT&T

AT&T is already offering fixed wireless service (also referred to as *Fixed Local Loop*) to test markets around the United States. This service provides customers with high-speed Internet service and telephone service without any wires coming into their homes.

AT&T Wireless Group began offering AT&T Digital Broadband technology to customers in Fort Worth, Texas in March, 2000. The service included always-on Internet service (no phone line or dialing) for a monthly flat fee. It also supports multiple telephone lines. Digital Broadband refers to the capability to send multiple channels of digitized data over one communication medium.

The Digital Broadband service is planned for several other major cities in the United States. AT&T's projections are to have the services available to more than 1.5 million households in 6 markets by the end of the year 2000.

To expand the Digital Broadband service, AT&T has partnered with Motorola. AT&T will license the service to Motorola, which will in turn supply the equipment to Internet providers outside of the United States. In most places outside of the United States, customers pay a per-minute rate for Internet service. AT&T sees Digital Broadband as a cost-effective alternative to dial-up around the world.

The AT&T Digital Broadband service offers

➤ Up to four high-quality voice lines

➤ A 512Kbps connection to the Internet (with that increasing to 1Mbps by the end of 2000)

According to AT&T, it is currently licensed to provide wireless service to 94% of the United States population. Combine that with AT&T's cable television (and related Internet services), and AT&T is capable of being reconnected with just about every household in the United States that it was divested of in the 1980s. The difference now is that there are many more companies fighting for those customers.

MCI WorldCom and Sprint Fixed Wireless with MMDS

In 1999, MCI WorldCom and Sprint each began buying fixed wireless companies in its strategy to reach the last few miles to their customers. The companies settled on a technology called Multipoint Multichannel Distributed Service (MMDS). Here are a few facts about MMDS Internet service:

➤ MMDS uses wireless frequencies between 2150–2162MHz and 2500–2690MHz that are licensed from the FCC.

➤ One transmitter can serve a 35-mile radius (a total area of more than 3,000 square miles).

➤ Transceivers (13.5×13.5-inch diamond-shaped units) must be placed on houses or businesses that have a line-of-sight to the transmitter.

➤ Transmitters are placed up as high as they can go (on mountains or Chicago's Sears Tower, for example).

➤ The transceiver communicates with a wireless modem (still no wires), which then connects to the customer's PC or LAN.

The FCC originally licensed the MMDS part of the spectrum (in other words, the transmission ranges in the sky that are shared by television, radio, and other broadcast communications) for transmission of educational television. Although schools and universities originally used this part of the spectrum for broadcasting, licenses were later sold to commercial companies attempting to use MMDS to compete with cable and satellite television providers. Those commercial companies lost the battle. MCI WorldCom and Sprint have now moved the MMDS battlefield to take on the same competitors (cable and satellite) for the Internet service market.

The FCC has recently been approving licenses to use the MMDS part of the spectrum for two-way communication (such as Internet service). It was originally intended for just one-way communication (such as broadcast educational television). MCI Worldcom and Sprint are currently looking to change licenses to allow two-way communication service for more than 100 markets. They hope to have those approvals before the end of 2000.

In early 2000, MCI WorldCom began testing fixed wireless Internet service in several markets. Business and residential customers signed up in Baton Rouge, LA; Memphis, TN; and Jackson, MS. The services are currently named WarpOne and Warp 310, although the final commercial names haven't been decided yet. Here are the differences between the two services:

➤ **WarpOne**   This is basically Internet service for small- and medium-sized businesses. Symmetrical data transmission (same speed in both directions) is available at speeds of about 1.5Mbps. (Prices haven't been set, but are expected to range between $300 and $600 per month.)

➤ **Warp 310**   This Internet service is intended for the home. Transmission speeds of 310Kbps are expected. The service should cost about $40 per month.

MCI WorldCom had relied on its merger with Sprint to provide broad, nationwide coverage of MMDS Internet service. Despite the fact that their merger was not approved, both companies are continuing to pursue MMDS strategies.

Techno Tip

You may not need to have Internet services that provide the same rate of transmission in both directions. Cable modem and DSL services typically offer products that let you download much faster than you can upload data. The assumption is that a home user will be downloading music, video, and data files, but not providing much data to others. A business, on the other hand, might have a Web server that requires more bandwidth to upload data to its customers.

Techno Tip

A competing technology to MMDS is Local Multipoint Distribution Services (LMDS). LMDS uses a higher band of the spectrum (28GHz) but covers shorter distances (about a 3-mile radius) than MMDS. So LMDS can be more expensive for companies to deploy because it takes more equipment to cover the same area as an MMDS transmitter. It also seems to be lagging behind MMDS in deployment.

LMDS works best in areas where there is concentrated traffic in a relatively small area. Because of a lack of standards, different vendors have taken different (and incompatible) approaches to producing LMDS equipment. Like MMDS, LMDS requires transceivers to have a line-of-sight to the transmitter and covers a 360-degree area around the transmitter.

LMDS does have some big guns behind it. Cisco Systems and Motorola set up a company called SpectraPoint Wireless (`http://www.spectrapoint.com`) to provide LMDS equipment.

Satellite

For years, satellite dishes have been able to bring television programming into homes in remote locations (or to people who were discontent with their local cable company). Soon satellites will be available to bring two-way Internet service to the home or business as well.

Broadband satellite Internet service works by transmitting Internet data from ground-based transmitters to a satellite. The satellite, in turn, transmits data to a satellite dish that has a clear line of sight to the ground-based satellite. The satellite connection can then serve multiple computers or other Internet devices at high speeds from a single dish.

Several different companies will be offering two-way satellite broadband service in the near future. Hughes Network Systems currently offers Internet service that combines modem and satellite Internet access. Soon, full two-way Internet service will be available from iSKY and Gilat-To-Home.

iSKY Satellite High Speed Internet

In 2001, iSKY (`http://www.isky.net`) expects to offer broadband satellite Internet service to customers in North America and Latin America. Using a high-speed modem, up to eight PCs or other Internet devices can connect to the Internet via a satellite dish. Figure 16.1 illustrates the iSKY service.

Figure 16.1

iSKY will bring Internet service to home and business via satellite.

Here are some of the features of iSKY's satellite service:

➤ Offers speed of up to 1.5Mbps, which is nearly 30 times faster than 56Kbps modems.

➤ Although they haven't yet been formally announced, equipment prices are expected to be comparable to the cost of mini-dish satellite television equipment ($200-$400). Plus, there will be a flat monthly fee for unlimited Internet access.

➤ In the future, iSKY hopes to offer interactive television.

Gilat-To-Home High-Speed Satellite Internet

High-speed satellite Internet is expected to be available from Gilat-To-Home (http://www.gilat2home.com) before the end of 2000. Gilat Satellite Networks and Microsoft are offering the service. With Gilat-To-Home (GTH), the same satellite dish can be used for television or Internet connections. Here's how it works:

1. You attach a 24×36-inch satellite disk to your roof, a pole, or any other location with an unobstructed view of the southern sky.

2. Attach the dish, via two standard coaxial cables, to either a PC (with a GTH transmit/receive card) or an external GTH satellite modem.

3. You transmit and receive data from the GTH satellite, which communicates with a GTH Hub, which communicates with the Internet.

4. The same satellite can also receive DISH Network television programming from the EchoStar DISH Network Broadcast Center, via the DISH Network satellite.

Transmission speeds are expected to be about 10 times faster than standard modem speeds for receiving content and twice as fast when sending it. Pricing for the service has not been determined yet. As with other satellite Internet services, its greatest benefit over DSL and cable is that it offers comparable always-on, high-speed service, but makes it available in remote areas.

Hughes Network Systems DirecPC Satellite Internet

Hughes Network Systems offers a combination satellite/phone line system that is available today for accessing the Internet. Incoming data is provided via the DirecPC satellite (http://www.direcpc.com), while outgoing data is sent out over standard telephone lines. This arrangement can be efficient if you download or view a lot of data, but don't send much. Here's how it works:

1. You request a Web address from your browser, which is sent out through your modem.

2. Using a "tunneling" technique, the request is forwarded past your ISP and directed to the DirecPC Network Operations Center (NOC). (Tunneling is when data passes through a public network without being interpreted along the way.)

3. The NOC requests the data from the Web site, and then uploads that data to the DirecPC satellite.

4. The satellite beams the information down to you.

Whatever I just said, Figure 16.2 from Hughes Network Systems shows it.

Figure 16.2

With DirecPC, data goes out over phone lines and comes in over high-speed satellite networks.

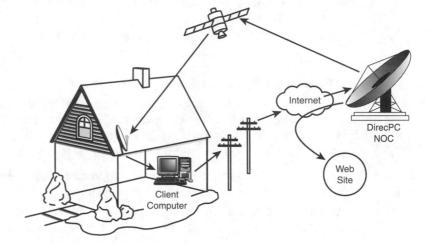

The advantage of using DirecPC is that you can get significantly faster downloads of information (up to 400Kbps). However, disadvantages are that you still need to have a dial-up ISP account and if you need to upload files, you are still limited by the speed of your dial-up connection. Prices for the service range from $19.99 to $49.99 per month.

Taking Your LAN Wireless

To Internet providers, the last mile stretches from their facilities to your home or office. To you, the end of your network includes the devices you connect to your own local network. For most of us, our present local network consists of wires, although the future might be wireless.

Without a doubt, there are a variety of network devices that are in the pipeline and coming our way. Unlike some of the fixed wireless technologies for using MMDS and LMDS spectrums, there are several accepted standards that are driving the development of home and office wireless devices. These include the initiatives discussed next.

Bluetooth (http://www.bluetooth.com) is a special interest group that is helping standardize how a variety of handheld and other mobile devices can connect to a Bluetooth-enabled wire-bound connection. You will not only be able to communicate between your wireless and wired devices, but you will also be able to easily synchronize your appointments, files, or other items.

For connecting home or office equipment without running wires, groups such as the Infrared Data Association (http://www.irda.org) and the HomeRF (http://www.homerf.org) have created several standards. IrDA set specifications for infrared communications among computers and peripheral devices. HomeRF specifies communication protocols between home-networked devices.

Preparing for the Next Generation Internet (IPv6)

Unlike the Y2K problem, no one is scrambling to figure out what needs to be done to overcome many of the shortcomings of the original design of the Internet. In the early 1990s, efforts began to set how the current Internet (based on Internet Protocol version 4—IPv4— protocols) will evolve into the next generation Internet (based on IPv6 protocols). By understanding what is in store for us with IPv6, you can understand some of the current flaws and future prospects for the Internet.

IPv6 stands for Internet Protocol Version 6. Limitations to the current IPv4 standard (don't worry about missing IPv5, because there is no such animal), were noted as Internet designers began projecting the growth of the Internet into the future.

Note

For more information on Bluetooth, IrDA, and HomeRF, see Chapter 18, "Networking Your Kitchen Appliances"

Huge growth has drained available IP addresses and caused routing tables to become too large be to handled efficiently. Routing tables are lists of information that describe where data needs to go to reach its destination. Security concerns have been raised about the large amounts of unencrypted data flowing across the Internet. Difficulties in assigning IP addresses and discovering the types of devices being connected is becoming cumbersome as more wireless devices connect to the Internet. IPv6 addresses these issues by creating new protocols and standards.

So, if IPv6 is so great and so well defined today, why has it not already been implemented on the entire Internet (or at least on a small part of it)? The simple reason is that to most Internet providers it ain't broke, so they don't want to fix it (yet). The more detailed reasons are described up ahead, right after I tell you what IPv6 is designed to do.

When TCP/IP (the suite of protocols that run the Internet) was first created by the United States Department of Defense in the 1960s, most computers were large mainframes. Many experts expected the trend of large machines handling more and more people to continue. As computers got smaller and more plentiful, and as the possibility of millions of handheld devices needing IP addresses appeared, TCP/IP gurus realized that IP addresses were going to run out.

Several stop-gap approaches were implemented to slow the consumption of IP addresses. Some of those measures include the following:

➤ **Classless Inter-Domain Routing (CIDR)**   The class-based system of handing out IP addresses was inefficient. Organizations that needed IP addresses tended to get too few or too many if they were given a whole class of IP numbers. CIDR allowed a finer granularity in assigning IP addresses, so organizations could more easily get the exact number they needed. In other words, an organization could get the right amount of IP addresses instead of being assigned a pool of numbers that was either too big or too small.

CIDR also helped make routing more efficient, by assigning the same type of hierarchy to IP addresses that is used with domain names. In other words, organizations that own a pool of IP addresses are responsible for maintaining routing information to the computers associated with that pool of addresses.

➤ **Private IP addresses**   Instead of having a public IP address for every computer on a local network, a network administrator would use (and reuse) a set of private IP addresses for the local computers. The addresses of the computers on the local network would only be visible to the router that acted as the gateway between the local network and the Internet. In that way, any private network in the world could reuse those private addresses.

Note

See Chapter 3, "Using a World-Wide Network (the Internet)," for a more complete description of CIDR and private IP addresses.

➤ **Proxy servers**   By having a proxy server on a LAN that is connected to the Internet, every computer on the LAN could have all requests for Internet access go through the proxy server. As with private IP addresses, the Internet has no direct knowledge of the computers on the LAN. As far as the Internet knows, all requests from that LAN come from the proxy server.

Although the techniques I just described have slowed consumption of IP addresses, they haven't stopped it. Today, the mobile telephone industry and makers of handheld devices are starting to ask for millions of IP addresses. The new IP addressing scheme for IPv6 is set to address this problem.

How IPv6 Addressing Works

Today's IP addresses (IPv4) use a 32-bit address space, which consists of four dot-separated numbers between 0 and 255. So a current IP address might look something like this:

123.123.12.12

The proposed IP address for the future (IPv6) uses a 128-bit address space. That's four times larger than the current IPv4 address. But hold on. That doesn't mean that there are four times as many addresses. You would have to multiply the number of 32-bit addresses by 32, then again by 32, and again by 32. I'm told (although I haven't done the math myself) that the number of possible addresses is:

340,282,366,920,938,463,463,374,607,431,768,211,456 (which is 2 to the 128th power)

In other words, a lot! Each IP address for IPv6 would contain a Format Prefix indicating the address type. There are three types of IPv6 addresses:

➤ **Unicast**   Identifies a single interface. The packet is sent to one and only one place.

➤ **Anycast**   Identifies a set of interfaces. The packet can be sent to any one of the interfaces identified by the address. In other words, there might be several different computers or network interfaces that could satisfy the request.

➤ **Multicast**   Identifies all computers or other types of equipment in a set of interfaces. A packet sent to a multicast address is sent to all interfaces in the set. There are no broadcast addresses in IPv6 because that feature can be handled by multicast addresses. In other words, instead of a computer just broadcasting information that is intended for all computers on a network, it can send a multicast packet that is directed to all computers on a network.

Many parts of the address structure are currently unassigned. In fact, only about 15% of the space is used initially, with the rest reserved for future use.

There are different ways of representing an IPv6 IP address. To get the 128-bit address, the number representing that address is split into 8 16-bit pieces. Instead of using dots, each piece is separated by a colon. So the preferred form of the address is:

x:x:x:x:x:x:x:x

So, an actual IPv6 address might look like:

1080:BA98:800:483:BA98:7654:200C:417A

To shorten the way of expressing the address, you can use several techniques. You could use "::" to compress one or more parts containing only zeros. The loopback address could be expressed as 0:0:0:0:0:0:0:1. (Loopback is when a computer requests its own address without going out on the network. This can be used for testing purposes.)

To route IP addresses, IPv6 would use basically the same routing method used by CIDR. This classless method is much more efficient than the original IPV4 class-based method of routing. Each organization that had a set of IP addresses would be responsible for all routing to those addresses. So, for example, if I were responsible for my company network and had a network address that contained 1,000 host addresses, any packets destined for any of my 1,000 hosts would come to my network router, and then be forwarded by my router to the correct host.

Secure from the Get Go

Secure transactions on today's Internet (IPv4) are done primarily using the Secure Sockets Layer (SSL) protocol. SSL provides authentication (verifying that the other computer is who it says it is) and confidentiality between two end systems (such as the computer you browse from and the Web server that serves the page).

IPv6 takes security to a lower layer, providing data encryption and authentication between the hosts and subnetworks that pass data along the way. In other words, there is security implemented between each hop along the way to a packet's destination. This makes transmission more secure.

Stopping Spoofing

The term for a computer impersonating another computer by using its IP address is called *spoofing*. Most denial-of-service attacks, where a computer is overloaded by requests that cause it to crash or at least become so slow that it's unusable, use spoofing to hide the identity of the attacker's computer. Although spoofing is hard to detect with IPv4, spoofing becomes very difficult to get away with in IPv6.

Security in IPv6 is implemented using security header extensions in each packet (that is, more information in the beginning of each packet to help make the data it contains more secure). The extensions can help ensure, with a good degree of certainty, that a packet came from the host it said it did. This level of security can help prevent malicious people from setting up a host computer to impersonate another computer.

Foiling Sniffers

Network traffic analyzers, also referred to as *sniffers*, can be used by malicious people to read the content of packets. By using encryption between each hop on a network, IPv6 can effectively foil (or at least severely slow down) anyone who is sniffing packets for private information (such as passwords or credit card numbers).

IPv6 packets have encryption headers that contain information on what encryption key to use, as well as providing various handshaking information (which is used to verify each computer along the way). So someone sniffing a packet would not be able to read its contents without knowing the encryption method used and having the ability to break that encryption.

Other IPv6 Features

There are other features in IPv6 that seem to get less airtime, but are very valuable in some cases:

➤ **Mobile Computing**   IPv4 was not set up well for finding and assessing mobile computers. Features have been added to IPv6 that allow mobile computers to be discovered and auto-configured. Basically, an IPv6 handheld device or portable PC could create a local IPv6 address for itself.

➤ **Real-time support**   If a computer on the Internet today needs a higher quality of service than other devices, it's basically out of luck. Real-time quality of services, which is necessary for such services as video conferencing, can be requested in IPv6 to create an end-to-end flow between the client and server that meets the application's needs.

Stepping Up to the Plate (When Will IPv6 Take Hold?)

Despite the fact that test versions of IPv6 have been up and running for several years now, the Internet community is not racing to upgrade its equipment to IPv6. Most deployment and testing so far of IPv6 has been done by scientific and non-profit organizations, many of which have their people test IPv6 in their spare time.

Being the first to upgrade to IPv6 is not something most network backbone providers or ISPs want to do. There is still a lot of networking equipment out there that does not support IPv6. And even though there are serious problems looming with IPv4, it still seems to work for the moment. Implementing IPv6 has still not been tried out in a large scale, making it a substantial risk to network providers that need to keep their networks up to survive.

So what will be the catalyst to getting IPv6 implemented on the commercial Internet? Some people believe that the wireless device industry might just be that catalyst.

The 3rd Generation Partnership Project (3GPP) is the standards forum for the 3G mobile system. Recently, a proposal by Nokia to use IPv6 as the protocol for future IP multimedia services was accepted by the 3GPP. The backing by this industry group, which is supported by members who expect to produce millions of devices in the coming years that will need to access the Internet, could be the first big step toward commercial implementations of IPv6.

IPv6 can remove roadblocks that are currently impeding the mass production of wireless devices. In particular, problems of limited IP addresses and the promise of support for self-configuring mobile devices are major features for vendors of mobile Internet devices. IPv6 networks that support mobile devices could give IPv6 the test bed it needs for acceptance by the wider Internet community.

Where To From Here?

Now that you know some of the enhancements on the horizon for the Internet, check out descriptions of applications that might take advantage of the coming Internet in

Chapter 17, "Prepare for an Explosion of Network Content." Then you might want to read about new network devices that will soon be available in Chapter 18.

The Least You Need to Know

Right now, the least you need to know about the future of the Internet is this:

➤ Fiber-optic networks have been expanding in both distance and capacity to carry long-haul Internet data.

➤ To connect the last few miles between network providers and home or small-business customers, a boom in fixed wireless networks is expected in the next few years.

➤ To offer Internet service to remote locations, satellite providers will soon begin offering two-way Internet service.

➤ Standards for connecting wireless devices in your home or office (such as IrDA and Bluetooth) have been put in place. There are some products already set to connect these devices. More are on the way.

➤ The next generation Internet specifications are already in place under the title Internet Protocol version 6 (IPv6).

➤ IPv6 offers several major enhancements, including a greatly expanded set of IP addresses and better security at the network level.

➤ Other enhancements to IPv6 include features that help discover and config-ure mobile devices, as well as features that allow improved quality of service for applications needing real-time service.

➤ Implementation of IPv6 has been slow to take hold. Adoption of IPv6 as the standard for future wireless Internet service by the 3GPP standards forum for mobile communicaiton could bring about the first commercial implementa-tions of IPv6 networks.

Preparing for an Explosion of Network Content

In This Chapter

➤ Learn about coming interactive television offerings

➤ Understand how content for handheld devices is expected to grow in the near future

➤ Learn what music, video, and virtual reality might gain from improved bandwidth and clearer business models

➤ See how Application Service Providers can deliver out-of-the-box Web-based solutions for your business

---

Big companies with big money are putting the network infrastructure in place to be able to pump a lot of information into your home or business. Millions of new mobile devices in coming years are going to be Internet-ready. You don't need all that just to look at your Aunt Betty's Web page.

The question is: How will "more" Internet translate into more content and what will that content be like? To make some guesses, here are two growth areas that are expected to result in new Internet content:

➤ **More bandwidth**   Applications that were once stifled by limited bandwidth will soon have the widespread network performance they need. In particular, content that requires a smooth flow of data or fast network response can benefit from more bandwidth.

➤ **More portable devices**   Most Web content is geared toward large screens. Especially in the business arena, content needs to be scaled down and targeted to fit on handheld and portable devices.

This chapter looks at some cool new ways that you will be able to use your home, office, and portable networks in the years to come. It also looks at how existing applications will become easier and more fun to use.

Merging Television and the Internet

The promise of broadband communications has brought a lot of new interest into the interactive television arena. Companies such as AT&T, AOL/Time Warner, Microsoft, and Cisco Systems have already made significant investments into interactive television.

One belief that most people who follow the interactive television industry can agree on is this: Whatever technologies survive will need a good business model. Earlier attempts to expand the reach of cable television and Internet services didn't do much to integrate the two types of services. On the TV side, simply expanding to hundreds of channels became expensive to maintain. On the Web side, products such as WebTV, which are predominantly Web-oriented, have not caught on significantly.

Plans for technologies that will bring together television and the Internet seem more focused on blending the two. Dozens of companies are scurrying around now to define what this new blended medium will look like. The following sections describe what some of the companies with the clout (and the wires) to make it happen are doing.

AT&T Interactive TV

AT&T, with its AT&T Broadband business unit, is putting technology in place that will synchronize interactive content with traditional television programming in its new Interactive Television (ITV) platform. Currently, AT&T Broadband offers cable television and high-speed Internet services to about 16 million customers in the United States. ITV could be incorporated to reach those customers.

AT&T's ITV will allow real-time interactions with television programming, e-commerce, targeted advertising, and customer feedback. On the consumer end of this platform will be new digital set-top boxes that manage television and data. Trials of the new technology have begun and the first commercial availability is expected by the end of 2000 or beginning of 2001.

To make interactive television a reality, AT&T has connected with several different companies to add pieces to its platform. It has announced that it will license TV Platform software (for set-top box and television server software) from Microsoft, add printing capabilities from Hewlett-Packard, and incorporate interactive television applications from RespondTV.

RespondTV Interactive Television Applications

RespondTV (http://www.respondtv.com) makes client and server products that let television operators, programmers, and advertisers create interactive television content. Content can include software for direct customer response, e-commerce, online polling, sales lead generation, and contests.

To create RespondTV content, the company relies on several different software standards, including HTML, JavaScript, and Advanced TV Enhancement Forum (ATVEF) content (see the sidebar on ATVEF, later in this chapter). According to RespondTV, here is how its service works:

1. The broadcaster sends video content to the cable television or satellite provider. Simultaneously, the broadcaster sends enhanced content over the Internet to RespondTV servers.

2. The cable or satellite provider sends the video content to the consumers' set-top boxes.

3. The RespondTV servers set up a two-way communication path between the servers and the client set-top boxes.

4. Sales leads and orders are transmitted from the set-top boxes to the RespondTV servers.

5. The results of the interactions are returned to the broadcaster.

The recent association with AT&T could bring RespondTV to millions of households. In the meantime, if you live in the San Francisco, California area you can receive RespondTV content from station KBHK. To get the content, you would need a set-top box from Liberate, Microsoft, PowerTV, or another company that sells standards-based set-top boxes.

Companies that currently provide RespondTV content include the World Wrestling Federation, CDNOW, Ralston Purina, Bloomberg Television, Domino's Pizza, Epicurious.com, Ford, and 1-800-Flowers.com. Here are some examples of some of the content being provided:

➤ **World Wrestling Federation (WWF) Smackdown**   Offered interactive sales of T-shirts during WWF programming.

➤ **CDNOW**   Offered a direct-response coupon campaign during a Melissa Etheridge concert.

➤ **Ralston Purina**   Offered a free "Incredible Puppy Care Kit" during its commercial for Puppy Chow.

Check This Out

Having all the players agree on standards for producing any new technology can increase its chances of being widely accepted. The Advanced TV Enhancement Forum (`http://www.atvef.com`) has set out to define the protocols used to create enhanced TV and a lot of industry leaders have signed on.

The ATVEF Enhanced Content Specification centers on HTML (the stuff Web pages are made from) to create enhanced TV content. The specification defines real-time events called "triggers" that alert users that enhanced content is available. Receivers can implement their own way of letting users turn enhanced content on or off.

ATVEF has more than 100 members that span different industries interested in enhanced TV: broadcasters, television programmers, platform providers, and transport providers. More than a dozen founding members include Intel Corporation, Microsoft (and WebTV), NBC Multimedia, Sony Corporation, Disney, and Warner Brothers (now Time Warner).

Liberate Technologies Enhanced Television Content

Liberate Technologies (`http://www.liberate.com`) produces products for delivering and producing Internet-enhanced broadcast content. To give you an idea of the clout behind this technology, Cisco Systems recently made a $100 million investment in the company. Also, Receivers for AOLTV from Phillips Electronics incorporates the Liberate TV platform.

Because Liberate's products rely heavily on HTML and JavaScript standards, Liberate claims that companies can reuse or quickly create content for enhanced TV. Web content can be reused and the same people that create Web pages can quickly get up to speed creating interactive television content. Figure 17.1 illustrates how enhanced TV information can appear on the screen with regular television content.

Cable & Wireless (CWIX) (http://www.cwix.net), a multinational Internet backbone provider, was one of the first major companies to roll out interactive content based on Liberate's enhanced TV software. CWIX's digital, two-way interactive cable television service is now being sold to customers in London, Manchester, and other parts of England.

Figure 17.1

Purchase a cookbook during a cooking show with Liberate enhanced TV.

By the year 2000, CWIX had more than 40 content providers offering enhanced television content. Content providers such as British Airways now allow customers to book flights and check flight schedules from their televisions.

AOLTV

Not to be left behind by the other heavyweights in the Internet industry, America Online is offering its own interactive television service called AOLTV. Essentially, AOLTV lets customers add AOL Internet services to their existing cable television connections.

Basically, AOLTV extends your AOL membership to the television screen. You will be able to use your AOL screen name to send email, do instant messaging, participate in chats, and browse the Web. You will be able to use many of these interactive features while your television show is still playing.

An AOLTV Program Guide will let you organize channels into content categories and view up to three days of television listings. Interactive features let you click on shows that interest you to see descriptions. Also, you will be able to store your favorite television stations in lists, much as you store bookmarks or favorites on your Web browser.

If you already have cable television service, you can purchase an AOLTV set-top box (manufactured by Philips Electronics) to connect to the service. This product includes the set-top box, a 56Kbps modem, a wireless keyboard (with batteries), coaxial cables, and telephone cords.

Booming Wireless Applications

Hold your portable telephone next to your computer screen and you will make a startling discovery: You can't fit as much stuff on your telephone screen. The small screen size is perhaps the most obvious, although not the only, challenge facing companies that want to sell you a multi-network phone or PDA that connects to the Internet. Other limitations include

➤ Limited hardware (memory, storage, and processors)

➤ Limited bandwidth

➤ Limited ability to input data

The solutions to these problems are new wireless applications.

So far, Internet applications for handheld devices tend to be practical and business oriented. Mobile people tend to travel, so there are weather, travel booking, and mapping applications. They also tend to be affluent, so there are applications for accessing financial information and shopping sites.

The following sections describe some of the companies offering Internet service to portable devices, as well as applications that are becoming available to use with these services.

Check This Out

The Wireless Application Protocol (WAP) is a standard for producing Web content for wireless devices. The WAP Forum (http://www.wapforum.com) and its ongoing work are described in Chapter 18, "Networking Your Kitchen Appliances?" A similar standard—the Handheld Device Markup Language (HDML)—is described in a sidebar, later in this chapter.

Digital PocketNet Service from AT&T

Wireless Internet access is available today using AT&T's Digital PocketNet Service
(http://www.att.com/pocketnet). You can use the same Internet-ready phone to
make telephone calls and access the Internet. Currently, you need either an Ericsson
R280LX or a Mitsubishi MobileAccess T250 phone to use the PocketNet service.

More than 40 Internet content providers are available to use with the AT&T
PocketNet service. The following is a list of the premier PocketNet content providers:

➤ **ABCNEWS.com**   Provides coverage of
news, sports, business, technology, and
entertainment. News stories are updated
continuously, 24 hours a day.

➤ **Barnes & Noble.com**   Lets you buy
books, software, and music online. It also
lets you check the status of your orders.

➤ **eBay**   Allows you to search for auction
items, make new bids, or check on existing bids on eBay.

➤ **ESPN.com**   Lets you access ESPN.com
to get the latest sports scores and information.

➤ **MapQuest**   Provides maps, directions,
and other travel services.

➤ **Travelocity.com**   Lets you make flight
arrangements and view flight schedules.

Figure 17.3 shows an example of a Mitsubishi
Mobile Access T250 wireless phone displaying
a menu for access to ABCNEWS.com information.

Check This Out

Digital PocketNet Internet service is
provided by a different network
than the network that provides the
wireless voice service. For that reason, there are places where phone
service will be available but not
Internet service. Click the
Coverage Map link from the
PocketNet home page to get more
information about Internet coverage
areas.

Mobile Web from Verizon Wireless

Verizon Wireless (http://www.verizonwireless.com) offers its Mobile Web service in
more than 60 cities across the United States. Like AT&T's PocketNet, you can trade
stock, purchase music and books, and get the weather. The uniting of Bell Atlantic
Mobile, AirTouch Cellular, PrimeCo, and GTE Wireless to form Verizon Wireless has
made it a formidable company in the wireless arena. Along with commercial content,
Mobile Web allows you to set up your own personal page. When you update content

from your desktop, you can see that content is immediately updated on your hand-set. This personal page, called MyVZW.com, lets you set alerts, manage email, and manage other information.

Using the Mobile Web phone, you can view any Web site that supports HDML markup. Some HDML sites will already appear on the Mobile Web browser from your handset.

Techno Tip

The Handheld Device Markup Language (HDML) is a standard for creating Web content for wireless devices. The World Wide Web Consortium (http://www.w3c.org) is responsible for defining the HDML standard. These are the same people who standardize HTML content.

HDML defines mechanisms for displaying information and navigating from hand-held devices. Like other wireless Internet protocols, HDML relies on navigation of discrete sets of information called cards.

Palm Handheld Internet Access

Using a Palm VII connected organizer, you can access the Internet via the Palm.Net Wireless Communication Service. Internet coverage is available in more than 260 cities in the United States, with most of that coverage concentrated in the East, Midwest, and along the West coast.

A technique called Web Clipping is used to develop Internet content for the Internet-enabled Palm VII devices. Web clipping applications are like little Web pages that can fit on Palm displays. Palm maintains a library of Web Clipping applications at http://www.palm.net/apps. There are Web clipping applications available for financial, news, travel, entertainment, shopping, and other types of content.

Improvements in Network Content

A decade ago, most computer network applications served corporate users, were built on many networking protocols, and relied on varied programming interfaces. Today's networking applications, and those of the near future, can be summed up with two acronyms:

> **TCP/IP**   The transport for the Internet and the Web.

> **HTML**   The language that provides the centerpiece of Web content.

Extensions to HTML have been created so developers can efficiently create the applications they need to access corporate databases and manage information resources. For the user, getting anything on the network from theater tickets to corporate reports can be just a Web address and, possibly, a password away. All that's needed is a connection to the Internet and a Web browser.

So, if everyone is agreeing on how to create and distribute networking applications, where will the great battles for the hearts and minds of users occur? Many future improvements on the Web might come from applications that have been around for a while, but have been waiting for bandwidth. Others will come from continuous small enhancements. And, yes, there probably will be some way-out new tools for using the Web.

New and Evolving Content

With every major category of Internet content, there are still significant challenges. Technologies exist today that could solve many of the technical issues facing the Internet. Rules to prevent abuses are more difficult to get everyone to agree on. In many cases, it is the rules that will govern how proprietary content (such as music and movies) is handled and how attacks against Internet sites are prevented that will set the direction of new Internet content.

Who Owns the Music?

You can find just about any popular musical recording on the Internet, download it, and play it without paying anyone a cent. Companies such as Napster (http://www.napster.com) believe they can provide a service that lets friends share music digitally that they copy from their CDs to the Internet. The recording industry calls this piracy. The two sides have taken their battle into the courts (with judges, at the time of this writing, leaning toward the side of the record companies).

Technologies for distributing and using digital music content are well accepted and understood today. MP3 is the predominant format for storing music on the Internet. Not only can these files be played on computers, but they can also be played on a wide variety of portable and stationary MP3 players.

Change in how music is distributed on the Internet in the near future will probably relate more to the business models that grow up around this technology than in the technology itself. On thing is for sure: Digital music on the Internet is not going away.

At some point, those who hold the copyrights to music will find a way to make a profit from music that is distributed from the Internet. Here are some of the ways that the Internet might evolve to allow you to legally get music on the Web:

➤ **Subscription services** Some people have suggested that music might be offered as a subscription service, simply charging you for every song that is downloaded. This model is similar to the one used by ISPs to sell Internet subscriptions. At first, ISPs charged a per-hour connect fee for Internet Service (just as long distance phone companies still do). Now all but a few simply charge a monthly subscription fee and try to make up the cost by having more subscribers.

➤ **Secure content**   Because it is difficult to control the distribution of music online, some record companies are looking at ways of encoding music so that it can only be played by those who own rights to play it. InterTrust Technologies (`http://www.intertrust.com`) produces digital rights management (DRM) tools for controlling the playback of protected material.

Another approach that could be used to deter the unauthorized sharing of protected material is a bit more complicated. Some media companies have suggested the possibility of having Internet backbone and service providers use monitoring techniques to only allow legally protected digital content to pass through their networks and block illegal content.

Video on the Web

Video was a prime candidate for content on the Web long before it was very practical. Using *streaming* technology, video content providers can direct live or stored video to your desktop and have it begin playing as it arrives.

The problem with the first videos delivered on the Internet had to do with limited bandwidth and poor playback tools. With low-speed modems, even small video clips could take minutes or hours to download. To conserve download times, images were usually only a few inches in size. Slow Internet connections would make playback bumpy and full of drop-outs. Even the best quality Web video couldn't approach the quality of cable television.

Video is an area that is expected to benefit mightily from increased bandwidth. As the new Internet standard (IPv6, described in Chapter 16, "To the Internet and Beyond") takes effect, transmission of video content should also improve because of quality of service features that will prevent packets of streaming data from being split up.

Many independent producers of short films and video clips have already started distributing video on the Web. These producers should be able to more efficiently deliver their content in the future. Here are some examples of Web sites that offer independent film and video content:

➤ **AtomFilms (`http://www.atomfilms.com`)**   Lets you play short independent films over the Web. Choose from its most popular and most highly rated films. View interviews with the directors and actors.

➤ **Ifilm (`http://www.ifilm.com`)**   Play and review independent films from this site or submit your own films.

As with music content, video and film clips distributed on the Internet can provide a venue for filmmakers who don't have access to the commercial television or film industry. As tools for creating video improve (and come down in price) and distribution methods become faster, you can expect more and higher quality video content on the Web in coming years.

Exploring Virtual Worlds

A few years ago, predictions for the future of the Internet usually included virtual reality. The belief was that some day, instead of using a Web browser people would enter virtual worlds to browse the Web. Imagine walking down virtual store aisles to choose products or walking through a virtual zoo to learn about animals. Instead of plain links, you could exit a world through a door and join another world on the other side.

Virtual Reality Modeling Language (VRML) was a standard developed to create virtual reality content. Content could be viewed by a separate VRML viewer or by using plug-ins within your Web browser. You could move around in the virtual world using your mouse and keyboard. Here are some features of VRML worlds:

➤ **Viewpoints**   Lets you move directly to a preset location in the virtual world.

➤ **Links**   Provides links to other Web locations by selecting objects in the virtual world.

➤ **Live action/animation**   Allows objects to move (walk, drive, dance, and so on) by themselves or in response to actions by the user.

➤ **Multi-user capability**   Lets several users be in a virtual space simultaneously.

➤ **Streaming media**   Supports the playing of live audio, video, or other multimedia effects to stream (play continuously) in the virtual world.

➤ **Java**   Lets Java code be used in virtual worlds. (Java and JavaScript are programming languages developed by Sun Microsystems for creating secure, Web-based applications that can be displayed and used by all major Web browsers.)

➤ **Internationalized capability**   Lets text in different languages be available in the virtual worlds.

➤ **Cross-platform capability**   Allows virtual worlds to play on different computer platforms (PCs, workstations, and so on).

VRML has not caught on as a Web navigation medium. Probably the biggest reason for this is that it takes up so many resources. It takes resources to create VRML worlds, bandwidth to deliver it to desktops over the Web, and powerful video hardware to render it smoothly. You never know. With more powerful networks and workstations, virtual worlds might still catch on.

It's easy to try out virtual reality from your browser. Start by downloading a VRML plug-in from http://www.netscape.com/plugins. Click the link to 3D & Animation plug-ins. I selected the Cortona VRML client from Parallel Graphics (http://www.parallelgraphics.com). Follow the instructions for installing the plug-in within your browser. (Plug-ins are compatible with Internet Explorer as well.)

Here are some of the things you can do in a typical virtual world:

➤ **Move around**   Hold down the left mouse button on the scene and move the mouse to navigate the world. Some virtual worlds also let you swim or fly through them. Right-click the world to see a list of navigation. Click viewpoints to jump to a particular place in the scene.

➤ **Select objects**   Some objects have links or other objects associated with them. The selection might result in a video playing, a sound playing, a Web page being displayed, or the object playing some sort of animation.

➤ **Examine objects**   You can look at an object from all sides.

Some practical uses for VRML-based virtual worlds include anything in which a 3D view of an area or object could benefit someone. For example, a virtual tour of a city could give prospective tourists an idea of what a vacation would be like. A virtual house could show a prospective homeowner what a home would look like before it was built.

If you want to keep up with the latest initiatives to bring VRML virtual worlds to the Web, visit the 3DWeb home page at `http://www.vrml.org`.

Applications in a Box?

The focus on Web-based everything has helped create a new category of vendors called Application Service Providers (ASPs). If you have a medium-sized business without the resources to develop your own applications, ASPs can provide a fast and inexpensive way to get Web-based applications to suit your business needs.

Here are some of the prepackaged Web-based services you can connect with:

➤ **Web Portals**   There are ASPs that sell software to quickly get your business up and running on the Web with your own portal. For example, the 2Bridge (`http://www.2bridge.com`) 2Share out-of-the-box e-business portal software helps create a single gateway for employees, partners, and customers to collaborate in real time.

➤ **Personal Information Managers (PIMs)**   To make it easier to manage a business, Web-based information management software has been created. For example, CoolSync (`http://bookmarks.coolsync.com`) lets you store and access personal bookmarks from anywhere on the Web. EntryPoint (`http://www.entrypoint.com`) provides customized news and information service to your computer.

➤ **Desktops and Calendars**   A variety of companies offer Web-based desktops and calendars that you can use to organize yourself at work. One Web site to try is `http://www.desktop.com`.

To find more information about ASPs that might be able to help you going forward with your own instant Web applications, check out the Yahoo! listing of ASPs. You can reach it from the Yahoo! home page (`http://www.yahoo.com`) by selecting **Home**, **Business and Economy**, **Business to Business**, **Communications and Networking**.

Techno Tip

A *Web Portal* acts as a focal point for a business's communications needs. From the portal, employees, partners, and customers can find the communication path they need to connect with each other and share a common understanding of the business. A business can use its portal to align its business and technology strategies.

Where To From Here?

This chapter helped you understand the kinds of networking applications that are either just coming available or will soon be available. The next chapter, "Networking Your Kitchen Appliances?" describes a variety of network devices that are on the horizon for connecting to a local network or the Internet.

The Least You Need to Know

Right now, the least you need to know about the coming network applications is this:

➤ New interactive television initiatives are focusing on blending television and Internet content.

➤ Interactive television products, such as RespondTV, will synchronize e-commerce features with television programming.

➤ Limited hardware, bandwidth, and data entry poses challenges for new, scaled-down Internet content on handheld devices.

➤ Improved bandwidth could help video and virtual reality applications become more popular on the Web.

➤ The convergence of Web technologies had given rise to Application Service Providers. These ASPs can often provide out-of-the box solutions to business portal and information management needs.

Chapter 18

Networking Your Kitchen Appliances?

In This Chapter

➤ Learn who is charting the future of network appliances

➤ Learn about next generation wireless devices

➤ Understand initiatives to network household appliances

➤ Learn how home entertainment systems will benefit from Internet connections

"Coffee brewing is an art, but the distributed intelligence of the Web-connected world transcends art. Thus there is a strong, dark, rich requirement for a protocol designed expressly for the brewing of coffee. Coffee is brewed using coffee pots. Networked coffee pots require a control protocol if they are to be controlled."

Hyper Text Coffee Pot Control Protocol (HTCPCP/1.0), RFC 1324

Network Appliances of the Future

The idea of connecting something other than your personal computer to the Internet is not a new one. The somewhat-tongue-in-cheek Hyper Text Coffee Pot Control Protocol was inspired by other networked appliances: a Coke machine status monitor and a remotely operated Internet toaster. From all indications, there will be a lot more serious, and some not so serious, network appliances on the horizon.

Network appliances are a natural extension of today's explosive Internet growth. Why incur the overhead of a full-blown PC to do one specific task? Use scaled-down hardware, simplified software, and do one or two jobs very well. The first network appliances to hit the market do just that: They take a task that was formerly done on a computer and do it simply and efficiently on a more streamlined piece of hardware.

The idea of a networked coffee maker, however, is not relegated only to the network programmer with a sense of humor and too much time on his hands. There are several efforts underway to network common household appliances to make them more efficient and user friendly.

Charting the Course

Nobody wants to make a device that nothing else can talk to. For that reason, software and hardware vendors, research organizations, and consumer products manufactures are joining forces to set the course for the next generation of network devices. Some of the initiatives underway today include the following:

➤ **Bluetooth SIG** (`http://www.bluetooth.com`)   The Bluetooth special interest group is working toward standardizing wireless communications for mobile devices. This includes specifications for connectivity to the Internet.

➤ **Infrared Data Association** (`http://www.irda.org`)   IrDA is a non-profit group that creates specifications for infrared communications among computers and peripheral devices.

➤ **HomeRF** (`http://www.homerf.org`)   This organization specifies how wireless communication can be done between networked devices in the home.

➤ **Wireless Application Protocol Forum** (`http://www.wapforum.org`)   This group is developing standards for creating and displaying Web content on wireless devices. In particular, the WAP specification focuses on providing Web content to wireless phones, handheld devices, and other devices with small screens.

➤ **Jini Connection Technology** (http://www.sun.com/jini)   This is a specification from Sun Microsystems that provides a simple mechanism for devices to automatically connect on a network.

➤ **Universal Plug and Play** (`http://www.upnp.org`)   This is one of many Microsoft initiatives intended to set the course for the future of networking. UPnP is intended to standardize the hardware and protocols used for networked devices to Communicate.

These initiatives are discussed in the following sections.

Bluetooth Wireless Specification

The Bluetooth special interest group has set out to standardize how mobile computers, mobile phones, and portable handheld devices communicate. At the center of this group are "promoter companies," including 3Com, Ericsson, IBM, Intel, Lucent, Microsoft, Motorola, Nokia, and Toshiba. There are more than 1,700 Adopter and Associate member companies supporting the specification as well.

The Bluetooth motto is: "All the things that are connected by cable can now be connected without." Devices that incorporate Bluetooth technology include a radio transceiver microchip. The chip can transmit both voice and data. Bluetooth claims "Before year 2002, the Bluetooth technology will be built into hundreds of millions of electronic devices."

Bluetooth defines protocols and services for the following types of devices:

➤ Mobile phones

➤ Handheld devices

➤ Wirebound connections

➤ Headsets

Bluetooth devices can connect to a wide-area network either through a wire-bound connection (xDSL modem, Local Area Network, or ISDN) or through a mobile phone that is Bluetooth enabled. The Bluetooth specification also lets you connect a variety of office equipment (printers, scanners, faxes, mouse, keyboard, and digital cameras) to a Bluetooth-enabled computer without cables.

The Bluetooth specification was specifically designed to use a minimum amount of power. By adjusting the amount of power used, based on the exact amount needed to reach the distances required, significant power savings can be achieved. For example, Bluetooth claims that a Bluetooth radio uses less than 3% of the power used by a modern mobile phone.

IrDA Infrared Technology

Devices that are IrDA-compatible can use infrared technology to provide cable-less communications. For example, you can use an IrDA-enabled digital camera to transfer images to an IrDA-enabled computer quickly without wires connecting them. You just hold the camera near the IrDA-enabled computer and the infrared waves transmit data between the two units.

The non-profit Infrared Data Association (http://www.irda.org) provides specifications for infrared technology that have already been incorporated into many different types of devices. These devices include

➤ Notebook/Portables

➤ Handheld PDAs

➤ Adapters/Dongles

➤ Digital/Electronic Capture Devices

➤ Printers

➤ Telephony

➤ Network Access

➤ Cameras

Although development of the IrDA specification continues, there are already dozens of products available for the types of equipment mentioned previously that use IrDA-compatible infrared technology. Current projects include a special interest group formation to standardize inter-appliance MP3 audio data exchange (MP3 is the most common format for storing and exchanging music on the Internet). There are also efforts underway to dramatically increase current data transmission rates.

HomeRF Wireless Home Networks

The HomeRF Working Group (http://www.homerf.org) was created to help standardize how wireless communication could be accomplished between consumer devices used in the home. The result has been a specification for wireless communications called the Shared Wireless Access Protocol (SWAP).

SWAP was designed to create products that support sharing of resources between home electronic equipment. According to HomeRF, the following features can be implemented using SWAP:

➤ Shared voice and data among PCs, peripherals, PC-enhanced cordless phones, and portable devices

➤ Internet access from anywhere in, or near, the home using portable display devices

➤ Shared Internet connection among all PCs and other devices

➤ Shared computing resources for homes with multiple PCs (including file sharing, modem sharing, and printer sharing)

➤ Forwarding of incoming telephone calls to any of the following: cordless telephones, fax machines, and voice mailboxes

➤ Ability to use a cordless telephone to review incoming voice, fax, and email messages

➤ Ability to voice-activate electronic systems from a cordless telephone

➤ Multi-player game playing on a PC

There are HomeRF products that are currently available from Intel, Compaq, and Cayman Systems. Intel's AnyPoint wireless home networking products are based on HomeRF standards.

Wireless Application Protocol Forum

In case you hadn't noticed, the screens on those dinky little wireless hand-held devices are much smaller than most Web pages. Yet, everyone keeps talking about accessing the Internet from such things. How can that be? The Wireless Application Protocol Forum (http://www.wapforum.com) was created to handle just that issue.

The Wireless Application Protocol (WAP) is intended to allow Web-based applications to scale across different transport options and device types. Content providers can use the tag-based Wireless Markup Language (WML) to provide content to wireless devices that will allow them to navigate Web content, provide data input, connect to hyperlinks, appropriately display text and images, and present forms.

Whereas HTML content is viewed in Web pages, WML content is displayed in small cards. Each WML card contains a small amount of information and possibly an action to take. Using a hand-held device, you can navigate among these cards.

Sun Microsystem's Jini Connection Technology

Jini Connection Technology is designed to allow different kinds of network devices to start up and automatically connect to a network. When the Jini device starts up, it connects to the network and describes to the network the kind of device it is and the services it offers.

Sun Microsystems has teamed up with several major companies to partner in developing Jini products. In particular, companies such as Whirlpool Corporation have begun work with Sun to provide solutions for connecting household products in a way that they can communicate on a network.

Microsoft's Universal Plug and Play

Microsoft has its own ideas about how to connect network devices and appliances, and it has signed up some big name supporters. The Microsoft strategy centers on its Universal Plug and Play (UPnP) specifications. These specifications allow many different types of devices to talk to each other directly or through intermediary devices (including set-top boxes that connect to your television and personal computers).

Like the Plug and Play initiative from Intel, Microsoft, and Compaq Computer in 1992, Universal Plug and Play is designed to simplify how devices connect together. With UPnP, however, the focus is on networked devices. A UPnP device should be able to automatically

➤ Get a network address

➤ Become known to other devices on the network

➤ Describe its features to other network devices

UPnP attempts to include existing Internet protocols (TCP/IP, HTTP, and so on) as well as the underlying media used by the Internet (Ethernet, HomeRF, and so on). UPnP also tries to take into consideration existing ways of directly connecting devices to computer buses (ISA, PCI, and so on).

Dozens of the largest players in the computer systems industry, chip equipment makers, electronics vendors, and others have signed on to support UPnP. Companies participating in the development and/or use of UPnP include 3Com Corp., Advanced Micro Devices, AT&T, Diamond-Multimedia Systems, Hewlett-Packard, Intel, Samsung, Gateway, IBM, and Sony Corp.

Next Generation Wireless Devices

A host of wireless devices have burst into the world of communications in the past few years. According to industry experts, that trend is expected to continue in full force.

Wireless versions of some office equipment have been available for some time now. These include printers, computer network adapters, and digital cameras. Although typically slower and more expensive than their wired counterparts, wireless devices can save you from the mess of running wires all over your office.

Some technological breakthroughs in the wireless area are expected to overcome barriers encountered with portable wireless devices. In particular, improvements in microprocessor chips needed for portable communications are being developed in the following areas:

➤ **Power consumption**   For a hand-held device to be an effective Web browser, chips that manage communications and display Web content need to use less power than current chips.

➤ **Cost**   To add wireless communication features to a variety of devices, the microprocessor chips can't add a huge amount of cost to the product. This is especially true of household appliances in which networking might be nice, but not necessary.

➤ **Heat**   More powerful microprocessor chips typically need a fan to keep cool. Low-heat microprocessor chips need to be developed that still provide acceptable processing power.

Several companies are producing inexpensive chips that can be used in wireless devices. Besides Intel, companies such as Advanced Micro Devices (AMD) and a fairly new company called Transmeta are working on lower-power x86 (that is, PC-compatible) chips that can go into a variety of network appliances.

Wireless Phones

The future direction of networking features in wireless phones and handheld devices is linked to several major areas:

➤ Improvements in wireless hardware

➤ Internet content

➤ Improvements in wireless network capacity and services

In the hardware area, handheld devices are limited by having slow transmission rates, limited memory and CPU, small screens, and a limited means of data input. There are many different efforts underway to improve the hardware.

Transmeta Makes a Run at Intel

After spending five years in highly secretive research and development, Transmeta (`http://www.transmeta.com`) emerged in 2000 with a viable contender in the portable x86-compatible chip market. The company's Crusoe chips take aim at portable devices. In particular, the 3200 family of chips were designed for use in Web pads (wireless Internet access devices), although the 5400 series is aimed at notebook computers.

As x86-compatible processors, the Crusoe chips will allow Web pads to offer a wide range of browser plug-ins and helper applications to work with different types of multimedia content. Power consumption is expected to be low and devices sporting the chip are expected to be thin and quiet.

Wireless Phone Hardware

More powerful and compact chips are driving improvements in mobile phone hardware. Ericsson is moving toward a single-chip solution for its devices. The company plans to incorporate functions that are done with several chips (radio, baseband, and flash) into a single chip. Battery life is improving all the time. Using new compression techniques, the maximum 14.4Kbps transmission speeds can be increased four times to 64Kbps.

Wireless Phone Content

One initiative underway to create a standard for producing and distributing content that can be used for wireless Internet access is the Wireless Access Protocol (described earlier). Today, data content that can be delivered to wireless phones is usually limited to email, paging, and faxes. Many other types of content, however, are being developed and are available by some wireless providers.

Improved Wireless Transmission

As for the transmission methods, Code Division Multiple Access (CDMA) has emerged as a future standard for high-capacity, global mobile networks. CDMA, which is licensed by Qualcomm, is built on standard IP packet data protocols. This gives CDMA advantages over other wireless technologies because TCP/IP and PPP protocols are already built in. (TCP/IP and PPP are described in Chapter 3.)

Wireless Phones that Support Data

Some wireless phones available today can access some data, as long as data service is available from the wireless provider. Here are a few examples of data-enabled wireless phones:

➤ **Nokia 6100 and 5100 Series**   The Nokia 6120, 6160, 6161, 6162, 5120, and 5160 wireless phones are data capable if you have access to an analog network. Transmission rates are very slow (maximum of 9,600bps or less). Additional hardware needs to be provided by an outside company (3Com) to enable data transmission. The Nokia 6190 and 5190 phones support transmission of data over a digital network, using Nokia data accessories.

You also need the Nokia data suite software package to send and receive email and faxes on your Nokia 6190 or 5190 phones. (Because of slow transmission rates, you should check with your service provider to see if it supports data transmissions to these phones.)

➤ **Ericsson KF 788**   The KF 788 has a lot of extras, including support for data and fax transmission, if those services are provided by your wireless provider.

➤ **Qualcomm QCP-860**   The QCP-860 offers a five-line display area. Data features include text messages, voicemail, pages, and a scratch pad for taking notes.

➤ **Motorola StarTAC ST7760**   The StarTAC ST7760 phone can switch between CDMA and digital networks. It offers a two-line text display.

Personal Handheld Computers

Palm Inc. (which was recently spun off from 3Com Corporation) is the leader in producing personal handheld computers. Besides managing such things as address books, planners, and other personal productivity tools, the popular Palm computers can be expanded to provide Internet access.

In mid-2000, Palm released the Palm Mobile Internet Kit. This kit provides access to email, messaging services, and a variety of Internet and Web content. The Palm Mobile Internet Kit uses a technology called *Web clipping*.

In lieu of coming standards for producing content that is geared toward mobile devices, Palm's Web clipping cuts out graphics and other extraneous information. Palm encourages the development of Web clipping applications. You can learn more about how to develop Web clipping applications from the PalmOS Web site: `http://palmos.com/dev/tech/webclipping`.

Other vendors offering handheld computing devices that are looking toward connectivity to the Internet include the following:

➤ **Casio**   This company offers the Casiopeia line of handheld devices. For networking capabilities, some models in this line offer optional modems and IrDA support (for infrared connectivity to your network).

➤ **Compaq**   The Aero and IPAQ lines of hand-held computers are offered by Compaq. Add PC cards to connect a modem or LAN. Infrared connectivity is also built in.

➤ **Hewlett-Packard**   HP offers the Jornada line of pocket PCs. There are more than a dozen models, ranging from the palm-size 540 series to the 820 mobile email companion.

Wireless Watches

With everything getting smaller these days, it shouldn't be surprising to find a company trying to put a portable computer on a wristwatch. One example of this technology is the IBM WatchPad.

IBM recently unveiled the IBM WatchPad. The WatchPad is about the size of a deck of cards. Although not yet on the market, the WatchPad includes a watch-size VGA screen that will let you display text, photographs, and animations. The device lets you synchronize data and images with a portable computer or PC via wireless connections. The wireless technology is Bluetooth-compatible. Dick Tracy would be proud.

Web Access Appliances

To reduce the cost of connecting to the Internet, as well as make the Internet less intimidating to new users, Web access appliances have been appearing recently. Here are a few entries into the Web access appliance market:

➤ **Intel Dot.Station**   Intel's first Web appliance product, the Dot.Station, is aimed at distribution through Internet service providers. This appliance offers integrated Internet access, email, built-in telephone, and applications for home organization. The Dot.Station is based on the Linux operating system. Prices are expected to compare to low-end PCs ($500–$700).

To simplify Internet start-up, Intel is encouraging ISPs to integrate their services into each Dot.Station. The appliance also includes the Intel System Management Suite, to let ISPs manage each Dot.Station remotely. Figure 18.1 is an example of the Intel Dot.Station.

➤ **Netpliance I-opener**   The I-opener Internet appliance has gone from a very inexpensive Internet access machine ($99) to just a fairly expensive machine ($299–$499). Some nice communications-specific features are built into the hardware, such as an email waiting light and a phone-in-use light.

➤ **eMachines MSN Web Companion**   eMachines, which already produces sub-$1,000 computers, plans to add a low-cost start-up computer for accessing the MSN network to its line. The MSN Web Companion (expected out near the end of 2000) is being designed for users who are new to email and the Internet. The machine will feature a 15-inch monitor (17- and 19-inch monitors also available), a keyboard with additional one-touch keys for Internet browsing, and a mouse.

Improvements in low-power, low-cost microprocessor chips are leading to new kinds of Web appliances. In particular, Transmeta is set to produce a Web Pad, in conjunction with S3 Inc., which contains a hard disk and offers wireless Internet connectivity. The Web Pad will include Transmeta's new Crusoe chip. It will also feature a 10.4-inch LCD display, a touch-activated interface, and long battery life. Figure 18.2 shows an example of the Transmeta Web Pad.

331

America Online has already signed up with Transmeta to produce a line of network-ready Internet Appliances. These devices will be based on the Mobile Linux operating system and will offer wireless communication for use around the house or office.

Meet George Jetson!

If companies such as Sunbeam Corporation, Microsoft, Sun Microsystems, and emWare have their way, having a home like the Jetsons' is not too far off. Several different efforts are currently underway to provide standards by which home appliances can be networked and controlled. Actual networked home appliances, in fact, are just around the corner.

Sunbeam's Home Linking Technology

Sunbeam Corporation has set out to become one of the leaders in networking home appliances. With products such as Mister Coffee coffee maker, First Alert smoke detectors, and a variety of Oster kitchen appliances, Sunbeam already has a range of products waiting to be networked.

In conjunction with Thalia Products Inc., which is owned by Sunbeam, and several computer industry companies, Sunbeam has developed Home Linking Technology (HLT). The goal of HLT is to provide a low-cost standard for connecting common household appliances to networks. In particular, Sunbeam is going for appliances that are used during high-stress periods (morning before work and evening dinner times). Any appliance that could gain through some level of automation or monitoring could be a potential target.

Everything from Coffee Pots to Electric Blankets

Sunbeam's first products to use HLT technology will be several HLT-Smart enabled appliances: an electric blanket, bathroom scale, blood pressure monitor, coffeemaker, and Mixmaster. These products are expected to roll out near the end of 2000.

To manage these appliances, Thalia Products Inc. is developing what it calls "gateway appliances." These gateway appliances include the following:

➤ **HomeHelper Kitchen Console**   A screen and controls for monitoring other networked devices.

➤ **HandHelper PDA**   A portable device for monitoring your networked devices from anywhere in the home. This device also can double as a cordless phone.

➤ **TimeHelper Alarm Clock**   Acts as the master time keeper for your networked appliances. It can also control and monitor your appliances (coffee maker, electric blanket, and so on).

The gateway appliances act as a central point for managing the appliances in the home. However, the gateway appliances can also act as gateways to outside networks. This can allow communications between the home appliances from the Internet or other networks.

To help promote HLT as a standard for connecting home appliances, Sunbeam and Thalia are making the HLT specifications available to other home appliance manufacturers. Thalia will license the technology. HLT is also designed to be compatible with other upcoming home appliance specifications, such as the Microsoft UPnP, emWare e-Smart, and Sun Microsoft Jini technologies.

How Home Linking Technology Works

Cost and convenience are cited as two challenges to overcome with networked household appliances. If people have to add the price of a full computer to the cost of a coffee maker or run cables around their houses, not many units are going to be sold.

To provide the networking features, Sunbeam's appliances will include low-cost memory and microprocessors. Communications is based on Radio Frequency (RF) technology, which doesn't require special wiring, or even need to be plugged in. This can allow control of appliances from hand-held PDAs.

Partners working with Sunbeam include SundBerg-Ferar (a product development company based in Detroit, Michigan) and emWare (a Salt Lake City-based company that provides embedded technology solutions). Zilog, Inc. was brought in to produce the low-cost microprocessors needed.

The result of the HLT effort is expected to be a wide range of household appliances that are only slightly more expensive than their less intelligent counterparts. Likewise, Sunbeam and their partners hope that HLT will become a standard that is used by other home appliance vendors.

Microwave Cooking from the Internet

How about connecting your microwave to the Internet? Sharp Electronics Corp. and Samsung Electronics are two companies that think you can improve your microwave roasts and casseroles by hooking them to the Web.

Sharp's RE-M210 Convention/Microwave Oven

Sharp has developed a microwave oven (RE-M210) that lets you download data for more than 400 recipes from the Web. That data can then be sent to the microwave to automatically prepare the food from any of those selected recipes.

To choose recipes for the Sharp RE-M210, you start by downloading recipes from Sharp's Web site. Included with these recipes are

➤ A list of ingredients

➤ Heating instructions

➤ Steps for preparing the food

The information is transferred to the optional Cooking Data Box, which places the information into the microwave's memory. From there, the microwave can automatically select temperature, time, and power levels, as well as any necessary cooking sequences.

Currently, the RE-M210 is only being marketed in Japan. However, Sharp has been researching a potential market for the product in the United State as well.

Samsung's Intelligent Microwave Oven

The Samsung Intelligent Microwave Oven is designed to gather different kinds of food and cooking information from the Web. Connect the microwave to your computer and it can download information on preparing a variety of foods.

Besides temperature settings, the microwave is also designed to download related information, such as nutrition and preparation information. Other features of the Intelligent Microwave Oven include a bar code reader that could allow a product package to be scanned for information on cooking.

Internet Server Appliances

The progression of small office computing has evolved from single PCs, to simple LAN connections (with file and print sharing), to LANs with outside connections to the Internet. Mail servers, Web hosting, email servers, and other Internet services were typically handled by the ISP for small businesses. Internet server appliances have set out to change that.

Internet appliances are designed to be popped out of the box, plugged in, and fired up in a short period of time. Because they are intended for locations where there might not be a computer room, these appliances typically come in sleek designs and attractive colors. Server appliances usually handle one or more of the following features:

➤ **Firewalls** Contains features for filtering traffic between the office LAN and the Internet.

➤ **Dial-up Access** Allows users to dial in to the office network or dial out from the network.

➤ **Virtual Private Network (VPN)** Allows secure connections between public networks and your private network.

➤ **Mail** Stores and distributes email.

➤ **Routing**   Routes information between your private network and the Internet.

➤ **Web Server**   Allows for publishing of Web pages and related content.

➤ **File Sharing**   Provides dedicated file sharing services.

There are several different companies offering Internet Server Appliances. Most of these appliances rely on the Linux operating system to provide the underlying network connectivity. Then, each vendor typically adds its own simplified user interfaces. Here are a few of those companies and the products they offer:

➤ **Cobalt Qube Internet Appliance** (`http://www.cobalt.com`)   Offers email server and Web server features for Internet or Intranet use.

➤ **WebRamp Communications Appliance** (`http://www.webramp.com`) Device for sharing Internet Access among an entire office. Contains access control features, VPN support, and Remote Dial-in features.

➤ **NetWinder OfficeServer** (`http://www.rebel.com`)   An Internet server appliance the can be used as an email server, file server, and print server. It can be used to support up to 100 users simultaneously.

➤ **EncantoWeb Server** (`http://www.encanto.com`)   Allows Internet access and email to the entire office. Lets you create your own Web site and build e-commerce applications.

➤ **Technauts eServer** (`http://www.technauts.com`)   Contains the following Web server features: email, Web publishing, file sharing, and communications.

➤ **Internet Appliance Small Enterprise Server** (`http:// internetappliance.com`)   Provides secure server communications, including firewall, routing, virtual private networking (VPN), and email. System administration is done through a Web browser interface.

The Multimedia Experience

Never in human history has it been so easy for so many to download so much stuff. Low-fidelity computer audio hardware and low-resolution video players haven't done much to enhance the playback of otherwise perfect digital music and video. That's about to change.

Some neat new devices are being produced these days to move our digital entertainment from the PC and back to where it belongs: dedicated entertainment devices. On the video front, there are Web-enabled televisions. For audio, there are some cool, networked audio systems.

Interactive Televisions

Televisions of the future will be less passive. Using interactive television features, you will be able to interact with shows that are set up to provide interactive features. One such product that is available today is WebTV Plus.

Some television shows from NBC and MSNBC networks are already interactive capable. All you need to do is look for an "i" to appear on the screen during a television show. When it does, you push the Go button. From that point on, you can interact with the show. Several news and sports shows already support interactive TV.

WebTV Plus relies on your existing television set and a telephone line. You need to add a WebTV Plus receiver and subscribe to the WebTV Plus Interactive service. Using this same setup, you can also surf the Web, For more information, visit http://www.webtv.com/itv.

Networked Audio Equipment

Thousands of hours of the world's most popular music has already been digitized and stored on the Internet. As recording companies and music service providers, such as MP3.com and Napster.com, struggle with copyright issues, one thing is for sure: Recorded music from the Internet is here to stay.

To this point, music downloading from the Web has been most popular with young people, with PCs and portable MP3 players being the playback devices of choice. For digital music to move more into the mainstream, however, playback equipment needs to be of better quality and more focused on convenience. That kind of equipment is on its way.

Audio equipment being developed to play music that can be downloaded from the Web, or any network device, can offer great advantages over traditional CD players. Here are some of the advantages that a networked stereo system can offer:

➤ No need to change CDs every time you want to change a song.

➤ You can search music databases for the music you want. Searches can be based on any parameters you can think of: artist, song title, CD title, record label, or any other information that can be stored and searched.

➤ There is virtually no limit to the songs you can select from. After legal rights are obtained to play the music, bringing it to your player can be just a click away.

➤ Other information can be linked to the music. With display screens that come with some players, you can access information about a band, concert tours, or related products such as t-shirts or posters.

Here are some products for downloading and playing music from the Web that are either new or on their way soon.

RCA MP3 Audio Players

RCA is adding to its Lyra MP3 players line (http://www.lyrazone.com), which now contains only portable players, to include high-end home component MP3 players. High-end home component systems are expected to hit the market by the end of 2000. These units are said to have Internet capabilities.

Techno Tip

If you plan to download or otherwise store a lot of digital music on your PC or new audio equipment, be prepared to use a lot of hard disk space. On average, each hour of MP3 music consumes about 120MB of hard disk space. Although that's a lot better than WAV files (which use about 600MB to store one hour of music), it still means that you will need massive hard disks to store more than a few CDs.

Dell Digital Audio Receiver

In partnership with S3 Inc., Dell Computer has announced that it will market a Digital Audio Receiver that can play MP3 files at home. A person will be able to download a song from a PC and distribute the song to the MP3 player. The new receiver is expected out before the end of 2000.

Fun e-Business Wurlitzer Internet Jukebox

A company called Fun e-Business (http://www.fune-business.com) is marketing its Wurlitzer Internet Jukebox in conjunction with MP3.com. The jukebox is expected to have 14GB of hard disk storage space and feature DSL hardware to connect to the Internet.

The Wurlitzer Internet Jukebox will look and act a lot like traditional jukeboxes. You still drop in quarters to play songs. However, the unit also offers video support by connecting a television monitor and will be able to immediately download songs that are not currently stored locally on the machine. Figure 18.3 shows an example of the Wurlitzer Internet Jukebox.

Lydstrom SongBank MZ Audio Player

The SongBank MZ Audio Player from Lydstrom (http://www.lydstrom.com) can store up to 900 hours of recorded music. Although the current model lets you record from CDs, there is an Ethernet connector for future Internet connection. With this unit, you can set up and play music from your own playlists.

Where To From Here?

I hope this book has provided you with the basic tools you need to use and administer a computer network. At this point, you should get your hands on a computer network and try out some of the tasks described in this book. And, of course, there is still the appendix, which should help you "Speak Like a Geek" (if you can't already).

The Least You Need to Know

Right now, the least you need to know about network appliances is

➤ There are different initiatives underway to aid in the proliferation of network devices (especially in the wireless area). These include Bluetooth (to network wireless devices), WAP (to provide Web content to wireless devices), and IrDA (to connect peripherals and appliances to a network with infrared technology).

➤ Wireless devices are expected to flood the market over the next few years, offering a wide range of Internet connectivity features.

➤ The first Internet appliances to reach the market are those that target specific Internet server functions. These include simplified Web servers, communications servers, email servers, and file servers.

➤ Although the idea of networking kitchen appliances might seem a bit funny, there are companies actually doing it. Look for a wide range of networked home appliances in the coming years.

➤ Digital music that is currently relegated to the PC or to portable MP3 players is expected to move toward home entertainment systems in the near future. With a network connection from your home audio system, you could download a new song from the Internet with the press of a button.

Part 6
Appendix

In case you haven't had enough networking words yet, we stuck this appendix at the back of the book. It's a glossary of networking terms. Following each networking word are a few more words describing what the word means. After all, that's what a glossary is.

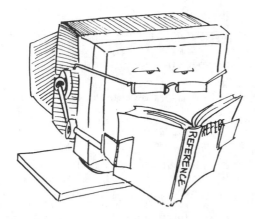

Speak Like a Geek: The Networking Bible

10Base2   Coaxial (thinnet) Ethernet capable of transmitting to distances of up to 185 meters per segment.

10Base5   Coaxial (thicknet) Ethernet that by default transports data to distances of 500 meters.

10BaseT   Twisted Pair Ethernet capable of transmitting to distances of up to 100 meters between the two farthest points on the network.

100Base-FX   Fast (100Mbps) Ethernet, typically strung via fiber-optic cable and capable of transmitting a distance of some 412 meters.

100BaseT   Fast (100Mbps) Ethernet, supporting various cabling schemes and capable of transmitting a distance of some 205 meters.

1000Base-CX   Extremely fast (1000Mbps) Ethernet, typically strung via copper wire and capable of transmitting a distance of some 25 meters.

1000Base-LX   Extremely fast (1000Mbps) Ethernet, typically strung via fiber-optic cable, and capable of transmitting a distance of between 440 meters and 3 kilometers (depending on the type of cabling used).

1000Base-SX   Extremely fast (1000Mbps) Ethernet, typically strung via fiber cable and capable of transmitting a distance of between 260 and 550 meters.

1000Base-TX   Extremely fast (1000Mbps) Ethernet, typically strung via copper wire and capable of transmitting a distance of up to 100 meters.

802.2   An Ethernet frame format (probably the most common) typically used in local area networks.

AARP   *See* AppleTalk Address Resolution Protocol

AAUI   Apple AUI. Apple Computer's version of the Attachment Unit Interface. *See also* attachment unit interface (AUI).

acceptable use policy (AUP)   Originally established by the National Science Foundation, AUP once forbade use of the Internet for commercial purposes. Today, AUP refers to rules a user must adhere to when using an ISP's services.

access control   Any tool or technique that allows you to selectively grant or deny users access to system resources.

access control list (ACL)   A list that stores information on users and what system resources they're allowed to access.

ACL   *See* access control list.

active hub   The main hub in a network. A hardware device that repeats and repropagates signals.

adapter   A hardware device used to connect devices. In networking context, an Ethernet adapter/card.

adaptive routing   Routing designed to adapt to the current network load. Adaptive routing routes data around bottlenecks and congested network areas.

adaptive pulse code modulation   A method of encoding voice into digital format over communication lines.

Address Resolution Protocol (ARP)   Maps IP addresses to physical addresses.

administrator   Either a human being charged with controlling a network or the supervisory account in Windows NT. Whoever has administrator privileges in Windows NT can—but need not necessarily—hold complete control over their network, workgroup, or domain.

ADSL   *See* Asymmetric Digital Subscriber Line.

ADSP   *See* AppleTalk Data Stream Protocol.

Advanced Server for Workgroups   An IBM GroupWare product featuring OS/2 and Lotus Notes.

AEP   *See* AppleTalk Echo Protocol.

AIM   *See* Ascend Inverse Multiplexing.

AIS   *See* Automated Information System.

AIX   A flavor of UNIX from International Business Machines (IBM). AIX runs on RISC workstations and the PowerPC.

American National Standards Institute   *See* ANSI.

American Standard Code for Information Interchange   *See* ASCII.

analog system   This term is generally used to describe the telephone system, which uses analog technology to convert voice to electronic signals.

Anonymous FTP   FTP service available to the public that allows anonymous logins. Anyone can access anonymous FTP with the username anonymous and their email address as a password.

ANSI   The American National Standards Institute. Check them out at http://www.ansi/org.

answer-only modem   A modem that answers but cannot dial out. These are useful for preventing users from initiating calls from your system via out-dials.

applet   A small Java program that runs in a Web browser environment. Applets can add graphics, animation, and dynamic text to otherwise lifeless Web pages.

AppleShare   Specialized Apple Computer software used to establish and maintain Macintosh file servers.

AppleTalk   Apple Computer's networking suite that supports Ethernet and Token Ring.

AppleTalk Address Resolution Protocol (AARP) Apple's version of ARP, this protocol maps IP addresses to physical addresses.

AppleTalk Data Stream Protocol (ADSP) Apple's peer-to-peer streamed communication protocol for transporting large amounts of data over a network.

AppleTalk Echo Protocol (AEP) Apple's version of the Echo protocol, used to test
the network by having a remote server echo back packets you send.

AppleTalk Remote Access Protocol (ARAP) Enabling this protocol turns your Mac
server into a remote access server, allowing others to access your network from remote
locations.

application gateways Firewall devices that disallow direct communication between
the Internet and an internal, private network. Data flow is controlled by proxy servers that
screen out undesirable information or hosts.

Application layer Layer 7 of the OSI reference model, the highest layer of the model.
The application layer defines how applications interact over the network. This is the layer
of communications that occurs (and is conspicuous) at the user level. (For example: File
Transfer Protocol interfaces with the user at the Application layer.)

ARAP *See* AppleTalk Remote Access Protocol.

ARCnet The Attached Resource Computer Network, a LAN system by Datapoint
Corporation. It supports 255 workstations in a star topology at speeds of 2.5Mbps.

ARP *See* Address Resolution Protocol.

ARPAnet Advanced Research Projects Agency Network. This was the original Internet,
which, for many years, was controlled by the Department of Defense.

Ascend Inverse Multiplexing (AIM) Proprietary protocol created by Ascend
Communications (router manufacturer) for managing multiplexers. To learn more, go to
`http://www.ascend.com`.

ASCII American Standard Code for Information Interchange, ASCII is a common standard by which all operating systems treat simple text.

Asymmetric Digital Subscriber Line (ADSL) A high-speed, digital telephone technology with fast downloading (nearly 6MBps) but much slower uploading (about 65KBps).
Unfortunately, ADSL is a new technology that is available only in major metropolitan
areas.

asynchronous data transmission The transmission of data one character at a time.

asynchronous PPP Run-of-the-mill PPP; the kind generally used by PPP dial-up customers.

asynchronous transfer mode (ATM) An ATM network is one type of circuit-
switched packet network that can transfer information in standard blocks at high speed.
These are not to be confused with automatic teller networks.

attachment unit interface (AUI) A 15-pin, twisted-pair Ethernet connection or connector.

attribute The state of a given resource (whether file or directory), and whether that
resource is readable, hidden, system, or other.

ATM *See* Asynchronous transfer mode.

AUI *See* attachment unit interface.

AUP *See* acceptable use policy.

authenticate   When you authenticate a particular user or host, you are verifying its identity.

authentication   The process of authenticating either a user or host. Such authentication may be simple and applied at the application level (demanding a password), or may be complex (as in challenge-response dialog boxes between machines, which generally rely on algorithms or encryption at a discrete level of the system).

Authentication Server Protocol   A TCP-based authentication service that can verify the identity of a user. (Please see RFC 931.)

Automated Information System (AIS)   Any system (composed of hardware and software) that allows the maintenance, storage, and processing of information.

automounting   The practice of automatically mounting network drives at boot.

back door   A hidden program, left behind by an intruder (or perhaps a disgruntled employee), that allows future access to a victim host. This term is synonymous with the more antiquated term *trap door*.

backbone   The fastest and most centralized feed on your network. The heart of your network to which all other systems are connected.

BackOffice   A networking suite from Microsoft that packages together database, mail, and network management.

back up   To preserve a file system or files, usually for disaster recovery. Generally, back-up is done to tape, floppy disk, or other portable media that can be safely stored for later use.

bandwidth   The transmission capacity of your network medium, measured in bits per second.

baseband   Audio and video signals sent over coaxial cable, typically used in cable television transmissions.

bastion host   A server that is hardened against attack and can therefore be used outside the firewall as your "face to the world." These are often sacrificial (in other words, they are expected to be attacked by hackers so they provide no connections to your internal network).

biometric access controls   Systems that authenticate users by physical characteristics, such as their face, fingerprints, retinal pattern, or voice.

BNC   A coaxial cable or connection used in older Ethernet networks. (BNC connectors look exactly like cable television wire connectors.)

bottleneck   An area of your network that demonstrates sluggish transfer rates, usually due to network congestion or misconfiguration.

bootp   See bootstrap protocol.

bootstrap protocol (bootp)   A network protocol used for remote booting. (Diskless workstations often use a bootstrap protocol to contact a boot server. In response, the boot server sends boot commands.)

border gateway protocol   A protocol that facilitates communication between routers serving as gateways.

bridge   A network hardware device that connects local area network segments together.

broadband   A very high-speed data transmission system, capable of supporting large transfers of media such as sound, video, and other data.

broadcast/broadcasting   Any network message sent to all network hosts, or the practice of sending such a message.

bug   A hole or weakness in a computer program. *See also* vulnerability.

cable modem   A modem that negotiates Internet access over cable television networks. Cable modems provide blazing speeds.

call back   Call-back systems ensure that a trusted host initiated the current connection. The host connects, a brief exchange is made, and the connection is cut. Then the server calls back the requesting host.

Carrier Sense Multiple Access with Collision Avoidance (CSMA/CA)   A traffic-management technique used by Ethernet. In CSMA/CA, workstations announce to the network that they're about to transmit data.

Carrier Sense Multiple Access with Collision Detection (CSMA/CD)   A traffic-management technique used by Ethernet. In CSMA/CD, workstations check the wire for traffic before transmitting data.

Cast-128   An encryption algorithm that uses large keys and can be incorporated into cryptographic applications. (You can learn more by obtaining RFC 2144.)

CA-Unicenter   Powerful database- and network-management software from Computer Associates. Typically used in very large, enterprise-based database serving, especially over wide area networks.

CERT   *See* Computer Emergency Response Team.

certificate authority   Trusted third-party clearing house that issues security certificates and ensures their authenticity. Probably the most renowned commercial certificate authority is VeriSign, which issues (among other things) certificates for Microsoft-compatible ActiveX components.

certification   Either the end-result of a successful security evaluation of a product or system or an academic honor bestowed on those who successfully complete courses in network engineering (such as certification as a Novell Network Engineer).

Certified NetWare Engineer   Person who has passed the certification tests for NetWare networks from Novell, Inc.

CGI   *See* common gateway interface.

Challenge Handshake Authentication Protocol (CHAP)   Protocol (often used with PPP) that challenges users to verify their identity. If the challenge is properly met, the user is authenticated. If not, the user is denied access. See RFC 1344 for further information.

channel   In networking, a communications path.

CHAP   *See* Challenge Handshake Authentication Protocol.

circuit   A connection that conducts electrical currents and, by doing so, transmits data.

client   Software designed to interact with a specific server application. For example, the Netscape Communicator and Internet Explorer browsers are WWW clients. They are specifically designed to interact with Web or HTTP servers.

client/server model   A programming model where a single server can distribute data to many clients (the relationship between a Web server and Web clients or browsers is a good example). Most network applications and protocols are based on the client/server model.

CNE Certified NetWare Engineer.

common carrier Any government-regulated utility that provides the public with communications (for example, a telephone company).

common gateway interface (CGI) A standard that specifies programming techniques through which you pass data from Web servers to Web clients. CGI is language neutral. You can write CGI programs in PERL, C, C++, Python, Visual Basic, BASIC, and shell languages.

compression The technique of reducing file size for the purposes of maximizing bandwidth. The smaller the file, the less bandwidth you need to send it.

COM Port A serial communications port, sometimes used to connect modems (and even mice).

Computer Emergency Response Team (CERT) A security organization that assists victims of cracker attacks. Find CERT at `http://www.cert.org`.

copy access When a user has copy access, it means that he or she has privileges to copy a particular file.

cracker Someone who, with malicious intent, unlawfully breaches security of computer systems or software.

CSMA/CA *See* Carrier Sense Multiple Access with Collision Avoidance.

CSMA/CD *See* Carrier Sense Multiple Access with Collision Detection.

DAC *See* discretionary access control.

Data Encryption Standard (DES) Encryption standard from IBM, developed in 1974 and published in 1977. DES is the U.S. government standard for encrypting non-classified data.

Data Link layer Layer 2 of the OSI reference model. This layer defines the rules for sending and receiving information between systems.

datagram A packet or "...a self-contained, independent entity of data carrying sufficient information to be routed from the source to the destination computer without reliance on earlier exchanges between this source and destination computer and the transporting network..." (RFC 1594).

DECnet An antiquated, proprietary protocol from Digital Equipment Corporation that runs chiefly over proprietary, Ethernet, and X.25 networks.

denial-of-service See DoS.

Department of Defense The government agency that originally developed ARPAnet (which was the predecessor of the Internet).

DES *See* Data Encryption Standard.

DHCP *See* dynamic host configuration protocol.

digest access authentication A security extension for HTTP that provides only basic (and not encrypted) user authentication. To learn more, see RFC 2069.

digital certificate Any digital value used in authentication. Digital certificates are typically numeric values, derived from cryptographic processes. (There are many values that can be used as the basis of a digital certificate, including but not limited to biometric values, such as retinal scans and thumbprints.)

discretionary access control (DAC) Provides means for a central authority on a computer system or network to either permit or deny access to all users, and do so incisively, based on time, date, file, directory, or host.

DNS *See* domain name service.

DoD Department of Defense.

domain name A host name or machine name, such as `gnss.com`. This is the non-numeric expression of a host's address. Numeric expressions are always in "dot" format, like this: `207.171.0.111`.

domain name service (DNS) A networked system that translates numeric IP addresses (`207.171.0.111`) into Internet host names (`traderights.pacificnet.net`).

DoS This refers to denial-of-service, a condition that results when a user maliciously renders an Internet information server inoperable, thereby denying computer service to legitimate users.

Dynamic host configuration protocol (DHCP) A technique for assigning IP addresses dynamically to computers as they connect to a network. Often used for dial-up Internet connections that only use IP addresses during connection times.

dual-homed gateway Configuration or machine that supports two or more disparate protocols or means of network transport, and provides packet screening between them.

EFT Electronic funds transfer.

encryption The process of scrambling data so it is unreadable by unauthorized parties. In most encryption schemes, you must have a password to reassemble the data into readable form. Encryption is primarily used to enhance privacy or to protect classified, secret, or top-secret information. (For example, many military and satellite transmissions are encrypted to prevent spies or hostile nations from analyzing them.)

Ethernet A local area network networking technology (originally developed by Xerox) that connects computers and transmits data between them. Data is packaged into frames and sent via wires.

Ethernet spoofing Any procedure that involves assuming another host's Ethernet address to gain unauthorized access to the target.

exabyte Approximately 1,000,000,000,000,000,000 bytes. (Abbreviated EB.)

FDDI *See* fiber optic data distribution interface.

Fiber-optic cable An extremely fast network cable that transmits data using light rather than electricity. Most commonly used for backbones.

fiber optic data distribution interface (FDDI) Fiber-optic cable that transfers data at very high speeds. Used to significantly stretch the distances available for a Local Area Network.

file server A computer that serves as a centralized source for files.

File Transfer Protocol (FTP) A protocol used to transfer files from one TCP/IP host to another.

filtering The process of examining network packets for integrity and security. Filtering is typically an automated process, performed by either routers or software.

firewall Loosely, any device that refuses unauthorized users access to a particular host. Less loosely, a device that examines each packet's source address. If that address is on an approved list, the packets gain entry. If not, they're rejected.

frame *See* packet.

frame relay Frame relay technology allows networks to transfer information in bursts. This is a cost-effective way of transferring data over networks because you pay for only the resources you use. (Unfortunately, you may also be sharing your frame relay connection with someone else. Standard frame relay connections run at 56Kbps.)

FTP   *See* File Transfer Protocol.

full duplex transmission   Any transmission in which data is transmitted in both directions simultaneously.

gateway   A point on a network where two (or more) network protocols are translated into other protocols. Typical examples of such translation include TCP/IP to basic Ethernet or even proprietary protocols.

General Switch Management Protocol (GSMP)   A protocol by Ipsilon that controls ATM switches and their ports.

gigabit   1,000,000,000 bits.

GOPHER   The Internet Gopher Protocol, a protocol for distributing documents over the Net. GOPHER preceded the World Wide Web as an information retrieval tool. (See RFC 1436 for more information.)

granularity   The degree to which you can incisively apply access controls. The more incisively a system allows controls to be set, the more granularity that system has.

group   A value denoting a collection of users. This value is used in network file permissions. All users belonging to this or that group share similar access privileges.

GroupWare   Application programs that are designed to make full use of a network, and often promote collaborative work.

GSMP   *See* General Switch Management Protocol.

hacker   Someone interested in operating systems, software, security, and the Internet, generally. Also called a *programmer*. Commonly used to refer to people who break into other people's computers (although real hackers generally object to that definition).

hardware address   The fixed physical address of a network adapter and, hence, the machine on which it was installed. Hardware addresses are hard-coded into the network adapter.

hole   *See* vulnerability.

host   A computer with a permanent hardware address, especially on a TCP/IP network.

host table   Any record of matching hostnames and network addresses. These tables are used to identify the name and location of each host on your network. Such tables are consulted before data is transmitted. (Think of a host table as a personal address book of machine addresses.)

HP-UX   A flavor of UNIX from Hewlett Packard.

HTML   See hypertext markup language.

HTTP   *See* hypertext transfer protocol.

hub   A device that is used to connect computers together on a LAN in a star topology.

hypertext   A text display format commonly used on Web pages. Hypertext is distinct from regular text because it's interactive. In a hypertext document, when you click or choose any highlighted word, other associated text appears. This allows powerful cross-referencing, and permits users to navigate a document.

hypertext markup language (HTML)   Document formatting language that is used to create Web pages. It is the core language for creating content on the Web.

hypertext transfer protocol (HTTP)   The protocol used to traffic hypertext across the Internet, and the underlying protocol of the WWW.

IDEA   *See* International Data Encryption Algorithm.

International Data Encryption Algorithm (IDEA)   IDEA is a powerful block-cipher encryption algorithm that operates with a 128-bit key. IDEA encrypts data faster than DES and is far more secure.

IDENT   *See* Identification Protocol.

Identification Protocol (IDENT)   A TCP-based protocol for identifying users. IDENT is a more modern, advanced version of the Authentication Protocol. You can find out more by obtaining RFC 1413.

IGMP   *See* Internet Group Management Protocol.

IMAP3   *See* Interactive Mail Access Protocol.

InPerson   A GroupWare product from Silicon Graphics.

Integrated Services Digital Network (ISDN)   Digital telephone service that offers data transfer rates upward of 128Kbps.

Interactive Mail Access Protocol (IMAP3)   A protocol that allows workstations to access Internet electronic mail from centralized servers. (See RFC 1176 for further information.)

Internet   In general, the conglomeration of computer networks now connected to the international switched packet telephone system that support TCP/IP. Less generally, any computer network that supports TCP/IP and is interconnected.

Internet Group Management Protocol (IGMP)   A protocol that controls broadcasts to multiple users.

Internet Protocol (IP)   The chief method of transporting data across the Internet.

Internet Protocol security option   IP security option, used to protect IP datagrams, according to U.S. classifications, whether unclassified, classified secret, or top secret. (See RFC 1038 and RFC 1108.)

Internet Worm   Also called the Morris Worm, a program that attacked the Internet in November 1988. To get a Worm overview, check out RFC 1135.

Internetwork Packet eXchange   See IPX.

Internetworking   The practice of using networks that run standard Internet protocols.

InterNIC   The Network Information Center located at `www.internic.net`.

intrusion detection   The practice of using automated systems to detect intrusion attempts. Intrusion detection typically involves intelligent systems or agents.

IP   *See* Internet Protocol.

IP Address   Numeric Internet address, such as `207.171.0.111`.

IP masquerading   A feature used on networks that use private IP addresses that allows computers on those networks to connect to the Internet. With this feature, all communication to the Internet is done through a proxy host, which maps private IP numbers into IP/port numbers.

IP spoofing   Any procedure where an attacker assumes another host's IP address to gain unauthorized access to the target.

IPX   Internetwork Packet eXchange. A proprietary data transport protocol from Novell, Inc. that loosely resembles Internet Protocol.

349

IRIX A flavor of UNIX from Silicon Graphics.

ISDN *See* Integrated Services Digital Network.

ISO International Standards Organization.

ISP Internet service provider.

Java A network programming language created by Sun Microsystems that marginally resembles C++. Java is object oriented, and is often used to generate graphics and multimedia applications, although it's most well known for its networking power.

JavaScript A scripting language developed by Netscape Communications Corporation. JavaScript runs in and manipulates Web browser environments, particularly Netscape Navigator and Communicator (but also Internet Explorer).

Kerberos An encryption and authentication system developed at the Massachusetts Institute of Technology. Kerberos is used in network applications, and relies on trusted third-party servers for authentication.

Kerberos Network Authentication Service Third-party, ticket-based authentication scheme that can be easily integrated into network applications. See RFC 1510 for details.

LAN *See* local area network.

Line Printer Daemon Protocol (LPDP) A protocol used to facilitate remote printing. (See RFC 1179 for more information.)

Linux A free UNIX clone that runs on widely disparate architecture, including X86 (Intel), Alpha, Sparc, and PowerPC processors. Linux is becoming increasingly popular as a Web server platform.

LISTSERV Listserv Distribute Protocol, a protocol used to deliver mass email. (See RFC 1429 for further information.)

local area network (LAN) LANs are small broadcast types of network. Most LANs incorporate Ethernet protocols, although Token Ring protocols are also used.

Lotus Notes A GroupWare product from Lotus.

LPDP *See* Line Printer Daemon Protocol.

maximum transmission unit (MTU) A value that denotes the largest packet that can be transmitted. (Many people adjust this value and often get better performance by either increasing or decreasing it.)

megabyte Approximately 1,000,000 bytes. (Abbreviated MB.)

Microsoft Exchange A GroupWare product from Microsoft Corporation.

modem A device that converts signals that the computer understands into signals that can be accurately transmitted over phone lines or other media, and that can convert the signals back into their original form.

Morris Worm *See* Internet Worm.

MTU *See* maximum transmission unit.

NE2000 A standard by which network interface cards are judged. Most cards use this standard.

NetBIOS Protocol A high-speed, lightweight transport protocol commonly used in local area networks, particularly those running LAN Manager.

netstat UNIX command (also available in Windows) that shows the current TCP/IP connections and the source addresses.

NetWare   A popular network operating system from Novell, Inc.

network file system (NFS)   A system that allows you to transparently import files from remote hosts (including those running different operating systems). These files appear and act as though they were installed on your local machine.

Network Information System (NIS)   A system developed by Sun Microsystems that allows Internet hosts to transfer information after authenticating themselves with a single password. NIS was once called the Yellow Pages system.

network interface card (NIC)   An adapter card that lets the computer attach to a network cable. Also known as a NIC.

Network layer   Layer 3 of the OSI reference model. This layer provides the routing information for data, opening and closing paths for the data to travel, and ensuring it reaches its destination.

Network News Transfer Protocol (NNTP)   The protocol that controls the transmission of Usenet news messages.

network operating system (NOS)   An operating system for networks, such as NetWare or Windows NT.

NFS   *See* network file system.

NIC   *See* network interface card.

NIS   *See* Network Information System.

NNTP   *See* Network News Transfer Protocol.

NOS   *See* network operating system.

offline   Not available on the network.

online   Available on the network.

one-time password   A password generated on-the-fly during a challenge-response exchange. Such passwords are generated using a predefined algorithm, but are extremely secure because they are good for the current session only.

Open Systems Interconnection reference model   See OSI reference model.

OpenLinux   A popular distribution of the Linux operating system that is produced by Caldera Systems, Inc.

OSI reference model   Open Systems Interconnection Reference Model. A seven-layer model of data communications protocols that make up the architecture of a network. The seven layers (from the bottom up) are Physical, Data Link, Network, Transport, Session, Presentation, and Application layers.

owner   The person (or process) with privileges to read, write, or otherwise access a given file, directory, or process. The system administrator assigns ownership. However, ownership may also be assigned automatically by the operating system in certain instances.

packet   Data that is sent over a network is broken into manageable chunks called *packets* or *frames*. The size is determined by the protocol used.

Password Authentication Protocol   A protocol used to authenticate PPP users.

PCI   *See* peripheral component interface.

PCM   *See* pulse code modulation.

penetration testing   The process of attacking a host from the outside to ascertain remote security vulnerabilities. This process is sometimes called *ice-pick testing*.

peripheral component interface (PCI)   An interface used for expansion slots in PCs and Macintosh computers. PCI slots are where you plug in new adapter cards, including Ethernet adapters, disk controller cards, and video cards to name a few.

PERL   Practical Extraction and Report Language. A programming language commonly used in network programming, text processing, and CGI programming.

petabyte   Approximately 1,000,000,000,000,000 bytes. (Abbreviated PB.)

phreaking   The process of (usually unlawfully) manipulating the telephone system.

physical layer   Layer 1 of the OSI reference model. This layer deals with hardware connections and transmissions and is the only layer that involves the physical transfer of data from system to system.

Point-to-Point Protocol (PPP)   A communication protocol used between machines that support serial interfaces, such as modems. PPP is commonly use to provide and access dial-up services to Internet service providers.

Point-to-Point Tunneling Protocol (PPTP)   A specialized form of PPP. Its unique design makes it possible to "encapsulate" or wrap non-TCP/IP protocols within PPP. Through this method, PPTP allows two or more LANs to connect using the Internet as a conduit. (PPTP is a great stride ahead because previously, expensive leased lines were used to perform this task which was cost-prohibitive in many instances. The IP Security standard, IPSec, is expected to eventually replace PPTP.)

POP2   *See* Post Office Protocol.

Post Office Protocol (POP)   A protocol that allows workstations to access Internet electronic mail from centralized servers. (See RFC 937 for further information.)

PPP   *See* Point to Point Protocol.

PPP Authentication Protocols   Set of protocols that can be used to enhance security of Point-to-Point Protocol. (See RFC 1334.)

PPP DES   The PPP DES Encryption Protocol, which applies the data encryption standard protection to point-to-point links. (This is one method to harden PPP traffic against sniffing.) To learn more, see RFC 1969.

PPTP   *See* Point-to-Point Tunneling Protocol.

Practical Extraction and Report Language   *See* PERL.

Presentation layer   Layer 6 of the OSI reference model. This layer manages the protocols of the operating system, formatting of data for display, encryption, and translation of characters.

ProShare   A GroupWare product from Intel.

protocol   A standardized set of rules that govern communication or the way that data is transmitted.

protocol analyzer   Hardware, software, or both that monitors network traffic and reduces that traffic to either datagrams or packets that can be humanly read.

protocol stack   A hierarchy of protocols used in data transport, usually arranged in a collection called a *suite* (such as the TCP/IP suite).

pulse code modulation (PCM)   A system of transforming signals from analog to digital. (Many high-speed Internet connections from the telephone company use PCM.)

RAID   *See* redundant array of inexpensive disks.

RARP   *See* Reverse Address Resolution Protocol.

read access   When a user has read access, it means that he or she has privileges to read a particular file.

Red Hat Linux   A popular commercial distribution of the Linux operating system.

redundant array of inexpensive disks (RAID)   A large number of hard drives connected together that act as one drive. The data is spread out across several disks, and one drive keeps checking information so that if one drive fails, the data can be rebuilt.

Referral WHOIS Protocol (RWHOIS)   A protocol that provides access to the WHOIS registration database, which stores Internet domain name registration information.

repeater   A device that strengthens a signal so it can travel further distances.

request for comments (RFC)   RFC documents are working notes of the Internet development community. These are often used to propose new standards. A huge depository of RFC documents can be found at `http://www.internic.net`.

Reverse Address Resolution Protocol (RARP)   A protocol that maps Ethernet addresses to IP addresses.

RFC   *See* request for comments.

RIP   *See* Routing Information Protocol.

rlogin   A UNIX program that allows you to connect your terminal to remote hosts. rlogin is much like Telnet except that rlogin allows you to dispense with entering your password each time you log in.

router   A device that routes packets in and out of a network. Many routers are sophisticated and can serve as firewalls.

Routing Information Protocol (RIP)   A protocol that allows Internet hosts to exchange routing information. (See RFC 1058 for more information.)

RSA   A a public-key encryption algorithm named after its creators, Rivest, Shamir, and Adleman. RSA is probably the most popular of such algorithms and has been incorporated into many commercial applications, including but not limited to Netscape Navigator, Communicator, and even Lotus Notes. Find out more about RSA at `http://www.rsa.com`.

RWHOIS   *See* Referral WHOIS Protocol.

Secure Socket Layer (SSL)   A security protocol (created by Netscape Communications Corporation) that allows client/server applications to communicate free of eavesdropping, tampering, or message forgery. SSL is now used for secure electronic commerce. To find out more, see `http://home.netscape.com/eng/ssl3/draft302.txt`.

secured electronic transaction (SET)   A standard of secure protocols associated with online commerce and credit-card transactions. (Visa and MasterCard are the chief players in development of the SET protocol.) Its purpose is ostensibly to make electronic commerce more secure.

security audit   An examination (often by third parties) of a server's security controls and disaster-recovery mechanisms.

Serial Line Internet Protocol (SLIP)   An Internet protocol designed for connections based on serial communications (for example, telephone connections or COM port/RS232 connections).

Session layer   Layer 5 of the OSI reference model. This layer handles the coordination of communication between systems, maintains sessions for as long as needed, and handles security, logging, and administrative functions.

SET   *See* secured electronic transaction.

sharing The process of allowing users on other machines to access files and directories on your own. File sharing is a fairly typical activity within local area networks, and can sometimes be a security risk.

shielded twisted pair A network cabling frequently used in IBM Token Ring networks. (STP now supports 100Mbps.)

Simple Mail Transfer Protocol (SMTP) The Internet's most commonly used electronic mail protocol (see RFC 821).

Simple Network Management Protocol (SNMP) A protocol that offers centralized management of TCP/IP-based networks (particularly those connected to the Internet).

Simple Network Paging Protocol (SNPP) A protocol used to transmit wireless messages from the Internet to pagers. (See RFC 1861 for more information.)

Simple Network Time Protocol (SNTP) A protocol used to negotiate synchronization of your system's clock with clocks on other hosts.

S/Key One-time password system to secure connections. In S/Key, passwords are never sent over the network and therefore cannot be sniffed. See RFC 1760 for more information.

SLIP *See* Serial Line Internet Protocol.

SMTP *See* Simple Mail Transfer Protocol.

sniffer Hardware or software that captures datagrams across a network. It can be used legitimately (by an engineer trying to diagnose network problems) or illegitimately (by a cracker).

SNMP *See* Simple Network Management Protocol.

SNMP Security Protocols Within the SNMP suite, there is a series of security-related protocols. You can find out about them by obtaining RFC 1352.

SNPP *See* Simple Network Paging Protocol.

SNTP *See* Simple Network Time Protocol.

SOCKS Protocol Protocol that provides unsecured firewall traversal for TCP-based services. (See RFC 1928.)

SONET Synchronous Optical Network. An extremely high-speed network standard. Compliant networks can transmit data at 2Gbps (gigabits per second) or even faster. (Yeah, you read that right! 2 gigabits or better!)

SP3 Network Layer Security Protocol.

SP4 Transport Layer Security Protocol.

spoofing Any procedure that involves impersonating another user or host to gain unauthorized access to the target.

SSL *See* Secure Socket Layer.

stack *See* protocol stack.

STP *See* shielded twisted pair.

suite A term used to describe a collection of similar protocols. This term is used primarily when describing TCP- and IP-based protocols (when talking about the TCP/IP suite).

switch A network device that can filter and forward data across segments of a LAN. Often used to connect different types of LAN technologies (such as 10BaseT and 100BaseT LAN segments). Switching is done on the mechanical level, as opposed to bridges that use slower software switching.

TCP/IP Transmission Control Protocol/Internet Protocol. The protocols used by the Internet.

Telnet A protocol and an application that allows you to control your system from remote locations. During a Telnet session, your machine responds precisely as it would if you were actually working on its console.

Telnet authentication option Protocol options for Telnet that add basic security to Telnet-based connections based on rules at the source routing level. See RFC 1409 for details.

TEMPEST Transient Electromagnetic Pulse Surveillance Technology. TEMPEST is the practice and study of capturing or eavesdropping on electromagnetic signals that emanate from any device, in this case a computer. TEMPEST shielding is any computer security system designed to defeat such eavesdropping.

terabyte Approximately 1,000,000,000,000 bytes. (Abbreviated TB.)

terminator A small plug that attaches to the end of a segment of coax Ethernet cable. This plug terminates the signal from the wire.

TFTP *See* Trivial File Transfer Protocol.

Token Ring A network that's connected in a ring topology, in which a special "token" is passed from computer to computer. A computer must wait until it receives this token before sending data over the network.

topology The method or system by which your network is physically laid out.

Traceroute A TCP/IP program common to UNIX that traces the route between your machine and a remote host.

traffic analysis The study of patterns in communication rather than the content of the communication. For example, studying when, where, and to whom particular messages are being sent, without actually studying the content of those messages.

transceiver An essential part of a network interface card (NIC) that connects the network cable to the card. Most 10BaseT cards have them built in, but in some cases you might have to get a transceiver for an AUI port to 10BaseT.

Transient Electromagnetic Pulse Surveillance Technology *See* TEMPEST.

Transmission Control Protocol/Internet Protocol *See* TCP/IP.

Transport layer Layer 4 of the OSI reference model. This layer controls the movement of data between systems, defines the protocols for messages, and does error checking.

trap door *See* back door.

Trivial File Transfer Protocol (TFTP) An antiquated file transfer protocol now seldom used on the Internet. (TFTP is a lot like FTP without authentication.)

Trojan Horse An application or code that, unbeknownst to the user, performs surreptitious and unauthorized tasks that can compromise system security. Also referred to as a *Trojan*.

trusted system An operating system or other system secure enough for use in environments in which classified information is warehoused.

tunneling The practice of employing encryption in data communication between two points, thus shielding that data from others who may be surreptitiously sniffing the wire. Tunneling procedures encrypt data within packets, making it extremely difficult for outsiders to access such data.

twisted pair A cable that is made up of one or more pairs of wires, twisted to improve their electrical performance.

355

UDP   *See* User Datagram Protocol.

UID   See user ID.

uninterruptible power supply (UPS)   A backup power supply for when your primary power is cut. These are typically huge batteries that can only support your network for several hours.

UNIX   A multi-user, multi-tasking computer operating system that is very popular in networked computing environments. UNIX was created and developed at AT&T, although many offshoots of UNIX have been created over the years. Many Web servers and file servers today run on UNIX operating systems.

Unshielded twisted pair (UTP)   Common type of copper wiring, used for telephone lines and Ethernet LANs. The name comes from the fact that one or more pair of wires are twisted together.

UPS   *See* uninterruptible power supply.

user   Anyone who uses a computer system or system resources.

User Datagram Protocol (UDP)   A connectionless protocol from the TCP/IP family. Connectionless protocols will transmit data between two hosts even though those hosts do not currently have an active session. Such protocols are considered unreliable because there is no absolute guarantee that the data will arrive as it as intended.

user ID   In general, any value by which a user is identified, including his or her username. More specifically, and in relation to UNIX and other multi-user environments, any process ID—usually a numeric value—that identifies the owner of a particular process. *See also* owner and user.

UTP   *See* Unshielded twisted pair. *See also* 10BaseT.

Vines   A network operating system made by Banyan.

virtual private network (VPN)   VPN technology allows companies with leased lines to form a closed and secure circuit over the Internet between themselves and with employees in the field. In this way, such companies ensure that data passed between them and their counterparts is secure (and usually encrypted).

virus   A self-replicating or propagating program (sometimes malicious) that attaches itself to other executables, drivers, or document templates, thus "infecting" the target host or file.

VPN   *See* virtual private network.

vulnerability   This term refers to any weakness in any system (either hardware or software) that allows intruders to gain unauthorized access or deny service.

WAN   wide area network. A network that spans more than a few kilometers of distance, often encompassing multiple LANs and other types of subnetworks.

Windows 2000   Microsoft's recent version of Windows, designed to merge Windows 95/98 and Windows NT systems, as well as expand the operating system's networking capabilities.

Windows NT   Microsoft's network operating system that was created for networked environments.

write access   When a user has write access, it means that he or she has privileges to write to a particular file.

yottabyte   Approximately 1,000,000,000,000,000,000,000,000 bytes. (Abbreviated YB.)

zettabyte   Approximately 1,000,000,000,000,000,000,000 bytes. (Abbreviated ZB.)

Index

365